— a memoir —

# The Great Life I've Had!

## David William Sinclair

THE GREAT LIFE I'VE HAD! : A MEMOIR. Copyright © 2006 by Sinclair Family Trust. All rights reserved. Printed in the United States of America. No part of this book may used or reproduced in any manner whatsoever without written permission from the publisher except in the case of brief quotations embodied in critical articles and reviews.

Published by Sinclair Family Trust, 4510 144th Avenue SE, Bellevue, Washington 98006-2325.

Sinclair, David William, 1915-

The great life I've had! : a memoir / David William Sinclair.

ISBN: 978-0-6152-3583-7

FIRST EDITION

# The Great Life I've Had!

### By David William Sinclair

**PREFACE.** My aim is to document my life for the interest of my family and descendants, with selected memories from the various phases of my life. Like in a play, the scenes change, and so it is as we go from birth to death. I will try to describe the "scenery" as the way things were in the world in which I lived, which was quite different than the world today.

Dave Sinclair
San Diego, California

This book is **dedicated** to **Mary Bond Sinclair**, my lovely and loving partner in life for over 60 years.

# Contents

SCENE 1: Infancy—1915 (Westward Ho!) ........................................................................... 9

SCENE 2: Early Childhood—1916-1924 (War & Revolution!) ................................................. 13

SCENE 3: Pre-Teens—1924-1927 (Six-Thirty-Eight) ............................................................. 20

SCENE 4: Visitations—1924-1929 (Bobbie) .......................................................................... 25

SCENE 5: Expanding Horizons—1925-1928 (Auto-Touring) ................................................... 31

SCENE 6: The Great Depression—1928-1930 ...................................................................... 39

SCENE 7: Boy Scouts, Sea Scouts, Eagle Scouts—1927-1932 ............................................. 43

SCENE 8: Jalopies—1932-1935 ........................................................................................... 52

SCENE 9: UCLA (Fraternity, Basketball, Uplifters Club) ......................................................... 57

SCENE 10: Coast Guard Academy—1935 (Swab Summer) ................................................... 63

SCENE 11: Coast Guard Academy—1935-1936 (Fourth Class Year) ..................................... 70

SCENE 12: Coast Guard Academy—1936-1937 (Third Class Year) ....................................... 76

SCENE 13: Coast Guard Academy—1937-1938 (Second Class Year / Academics) ............. 82

SCENE 14: Coast Guard Academy—1938-1939 (First Class Year) ........................................ 87

SCENE 15: Coast Guard Academy—1939 (Graduation) ........................................................ 94

SCENE 16: CG Cutter Duane—1939-1940 (Neutrality Patrol / Weather Patrol / Greenland Visitation) ........................................................................................................... 104

SCENE 17: CG Cutter North Star—1941-1942 (Greenland Patrol / Sledge Patrol / World War II) ..................................................................................................................... 113

SCENE 18: CG Cutter Mohawk—1941-1943 (Greenland Patrol / Convoy Duty) ................... 122

SCENE 19: Primary Flight Training—1943 NAAS Memphis ................................................. 130

SCENE 20: Advanced Flight Training—1943-1944 NAS Pensacola ..................................... 134

SCENE 21: CGAS St. Petersburg—1944-46 (Anti-Submarine Patrols / Marriage) ............... 137

SCENE 22: CGAS Port Angeles—1946-1949 (Search-and-Rescue) .................................... 144

SCENE 23: CGAS Elizabeth City—1949-1953 (International Ice Patrol) .............................. 152

SCENE 24: CGAS San Diego—1953-1956 (Search-and-Rescue) ........................................ 160

SCENE 25: CGAS Puerto Rico—1956-1958 (Search-and-Rescue) ................................. 165

SCENE 26: 11th CG District HQ, Long Beach—1958-1959 (Jet Fighter Qualification / Rotation to Sea Duty) ........................................................................................................ 171

SCENE 27: CG Icebreaker Northwind—1959-1960 (Bering Sea Patrol) .............................. 175

SCENE 28: CG Cutter Wachusett—1960-1961 (Weather Patrol) ......................................... 180

SCENE 29: Commander Far East Section, USCG—1961-64 ............................................... 186

SCENE 30: CG Headquarters—1964-1967 (Chief, Recreational Boating Safety) ................ 194

SCENE 31: 12th CG District HQ, San Francisco—1967-1969 (Chief-of-Staff / Retirement) .................................................................................................................... 197

SCENE 32: Retirement Years—1969 to present ................................................................. 201

SCENE 33: Sailing ................................................................................................................ 205

SCENE 34: Bargin' ............................................................................................................... 210

SCENE 35: Behind the Iron Curtain ..................................................................................... 217

SCENE 36: Coastal Cruising ................................................................................................ 223

SCENE 37: Bicycling—San Diego & Beyond ....................................................................... 227

SCENE 38: Birding Hither and Thither ................................................................................. 234

SCENE 39: Touring the British Isles—1975 ......................................................................... 239

SCENE 40: Vignettes of Animal Antics ................................................................................ 242

SCENE 41: Farewell ............................................................................................................. 244

Epilogue ................................................................................................................................ 246

# SCENE 1

## INFANCY—1915 (WESTWARD HO!)

I was born on August 20, 1915, in Redlands, California. Redlands is located about seventy miles inland from the Pacific Ocean, east of Los Angeles. Redlands lies at the foot of the forested San Bernardino Mountains and at the edge of the high desert known as the Bad Lands. It gets its name from the red earth. At the time of my birth, Redlands was surrounded by orange groves and was a principal shipping point for citrus fruit. It was an upscale winter resort catering to midwesterners tired of long cold winters. It was also a health spa where the dry clear air gave relief to those suffering respiratory problems. Many facilities were established in the southwestern states for treatment of tuberculosis, which was epidemic for many years before a cure was found. Redlands also had a reputation for very hot summers. The permanent residents built homes along Victorian lines with high ceilings and shaded porches to make it easier to survive the summer heat. Air conditioning was many years away.

My birth made the local newspaper! I quote in its entirety, "SINCLAIR—Born, in Redlands, Cal., August 20, 1915, to Mr. and Mrs. Fred W. Sinclair, a son."

And here is another quote, "AUGUST WAS RECORD BREAKER. Yesterday closed the hottest August on record—with one exception, that being in 1901. In the month just ending there were twenty days on which the mercury reached one hundred degrees or over, horrible as the truth may sound. These are official government figures and not doctored by chamber of commerce figures such as some not far distant cities' papers are wont to print to make the summer weather seem real nice to the tourist."

So—"Why Redlands?"

Stupid Question. Simple answer: "BECAUSE MY MOTHER WAS THERE!"

So—"Why was my mother there?" "BECAUSE MY FATHER WAS THERE."

And—"Why was my father there?" "BECAUSE HE AND MY FAMILY WERE PART OF WESTWARD HO!"

**My mother, Laura Louise Bird, as a young woman**

To trace the western movement of Europeans we have to go back to the Middle Ages. The incentive was to tap the riches of the Orient. The Silk Road caravans with up to one thousand camels (which incidentally passed through Baghdad) had been supplying eastern European markets, but there was a demand for much more. Europeans decided to establish their own overland "road" but the Muslim Turks would not allow them a step further than Alexandria. Historians know this as the Iron Curtain of the Middle Ages.

Portuguese Prince Henry-the-Navigator (who never left his lighthouse office) pushed for a sea route down and around Africa. That is a long story. India was finally reached by Vasco da Gama, but that was six years after Columbus showed the way to the west, and importantly, the ability to sail the oceans

**My mother with my brother, Porter Bird Sinclair, and me, 1915**

and return safely home. Columbus' voyages to the New World were the beginning of Westward Ho…and it continues to this day.

**My mother with Porter and me, 1915**

My father's parents (my staff side) came separately through Canada to Grand Rapids, Michigan, where they became a very prominent family. Alexander Porter Sinclair (Scottish) married Mary Ryan (Irish) and the family henceforth followed the Roman Catholic faith. They had four children, my father being the youngest. The family moved west to Salt Lake City between 1885 and 1890. I don't know the reason or my grandfather's occupation, but they apparently were in the upper strata of non-Mormon society.

My mother's parents (my distaff side) were early settlers in Salt Lake City. Her father, **Major William Harold Bird**, distinguished himself in the Civil War and retired as a Major, using his title the rest of his life. He completed his education and became a lawyer, helping the railroads acquire land for their westward routes. His first wife died, leaving him two children. He then married **Laura Jane Lapish**, who had come west with the last of Brigham Young's handcart companies. Laura's mother broke with the Mormon religion over the issue of educating her daughters. She found an Episcopal school for her daughters, and her family henceforth was Episcopalian. The marriage of Major Bird and Laura Lapish produced six more children. (They all, through the years, worked their ways to the West Coast.)

When these Salt Lake families arrived at the West Coast they were not Discoverers, not Explorers, not Farmers, not Very Early Settlers (except for my grandmother). They were Newcomers. And they were City Folks—educated, "white collar" workers, teachers, businessmen, professionals. My father is an example.

My father, **Frederick William Sinclair**, born in Grand Rapids, Michigan in 1880, quit school after the eighth grade (not uncommon in those years) and went to work in the Utah National Bank of Salt Lake City as a messenger boy. He became successively stenographer, bookkeeper, and general utility man. After several years of service with the Utah National, he accepted a position of trust with another commercial national bank. He remained for several years, then accepted a position

**Well-diapered, 1916**

with the Yampa Smelting Company in the Salt Lake City office. He next became assistant examiner of the Los Angeles Clearing House until he became examiner of the State Banking Department and in charge of the Los Angeles office. This led to being elected cashier of the Redlands Continental National Bank with a collateral position as Vice-President and Cashier of the Redlands Chamber of Commerce.

My mother, **Laura Louise Bird**, was born in Salt Lake City in 1881. After completing her education at the Episcopal school, she was sent to Washington, D.C., to a "finishing school for young ladies" where she was named the cheeriest girl in the class. Her great sense of humor stayed with her the rest of her life, and sustained her through many periods of grief.

In 1904, after a long and happy courtship, my mother and father were married in Salt Lake City.

**My father, Frederick William Sinclair, with Porter and me, 1916**

They had two children: my brother **Porter Bird Sinclair** born in 1910 and me in 1915. The family moved several times to be together near my father's banking assignments.

And now you know why, on August 20, 1915, I was born in Redlands, California.

The westward movement for my family was ending when I appeared

**Top row: my mother, Aunt Kathryn Sinclair, and Aunt Lillian (Sinclair) Gray**

**Front row: Porter, my Grandmother Mary Ryan Sinclair, and me**

on scene. Being a newborn infant, I, of course, do not personally remember any of this. But this heritage would imbue in me a love for the west, its clean and uncrowded cities, wide open spaces, casual living style, etc.

The final move in the Westward Ho was our move to Ocean Park, California, where we met the great Pacific Ocean barrier. I will remember plenty in Scene 2.

# SCENE 2

# EARLY CHILDHOOD—1916-1924 (WAR & REVOLUTION!)

Those early settlers **Back East** didn't have the slightest notion what was **Out West** when they defined the limits of the original thirteen colonies. They charted the northern, eastern, and southern limits but left the western boundaries open. But explorers like Daniel Boone, Lewis & Clark, and maritime explorers like Captain Gray and Captain Vancouver told of the wonders they had seen and the lure of the west drew people like a magnet. The California Gold Rush of 1849, together with the improved means of access, resulted in a flood of newcomers. Our great country was not a mystery any more. It was soon divided into states, railroads joined east and west, federal roads were built, steam vessels and motor cars and stage coach transportation became available.

The wonderful weather of Southern California's coast was also discovered. It had been quite isolated with inclement weather to the north, deserts to the east, unfriendly Mexico to the south, and the Pacific Ocean to the west. Long, sandy beaches with gentle surf, sunny days, and cooling breezes were just what midwesterners yearned for to escape long freezing winters, and inland southwesterners needed to cool off during hot summer months. To meet these needs, beach resorts were the answer. When my father left the banking business in 1916 to become a stock broker, my family moved to Los Angeles. But my parent's marriage was falling apart due to my father's infidelity. After about a year, we moved to Ocean Park, a resort section of the city of Santa Monica. That was in 1918 when I was three years old.

**Ocean Park** consisted of little wooden beach cottages with an occasional two story apartment house of good permanent construction, and a resort hotel or two. We moved into a cottage at 150 Hill Street. I remember this place had dining room chairs upholstered with horse hair that pricked. It is the only place where I recall my father living with us, at least one night anyway, because in the morning he rousted Porter and me out of bed and into the bathroom where we were to drink a full glass of water, and splash some cold water on our chests. I practice the water to this day, but the chest? No way.

A year later, my mother, brother and I moved to 114 Hill Street. It must have been a very old cottage for it still had gas light fixtures, although they were not in use. For light, a bare electric light hung from the ceiling.

Hill Street was a concrete paved walkway, not open to vehicles. It ran up from a boardwalk, where a tram ran alongside the sandy beach, to the train tracks of the Red Car Line. The electric Red Cars connected villages around the area with Los Angeles. Alongside our cottage, there was a narrow, two-lane paved road known as the Speedway. It originally was part of an auto racecourse for some very early road races run out of Los Angeles. They came down San Vicente Boulevard, down Ocean Boulevard, and eventually down this little alley. Barney Oldfield, a famous racer who was the first one to drive a car a mile-a-minute (60 mph), is said to have won on this course, and that the Oldsmobile car was named after him. This is

**Growing up in the Ocean Park community of Santa Monica**

not true. The name Oldsmobile comes from Ransom Eli Olds, a pioneer automobile inventor. And the early car named REO got its name from Ransom's initials.

The Speedway was quiet during the week, for only the affluent could afford an automobile. But on weekends the Los Angeles wealthy came down to show off their cars. (Henry Ford's assembly line of 1908 for mass production of autos would make them available to the middle class and change our lives forever.)

The neighbor behind us had a fence very close to our house. He raised fancy pigeons. Some were beautiful, but their pens smelled awful! Fortunately, we usually had a nice westerly breeze giving us fresh air. But the neighbor also raised chickens. I watched him kill them by chopping off their heads and turning them loose to run around the yard headless! Now <u>there</u> is a memory never to be forgotten!

From our front porch, we could look down Hill Street all the way to the beach and ocean beyond. Rosy sunsets were a common delight. I remember sitting on my mother's lap one evening while she sang me a lullaby. I remember fiddling with a little scar she had on her throat left there by surgery. She didn't mind. Her thoughts were elsewhere.

As I reflect back on this moment, I believe she was singing a lament, praying in song that my father would come home. It didn't happen. Here is the song, "Sweet and Low":

> Sweet and low, sweet and low,
> Wind of the western sea,
> Low, low, breathe and blow,
> Wind of the western sea!
>
> Over the rolling waters go,
> Come from the dying moon and blow,
> Blow him again to me,
>
> While my little one,
> While my pretty one,
> Sleeps.

**With Father**

Some months later, my mother came home from a trip to Los Angeles. I, of course, didn't know then what was going on. Now, I surmise she had been to Divorce Court. She knelt beside her bed and wept and prayed. I put my arm on her shoulder and said, "Don't cry, Mommy. We love you."

## World War I

World War I ranks second only to World War II as the bloodiest war in modern history. It started in July 1914 and ended in November 1918. The Central Powers (Austria-Hungary, Bulgaria, Germany, and Turkey) were out to annex territory and the Allies (France, Italy, Belgium, Russia, British Empire, and many others) were on the defense. The United States tried to remain neutral but American anger turned against the Central Powers with news of German submarines sinking unarmed passenger ships and with stories of German

atrocities against civilians. We entered the War in 1917.

I was a baby and didn't know what was going on until the end of the war and the years that followed. The government's committee on public information sent "Four Minute Men" to promote sale of Liberty Bonds and to support the draft of men between the ages of twenty-one and thirty. My father was exempt, being over the age limit. They also told us to hate Germans and everything German. German food disappeared from restaurant menus. German breeds of dogs were put down!

There was a modern four-apartment "flat" at the top of Hill Street run by an old lady as Germanic in features as a movie character. In front was a large flagpole. She proudly flew the American flag on top and beneath it the French flag. We all laughed at that, but Mrs. Schurer claimed she was from Alsace-Lorraine, a territory that had changed hands many times, and she was French, period!

War news was hard to come by. Europe was a long way off with no means of rapid transit. Long-range voice radio was not yet invented. The newspapers apparently got their reports by wireless telegraph, sent by radio operators dot by dash using Morse code. Area newspapers were the most reliable source available to the public. Home deliveries were rare. Most papers were sold on street corners or by vendors walking among crowds.

Porter decided to earn some money and the distributor gave him some papers to "hawk." I followed him. At the first corner, an adult said it was his corner and to "go away, boys, you bother me." The same at the next corner. Porter decided to work the streets. Newsboys called out, "EXTRA, EXTRA, READ ALL ABOUT IT" (whether it was an extra edition or not). Porter sold a few papers and seemed satisfied, but when we got home he appealed to Mom to "make Davy stay home! He embarrasses me!" Asked, "How does he embarrass you?" Porter said, "He yells too loud!"

I remember the fanfare given the returning "doughboys." Lots of flags. Lots of red, white, and blue bunting. But it was not all joy. There were many amputees. Many were shell-shocked. Many had lasting effects of poisonous gas attacks. For years to come, they would be seen standing on street corners begging, or just plain standing as in a daze. There is no real comparison of World War I with the War in Iraq which has just ended (2003), but to compare casualties is an eye opener. The Great War "to make the world safe for democracy" lasted two years. The major assault by the coalition forces in the Iraq War to rid the "evil empire of Saddam Hussein" lasted two weeks. In World War I, there were 325,018 U.S. casualties: 116,516 dead, 204,002 wounded, and 4,500 prisoners or missing. In the Iraq War, we bemoaned the loss of slightly under 200 Americans. (Since I wrote this, battles with insurgents have continued to cost lives, but the totals will never come close to the losses in the Civil War, World War I, or World War II).

Those exciting days soon passed and we settled into more childhood activities.

We kids prized military articles such as wrap-around puttees, canteens, and helmets. One favorite game was marbles. If you knocked another's marble out of the ring, you got to keep it, if playing "keepers." Likewise, when lagging pop-bottle caps at a goal line, the closest to the line won the other's bottle caps. We also played **mumbly-peg**. The knife used needed two blades at the same end to be set with one straight ahead and the other at right angles. By balancing on the angled blade, one could flip it and make it land in soft sand within a marked area. If it stuck upright, you could claim part of the marked area in accordance with changing rules among the contestants.

We played sand-lot games of softball and soccer with teams made up on the spot. Captains were chosen, usually the best players or the biggest guys (girls watched). There were no "little leagues" or uniforms. To help keep teams identified, we played "shirts versus skins." We played touch football. To settle arguments, we tucked a rag under our belts which had to be snagged to constitute a "touch" (tackle).

We younger boys "helped" our big brothers build coasters and scooters. I will not try to describe them except to mention their wheels. For coasters, they came from outgrown tricycles and wagons. For scooters, we used skates. In those days, the wheels were cast iron. There were no skate shoes; the skate clamped onto the sole of your street shoes. We fixed them to the front and back of the scooter board. These vehicles worked great on the paved Hill Street, but one soon got tired hauling them back uphill.

## Revolution! (Industrial Revolution)

This is a misnomer. It should be called the Industrial Evolution wherein new advances in engineering or science are achieved from earlier forms. It has been going on for eons and will continue as long as man is creative. I remember the expressed fear that new machinery would displace workers causing massive numbers of unemployed which, with loss of wages, would result in poverty, starvation, national depression, etc.

The development of steam engines, internal combustion engines (diesel, gasoline), and the electric motor resulted in rapid changes to modern living.

How did it affect me? In the big picture, the airplane grew from the Wright Bros. 1903 first powered flight to fighter planes in World War I and changed the outcome of the war. Henry Ford's assembly line production methods led to the first use of tanks in warfare. The greatest new weapon for trench fighting in World War I was the machine gun, part of the explosion of ideas that led to an expanded weapons industry.

On the home front, motors of all kinds were everywhere. I saw the first traffic signal in downtown Los Angeles. On a timed switch, a big arm like a railroad signal came out and said in red, "STOP." A few minutes later, the arms switched and a green one said, "GO."

The engine-powered tractor replaced the man behind the plow and happily also replaced the Mule Skinner, the brute driving a team of three big mules harnessed together clearing stumps and doing other heavy work, as the Mule Skinner cursed at them and whipped them mercilessly. A sickening sight.

Porter built a "peanut tube" radio equipped with an earphone headset. Loudspeakers were not yet available. One night, a few of us kids assembled on the front porch to try it out. When Porter found a station, he put the headset into an empty cigar box so we could all hear. Whoops of joy ! We had picked up San Francisco!

This is a good time to bring on stage **Uncle Bill Gray**, **Aunt Lill**, and **Aunt Kathryn**. They were part of the Salt Lake contingent. Bill married my father's sister Lill. Kathryn, an older sister, remained a spinster and lived with the Grays all her adult life, as far as I know.

Bill was also a Bank Examiner. Traveled a lot. Lived pretty high on the hog. Whether they were following my mother or she them, I don't know, but I am sure my mother was thankful they were near. They rented a flat from Madam Schurer.

They had a console Victrola phonograph. The turntable was on top. You placed a needle on the record and the sound traveled down an ever expanding horn to where it sent the sound through a porous screen. When the Grays went out of town, Aunt Lill stuffed her fox fur neck-piece into the mouth of the horn. Clever, huh?

Aunt Lill liked classical music, especially the sopranos, but Uncle Bill liked comedies. I remember one that must have been about a domestic quarrel for the words went: "He went in like a lion…a wild roaring lion. When she got through he came out like a lamb, ba-a-a-a-a! And a great big mug of mocha hit him on the cocoa, followed by some huckleberry jam!"

Also on the cutting edge, the Grays got a radio with loudspeakers when they became available in 1930. We all loved to gather around and listen to Amos and Andy, the Two Black Crows. (We could never have that mocking of blacks now.)

Another revolutionary development was motorizing the merry-go-round. No longer did a poor old nag walk in circles all day to turn it at country fairs. Not only did a motor drive it, the turning also produced the music, obvious as it speeded up and slowed down.

There were three piers spaced about two miles apart. The one at Venice had a big ballroom and not much else. The Ocean Park Pier was filled with fun concessions like shooting the wooden ducks as they traveled across. There were live monkeys dressed like jockeys riding on miniature horses around a ring. Bets were made on which would win by stopping closest to the goal. Uncle Bill loved this one because the Japanese concessionaire, when it stopped on #4, would call out, "Numba whore!"

The third pier was at Santa Monica, the farthest north, and used primarily for fishing.

Not having children, Uncle Bill enjoyed taking me to the Ocean Park Pier for a ride on the merry-go-round. On one occasion, when the ride ended, I got off and there was no Uncle Bill. I looked all around and not seeing him anywhere, I just walked home. Shortly, he showed up and was *frantic*. As it turns out, the merry-go-round stopped with me at the opposite side from where he put me on. When he looked for me, all he could see was a railing and beyond it a twenty-foot drop into the ocean!!

The neighborhood was going downhill from a nice beach village to a lower-middle-class bedroom community for Los Angeles. It was predominately white with no thought of segregation. I remember only one black family. They engaged in truck farming and ran produce counters in grocery stores. Their boy played with us. There were several Japanese families. Two Japanese boys went through the Boy Scout programs with my brother and me. Both served honorably in World War II.

Although we had never heard of drugs or gangs as we now know them, there was a tough element and it was growing. My mother knew it was time to find a better community in which to raise her sons. One Halloween made it clear when a bunch of older boys pulled a section of the boardwalk out of alignment and shut down the beach tram. Others hoisted a neighbor's gate up a telephone pole and left it there. Even worse, kids (us little ones included) sneaked into residents' properties and, if they hadn't taken in their garbage can, would dump the garbage onto their porch!

**Santa Monica** was opening new tracts of land north of Montana Avenue, plowing under wheat fields. Mom decided to have a home built one block north of Montana. (I have no idea the source of the money, although I believe it had to come from Grandma and my mother's sister Grace.) I can remember pouring over books of available house plans and Mom selecting one to be among the first to be built on Eleventh Street.

I will shift now to Scene 3 and the activity around 638 Eleventh Street, Santa Monica, California.

# SCENE 3

## PRE-TEENS—1924-1927 (SIX-THIRTY-EIGHT)

The year was 1924. Our newly built home sat lonesome, facing east at 638 Eleventh Street, just one-half block north of Montana Avenue, a major street with bus service. The land was recently cleared of wheat fields and zoned for single family dwellings. Vacant lots all around. No landscaping. But ready for my mother, my brother Porter, and me to move in.

The area south of Montana was zoned for multi-family dwellings. Happily, Uncle Bill with my aunts Lill and Kathryn rented an apartment just one half block south of Montana and also on Eleventh Street.

**Our home after my parents' divorce—638 Eleventh Street, Santa Monica**

Let's walk through the house now and check the floor plan. The front door opens directly into the living room. At the left end is a woodburning fireplace. To the right is a nice-sized dining room with a double-hinged door to the kitchen. Across from the front door, we enter a hallway. On the left is a bedroom that will be my mom's. Opposite the bedroom is an entrance to the kitchen.

At the end of the hall is the only bathroom. It has a lavatory, a toilet (of course), and a bathtub (but no shower—unheard of). To the left facing down the hall is a corner bedroom for Porter and me. To the right, another corner bedroom for Grandmother and/or Aunt Grace. We called it "Grandma's room."

Off the kitchen was a service porch for the laundry tub, ice box, and most importantly, another toilet (just a tiny closet without other facilities).

The driveway ran down the north side to the back of the lot where there was a double garage, but only one car door to the driveway. Two, however, to the alley.

So much for the floor plan.

## Furnishing 638

Grandmother must have sold that big house in Salt Lake. I imagine that it went for a tidy sum, and that is where the financing came from. When the van of furniture arrived, it was like unloading a museum. For the living room, there came a rosewood piano and a four-foot-round rosewood table for a lamp and reading material. A settee. Ornate chairs that rocked on their own bases, with heavily embossed leather seats and backs. And one roman-style chair with a half-round seat. (If you put an unwanted visitor in it, he wouldn't stay long!)

The dining room table was of walnut and, in addition to eight chairs, had leafs enough to extend it into the living room! At the far end of the dining room was a sideboard with a white marble counter. Above the counter was a little cabinet just right for a bottle of bootleg liquor. One time when no one was around I made myself a whiskey sour! It tasted darn good, too!

But the big problem was the book cabinet which came in three parts and completely covered one wall. It stood so high that a top railing had to be removed to fit under the ceiling.

Mother's room had a full-size bed. Porter and I had twins. But you should see what we squeezed into Grandma's room—a huge double bed with a bird's egg veneer on a six-foot headboard and a matching armoire.

The kitchen was modern with a mixing water faucet, an ironing board built into the wall, a breakfast table, and a city-gas stove. Disposals were not yet invented. There also was a cupboard to keep perishables cool. The bottom was open through a grid to the cool air under the house.

Santa Monica drinking water came from artesian wells and tasted awful. We had Arrowhead bottled water delivered. We left the backdoor unlocked for the delivery man and also for the iceman who carried blocks on his back from the wagon to the ice box. The milkman left his bottles on the porch outside and didn't go inside.

A story circulated about a young woman who was stripped for her bath when she remembered the soap was in the service porch. She heard what she thought was the milkman and who she knew would not enter the service porch so she walked right in stark naked. And there was the iceman! In her shock she said, "Oh, sorry, I thought you were the milkman!"

**The Bird sisters: Grace, Laura, and Fanny**

Although the Industrial Revolution was catching up with us, delivery wagons were still pulled, in many cases, by horses. Produce, milk, and ice I remember. For ice delivery, a card marked for different sizes was displayed in the front window. The driver would split with an axe the twenty-five-pound or fifty-pound block from a one-hundred-pound block, put it on his back over a leather drip back pad, and take it into the house. We kids would raid the wagon for chips of ice to suck on.

Garbage wagons were also pulled by tired old nags. Raw garbage from outside GI cans was dumped into the open back of the wagon and hauled away, flies, stench, and all! We had a song that went, "My old man's a garbage man. What the heck is your old man?"

## Landscaping

My mother took on the job of landscaping with enthusiasm. She put on old clothes (even pants) and a big straw hat. She would be down on hands and knees and when a little truck loaded with Japanese gardeners drove by, they would all smile broadly and wave! She liked that.

First, she had a curved walk put in from the front porch to the corner nearest Montana Avenue. Then, a grass lawn which typically was green most winters and brown every summer. But shrubs and flowers were her domain. The house was surrounded by shrubs and the backyard filled with flowers. Near the center of the yard she planted an avocado tree. I visited years later and it was <u>huge</u>, but never had fruit. My uncle Bill said it was an avocado and we should have also planted an avocado to pollinate it.

Porter had acquired an old Chevy which had been scrapped. I don't know the details, but I never saw the engine run. He parked it near the garage. To hide it from view, my mother planted a large shrub with a name I will never forget:

*Pittosporum rhombifolium.* How can anyone forget a name like that?

I learned a lot from that old car. We took the head off and tried to grind the valves. We took the drip pan off and removed connecting rods and pistons. I learned a little about the drip fuel system and the function of a spark plug. Schools had metal shop, wood shop, printing, but no auto shop.

My, how times have changed. My mother was always very religious. When we lived in Ocean Park, she enrolled us in the **Sunday School** of the Episcopal Church, which was located among the sand dunes in Venice, just across the line from Ocean Park and within walking distance. Before long, she was Superintendent. She continued this duty for a while after we moved to Santa Monica. But from there, we had to take the bus to church.

The bus route was on Montana Avenue. The driver stopped the bus at the nearest corner to where someone hailed it. It was like a paddy wagon! You boarded at the front. There was a bench seat on each side and an exit door at the rear. One Sunday, as Mother stepped aboard, she realized her Sunday School notes were still at home. She exclaimed, "Oh, dear. What can I do? The next bus will make me an hour late." The driver asked, "Where do you live?" She replied, "Just a half a block up this street." "No problem. Take a seat, lady." And, with that, he turned the corner and drove to our house and right up the driveway while Mom dashed in and retrieved her notes. And then back on Montana and off to the church on time!

## Great Depression

The Great Depression is usually dated from 1929 when the banks crashed. But we could feel it coming on. In our case, my father was unable to keep up alimony payments to my mother. One way I could help out was to raise rabbits for food. With help from Porter, we constructed a rabbit hutch. I had two or three pair. It was an eye opener for me to see the newborn babies and a responsibility to provide the necessary care. When they were big enough, I took them to our local butcher and he dressed them down for our dinner table!

**Raising rabbits during the Great Depression**

To help survive the Great Depression, my mother's sister Fannie and the Sterling family, consisting of husband Edward, daughter Virginia, and son Scott, moved in with us. Remember, our house had three bedrooms and <u>one</u> bathroom. To accommodate the overflow, my brother and I slept in a double-fly wall tent under a eucalyptus tree at the back of the yard, on a full-sized bed that completely filled it. My cousin, Scott, set up a cot in the garage amongst his family's possessions. Port-a-potties were unknown but we had "thunder mugs" just in case.

This crowd generated a lot of dirty dishes, for we couldn't afford paper plates. Dishwashing machines had not yet been invented, so Porter and I formed one of the dishwashing teams. To sweeten the chores, we sang songs of all kinds with campfire songs prevailing. When a new song would surface, Porter would say, "That's a song I almost forgot to remember!" Years later, I taped a collection of those songs and titled the tape "**Songs I Almost Forgot to Remember**."

When the Bird family home in Salt Lake City was sold, my grandmother went to Bakersfield, California, to share an apartment with her daughter, my aunt Grace. But the summer heat with no air conditioning was debilitating. They came to cool Santa Monica for a respite at 638, where they had a "vested interest." Where did they sleep? <u>Don't ask</u>!

# SCENE 4

## VISITATIONS—1924-1929 (BOBBIE)

I am going to *flash back* to 1924 when my mother, Porter, and I moved to our new home in Santa Monica. So many memorable events occurred in the next ten years that I could never put them in chronological order. So I will do them by category. The first one being **movies**.

Living on the edge of Hollywood, it follows that we were pretty much up to date on what was being offered to the public. It is amazing the changes that have occurred during my life.

I learned from a new friend that the **Criterion Theater** had a Saturday afternoon movie for kids. I got to go several times. It was great! First, they had a song-fest with the lyrics on the screen and the "bouncing ball" leading the audience through the words. Then, they raffled off some cheap china or toy using ticket stubs for numbers, no extra cost. Then, the black-and-white silent "flicker" came on with captions and live organ accompaniment.

The story was always exciting with the bad guys in black hats and the good guys in white hats. Or it might be Cowboys versus Indians. Or a snarling villain abducting the beautiful blonde heroine. The organists had scores of mood music to follow the action. The film always ended with the hero and villain in combat, often on the edge of a cliff, with one about to die. Hence the expression "cliffhanger."

"You must come next week to see what happened!"

We occasionally saw filming in the open with the cameraman actually cranking the camera and the property men adjusting big silver or gold reflective screens to get just the proper lighting effect.

I remember the first movie with sound. It was from a loud speaker behind the screen playing a sound effect record. It was called Movietone. And the first movie in color was called Kodachrome.

Years later, when there were talking movies, I got to go to Hollywood about once a year to see a premiere film in **Grauman's Egyptian Theater** (the predecessor of the famous Chinese Theater where famous movie stars have their hand prints imbedded in the cement entrance walk). The architecture included little gift shops in the atrium and a walkway on the roof with a guard in costume, turban, rifle, etc., pacing back and forth. What a thrill! On Saturdays, movie theaters often ran love stories for the ladies featuring a matinee idol like Nelson Eddie. I remember *Orange Blossom Time* only because they sent orange blossom perfume through the ventilator system!

**Pageants**. Before a premiere showing, there would be a short pageant on stage related to the story. One elaborate one I remember preceded the film *Long Trail*, an exciting film about the covered wagons bringing new settlers west.

When the curtain opened, there was a mountain in the background and miniature wagons were coming into sight. As the train of wagons disappeared, medium-sized wagons switched back across the stage coming closer. Finally, a full-size Conestoga wagon appeared on stage accompanied by a chorus of settlers in full voice.

I wonder if they sang "Sweet Betsy from Pike." I like the fourth verse, which goes:

> Out on the prairie one bright starry night,
> They broke out the whiskey and Betsy got tight.
> She sang and she shouted and danced o'er the plain,
> And showed her bare arse to the whole wagon train.

*The Iron Horse* movie was about the joining of the Union Pacific and Central Pacific at Promontory Summit, Utah. (Family lore has it that my grandmother, as a little girl, sat on a nearby fence and watched the "Driving of the Golden Spike" ceremony.)

Full-sized locomotives puffed on stage cowcatcher-to-cowcatcher, a chorus dressed as coolies accompanied the Central Pacific engine, and a tough-looking gang of Irish terriers accompanied the Union Pacific. Beautiful colors. Very dramatic. Over the recently completed telegraph line they flashed the message: "The last rail laid…The last spike driven…The Pacific Railroad is completed!"

*Wings*—there was no pageant before this movie but there was a breathtaking opening. When the curtain parted, the silent film was projected on a rather small square screen. The action and captions set the scene as World War I, with a squadron of fighter airplanes preparing for action. This would be the first war for airplanes and even seeing an aircraft take off on the screen was a thrill. Suddenly, the sound went to roaring engines and, as the planes took off, the curtain was drawn wider to a full, huge, square screen. (Widescreens as we know them didn't exist.) One felt as though being sucked right along with the planes!

**Sunday Visitations**. My father began exercising his visitation rights under the terms of the divorce shortly after we moved to Santa Monica. On Sundays, he would drive down from Los Angeles in his Marmon touring car. He would visit in private with my mother (we never heard an uncivilized word between them) and then he would take Porter and me to the beach near the Santa Monica Pier. At a little coffee shop, he would have a cup of Maxwell House Coffee ("good to the last drop") and we would have something to eat and drink. Most of these visits were boring to me for the conversation was usually over my head, and I would rather have been out playing with my friends. One thing of interest, though, was that we were at "Muscle Beach," where professional wrestlers practiced in an outdoor ring and weightlifters showed off their muscles.

We sometimes went for a sightseeing ride. A favorite was to go up the coast road as far as we could. The limit was at Point Dume where the road was blocked by Mrs. May K. Rindge, who owned the Rancho Topanga Malibu Sequit, a former Spanish Land Grant. She had mounted rangers keeping trespassers off her property because she used the beach at night for bootleggers to bring illegal liquor ashore in violation of the National Prohibition Act (1919).

There were two special Sunday trips I will never forget.

One Sunday, after a stormy cold front passed through the area, we drove to Mount Baldy, the tallest peak in the range just east of Los Angeles. We drove to where there were fields of *snow.* This was my first experience with snow. Yes, Porter and I had a snow fight. And, yes, a couple of snowballs "accidentally" hit my dad!

The other special Sunday trip was to Clover Field Airport in Santa Monica, the home of Douglas Aircraft. We had been there before because it was exciting to watch the private little biplanes as pilots practiced takeoffs and landings. The planes had tail skids and no brakes. Ground crewmen rushed out and grabbed a wing to spin the aircraft to a stop. The <u>special event</u> one Sunday was to be at the field to watch two Army Air Service planes land, completing the first-ever around-the-world flight!! (The Army Air Service became the Army Air Corps and now the U.S. Air Force.) The landing gear wheels were replaced by floats for some open water areas they crossed. Four aircraft had started. Just the two we saw finished. They made the 26,345-mile flight in 175 days. Their total flying time was 363 hours. It was great to witness history being made!

**Saturday Visitations**. We didn't have visitations every week, and I don't know what pattern they had, if any. But the Saturday trips were usually to downtown Los Angeles starting at my father's office. Porter and I would take the Red Car from Santa Monica. My father would be waiting at the designated stop and take us directly to his office. After meeting the staff, we would be joined by two or three men and have lunch at the Piggly Wiggly Restaurant. It was upscale. The men catered to Porter and me, and that made it a very pleasant experience.

We three left the others and went to the Orpheum Theater for a top-notch variety show. I can remember some of the acts to this day. There were acrobats and jugglers. Crooners who sang through megaphones (no microphones yet). A man named Lewis (not Jerry) wore a top hat and carried a gold-tipped swagger stick as he sang "Me and My Shadow" while strutting with style and did a little tricky step and twirled the hat and stick. There were lovers "Strolling through the Park One Day…" A world-class banjo player. Lots of tap and soft shoe dancers. Teams of hoofers produced Bing Crosby, Bob Hope, and many others who became motion movie stars. Variety show theaters began their decline when sound pictures came to the screen in 1927.

On one Saturday trip to Los Angeles, Porter and I were met as usual, but we spotted our father with a dog on a leash. What's up? (Our mother never spilled the beans. It was a complete surprise.) Yes, the dog was for us! It was a fox terrier, a year-and-a-half old. Housebroken. His name was **Bobbie**. His owner had to sell him due to a business transfer Back East. The year was probably 1925 when I was ten years old. He was my pal up until I left for the Academy in 1935.

**Bobbie demonstrating his athleticism**

Bobbie was as smart as a fox, but not purebred. We thought he had bulldog blood in him for his body was sturdy and his face rounded by strong jaw muscles. His tendency to roam suggests beagle blood. We found out years later that he had a regular early morning route to go begging at backdoors of two neighbors and to the local butcher shop a block down Montana Avenue. When we children were in school and all was quiet he went to the plumber's shop and took a nap in the display window. Two or three times, he stayed out all night. We decided he must have had a girlfriend. That was the "private life" of Bobbie.

There were no leash laws in those days. We had four loose dogs on our block, including Bobbie. A big strong airedale lived at the north end of Eleventh Street. Directly across from us was a big, sleek, tan great dane named Lucky. And down our side halfway to Montana was a large chow. It stayed home to guard its property, but the airedale came down occasionally for a romp around the lawn with Bobbie. Bobbie crossed over to

**At Boy Scout camp**

**Expert beggar**

Lucky's front lawn where they raced around in circles. It was hilarious to see that big floppy dog galloping after that little bullet. One paw tag would send Bobbie sprawling.

One day Bobbie strayed onto the chow's lawn. The chow grabbed him in the back of his neck and nearly killed him. As though told of this atrocity, the airedale came down and thrashed the chow. He couldn't hurt him with that heavy coat of hair, but it settled the score!

I played pretty roughly with Bobbie. He would mouth my hand until it raised welts, but he never bit hard unless I started to hurt him. I had a chunk of rubber tire tread I would hold about shoulder height. He would jump up and grab it and I would swing him in a circle. He would hang on until I gave up.

When Bobbie wanted something he would make eye-contact or sit up. Either was very persuasive. If there was a social gathering in the house, he would be the center of attention. If a lady was having a bite of cake with her tea and was careless how she held it—zip—it would be snatched out of her hand.

One of the funniest things was when he wanted attention and his brown eyes and sit-ups didn't work. He would pick out a lady, let's say, for his victim. He would put his front paws on her thigh and pump as fast and hard as he could. The choice was give in or get bruised.

Bobbie got his exercise chasing cars down our street. There weren't very many, and slowing for the Montana stop, they probably weren't going more than about 15 mph. He would charge out with a vengeance and bark with his mouth about six inches from the right front wheel. The driver not being able to see him would slow even more. We would be screaming "NO! NO! BOBBIE!" Lucky, Bobbie's great dane pal would think chasing was the thing to do and would join in on the other side, galloping and woofing into the driver's face. With the cars drawn to a halt, the dogs would peel off happily wagging their tails!

Porter got permission from the Boy Scout Camp Director to have Bobbie in camp with us one summer. The boys loved him. And he never missed morning or evening colors for which we Scouts lined up on the parade grounds. More often than not, he performed the "male dog salute" on the flag pole!!

My horizons are going to be geographically expanded to beyond Southern California in Scene 5. I hope you will join me.

**Bobbie with Porter and me**

# SCENE 5

## EXPANDING HORIZONS—1925-1928 (AUTO-TOURING)

Californians <u>love</u> their autos. When the Industrial Revolution caught up to the auto industry, assembly line production of cars reduced the price so that almost every family could afford one. Maybe not a new one, but cars only lasted six years and after that they were jalopies which the young and the poor kept running somehow.

Owners complained about registration fees, fuel taxes, road conditions, property tax, etc. But not even high fuel cost would stop them commuting one to a car. There are reasons cars are so important in California. Urban spread is one. That, in turn, makes mass public transportation lacking. And there are places to go that make California special—the mountains, the deserts, the beaches, the ski slopes, wonderful places for recreation not easily available without a car. And those places are partly why we are here in this Golden State.

My father had a driving experience that seems would have turned him off instead of on to touring by car. It was from Portland to Los Angeles in 1913. There were two other men, one of whom owned the car. It took them from September 2 to September 15. The roads were sometimes just the width of a car. The roads had what was called a crown for drainage, meaning higher in the center than at the sides. There was little auto traffic, but they had to share the road with teams of horses. There were differences of opinions as to whether cars or horses should have the outside on curves! The roads were rutted dirt and slippery when wet from rain. My father and friends slid off into a ditch. Here is the newspaper report:

"Where we went over, there is a drop of 600 to 800 feet, and had it not been for a small tree which caught the machine on the first roll, leaving us upside down fourteen feet below the road, we would have surely gone to the bottom. We were going about seven miles per hour, but the spill was so quick we couldn't even jump. None of us was even bruised, and after we had brought block and tackle from Drain, sixteen men worked for four hours to haul the car up the grade. Even with this extreme strain on the axles, the car was pulled up without the slightest injury, and ten minutes later we were on our way rejoicing!" The report went on to say "Among the many pleasant features of our run down to Los Angeles, one that occasioned genuine satisfaction, was the unfailing courtesy we received at the hands of the people living along the road, and especially those we met or passed driving teams en route. Everyone we met had a greeting for us, and on the occasion of the spill near Drain, Oregon, the men who came to help us back on the road turned to with a willing hand, and declined any remuneration whatever for their services."

*My, how times have changed!*

## Big Bear Lake, 1925

When I was ten years old and brother Porter was fourteen-and-a-half, our father asked, "How would you like a drive up to Big Bear Lake where we can spend the night in a real log cabin?" Porter said, "That would be keen!" I said, "Neat!" (or words to that effect). Dad said he would see if it was okay with our mother.

By this time, our father had remarried. He married a woman named Lydia Browning, known to everyone as Brownie (who may have been the third party in the divorce). I am sure my mother made it *perfectly clear* to my father that Brownie was not to accompany us on <u>any</u> overnight trip. And my mother made it *perfectly clear* to Porter and me that we could call her Brownie, because she was our father's wife and <u>not our mother</u>.

**The day's catch**

And so the trip was laid on. This was my first time "out of the box." I got an eyeful of variable terrain from bolder strewn hills to barren desert to orange groves and a fast pass through Redlands, where I was born. From there, we took the thirty-mile mountain road to Big Bear Lake.

Big Bear was a ski resort. To enter the road in winter, you must have tire chains. But we were entering in late summer and during the forest fire season. We were required to have a shovel or pickaxe, water, and food, as we were subject to being ordered to fight a forest fire! I guess my dad knew this, for we were equipped.

There were no fires when we were there, but there had been thunderstorms and the rutted, slimy, rocky, one-lane road must have brought memories back to my dad.

The one lane served two-way traffic, what little there was. The rule was that cars going up hill must make way for a downhill car to pass. That was easier said than done. Because of the heavy weekend traffic, we had to join an escorted convoy led by a man on a motorcycle. Because the flagmen didn't have radios like they do today, the last car carried a flag which, when it reached the other end, meant the road was clear for the waiting convoy to start their run.

I don't remember the cabin. I do remember renting a rowboat, but I don't think we tried fishing. And I remember visiting the vacation cabin of a friend that had a wonderful view of the lake, and in the living room there was a balcony or mezzanine for sleeping. And I remember the big evergreen trees and the sweet smell of the pines.

So much for the Big Bear Lake trip.

## The Great Northwest (a tragic ending), 1926

With Porter away to Boy Scout camp, it was an opportunity for my mother and my aunt Grace to visit their younger brother, Scott Elliot Bird, in Seattle. They would have to take me with them, but I was eager to go. The three of us boarded the overnight express train in Los Angeles. We were assigned to a Pullman car which had double-tiered berths by night converted to seats by day. Heavy curtains provided privacy. The wash basins and toilets (that dumped onto the tracks) were located at the ends of the cars. One wore a "Pullman robe" for modesty if nature called in the middle of the night.

A parody song comes to mind:

> Passengers will please refrain from flushing toilets while the train is
> standing in the station, I love you!
> When the train is in the station, we encourage constipation,
> California skies are always blue!

Sleeping was a little restless as the car jerked back and forth and the wheels clickety-clacked endlessly at the rail seams. But there was a diner, and when the black porter (sorry big brother) in the white jacket and French Foreign Legion cap sounded his gong, we were served a nice breakfast.

When we arrived at the San Francisco railhead, the engine was dismissed and the cars were hauled onto a barge and floated across the bay to the Richmond railhead, where two engines coupled on to take us through the mountains to Seattle.

Uncle Scott met us and showed us the way to his home on Bainbridge Island. There I met my cousins Bonnie (older), Bill (my age), and Scott (much younger).

We stayed about a week during which they had a big Pirate Day Party for all the local kids. When not doing that, we kids straddled logs and paddled around until our legs froze in that Puget Sound ice water. And special fun was getting inside large shipping cartons and rolling down the slope of their lawn!

Uncle Scott owned the Dodge agency. Aunt Grace had arranged to purchase the car he selected for her, which was a small four-door sedan. Autos in those days all were stick-shift drive (automatic transmissions were twenty-five years off). But not all cars followed the same pattern for shifting gears. The Dodge was different than the cars Grace had driven, but she caught on quickly and when our week was up was ready to drive us all the way to Santa Monica.

I draw a complete blank as to how far we went in a day, what we did for meals, or where we slept. But I do remember we stopped at a restaurant in a small town that had angle parking to the curb. When Grace engaged the clutch we leaped forward instead of back. The brakes worked <u>fine</u>—we stopped about three feet from the restaurant's big glass window!

Somewhere on about the third day, my mother and I were riding in the backseat when we encountered construction work that muddied the road. We were going very slowly when the car started skidding. It did a one-eighty and went broadside into a ditch. The car rolled onto its side but not all the way over. It was kind of like slow motion. My mother hugged me to protect me. It was frightening to Mom and Grace, but to me just like rolling down the lawn in those shipping crates.

There were some bruises but no broken bones. I don't remember how we got home. The *tragic ending*, if true, is the belief that my mother's left breast got badly bruised protecting me, which led to breast cancer from which she suffered for some eleven years.

Reprise: In Scene 3, I said the Sterling family was welcomed into our home to help them survive the Great Depression. While that is true, we see now that there was an even more compelling reason—for my aunt Fannie to nurse my mother back to health. While that was impossible, Fannie held our two families together under most trying conditions. She was an angel.

### Santa Catalina Island, 1927

The following summer, Porter was made a member of the staff at the Boy Scout camp located at Emerald Bay, Catalina Island. He was in charge of the Handicraft Lodge and of the little Snack Window that sold candy bars after the evening meal.

**My father, 1927**

As a popular song said, "Twenty-six miles across the sea, Santa Catalina is a-waitin' for me!" It has charm with ocean fresh air, sparkling clear water, warm sunshine, and unspoiled hills. It has a romantic history of Indian tribes, Spanish explorers, silver miners, goat hunters, the ocean cruise to get there, and as a place for lovers. And now for Dad and me to see Porter in camp was an opportunity not to be missed.

We drove to the Catalina Steamship terminal in Wilmington where we embarked for the three-hour passage to Avalon, the only city on Catalina. The ship was the SS *Catalina*, known by some as "the big white ship." It had a dance floor and a jazz band in the main hold, which put the passengers in holiday spirits (and offered opportunities to make pick-ups for further pursuit ashore!).

I don't remember where Dad and I spent the night, but we had supper at John's Café. We had no idea how we were going to get to the camp at the other end of the twenty-two-mile island, but Dad was good at asking questions. At John's, we learned that the Camp Director was in town buying supplies and would be going to the camp in the morning, and he always ate breakfast at John's. He would be traveling in the camp boat named *Mischief*, a retired racing sloop.

**My dad and I took the ferry to Santa Catalina to visit the Scout camp that Porter was attending, 1927**

We met the Director at breakfast. He was the Crescent Bay Council Executive Officer Bob Hill. A wonderful man. We all loved him and called him "Uncle Bob." I served under him for several years when I was on the camp staff. His confidence in us boys made us into reliable men. There is a saying that "There is no greater incentive to be trustworthy than to be trusted." He worked that on us.

We knew he trusted us, and it paid off.

The camp was full, but there was no place else to go, so my dad and I were assigned to the first-aid tent which was located at the edge of the parade ground! We visited the Isthmus and hiked across to Cat Harbor, which the movies had made into a tropical jungle village with fake trees, etc. A Chinese junk named *Ning Po*, believed to have been a slave ship, was left at anchor to rot away. Her hull was seen slowly disappearing over the next half century. We probably took a small passenger vessel named *Betty O* from the Isthmus back to Avalon to catch the steamer back to Wilmington. I have a picture of me on her deck dressed like for golf with a big cap and "plus four" pants.

It was a trip that broadened my horizons both figuratively and literally.

Porter?? Oh, you mean Porter, my big brother? We found him healthy and happy, and he wore the deepest tan I had ever seen on him. Except his knees were sunburned badly. He pinned handkerchiefs to his shorts to shade them. Sunscreen cremes? Never heard of them. Coco butter made you smell good as you simmered in the sun.

## June Lake (Bodie), 1928

This trip would be the longest one that Porter and I would make with our father, and the most interesting due to the varied terrain, camping and fishing activities, and the Wild West history of the region. We traveled in Dad's Marmon touring car, four-door, open

**My father's Marmon, which we took on auto touring trips**

except for fabric roof. Loaded for camping with a big frying pan and pot for cooking. Food, which included a side of bacon, unsliced. I don't remember what else. These went into the trunk attached to the rear of the car body. On the running board there was a kit of three five-gallon cans colored red, white, and blue. Red gasoline, white water, blue oil. Blankets, clothing, and miscellaneous items went mostly in the backseat. At June Lake, we stayed in a little rustic log cabin. The rental included fishing gear and a rowboat.

It was over 300 miles from Santa Monica to June Lake and it meant crossing a long stretch of the Mojave Desert. With a maximum speed of 45 mph, and often much less, that is a long day! Air conditioning was unheard of. The best you could do was holding a hand out to scoop the wind towards your face. But there was another way to survive the heat, one we used—we got a late afternoon start and drove in the cool of the evening, slept on the open desert sand, and traveled on early in the morning.

There was a problem to that method, however: desert animals! Little kangaroo rats hopped over us all night. To guard against snakes, we used the tow rope to encircle us for it is said a snake will not cross a scratchy line.

The main activity at June Lake, besides "survival," was trolling from the rowboat. I remember that we did catch a few fish but nothing spectacular, except that I caught the biggest one right in the reeds as we approached the end of our row.

June Lake is located on the eastern side of the Sierra Nevada range. To get there, we had driven up Owens Valley to the east of Sequoia, Kings Canyon, and Yosemite national parks. It is beautiful, so from June Lake we made an all day loop to enjoy it in more depth.

**Convict Lake**. It got its name from the 1871 Nevada State Penitentiary break when twenty-nine outlaws escaped and fled 250 miles from Carson City to the mountains. Along their route they killed anyone who got in their way. Convict Lake is open to the south, but the north end is surrounded by a vertical wall of rock cliffs. There the outlaws were cornered by a posse. Two posse members were killed. Two of the convicts were hanged. We saw what is said to be the "Hangin' Tree."

**Ghost Town, Bodie, California**. The Wild, Wild West wouldn't have been so wild if it weren't for gold mining camps. The beckoning call "Thar's Gold in Them Thar Hills" echoed throughout our nation, and drew thousands of prospectors in a rush for gold. In the 1800s, they traveled on foot, on horseback, and even to the isthmus of Panama by windjammer, where they portaged across for primitive west coast steamers to take them to California.

**Bodie Ghost Town, 1928**

Hardened by pick and shovel labor and harsh weather living, the men became tough and daring. The scarcity of supply support led to claim jumping, horse stealing, cattle rustling, robberies, stagecoach holdups, street fights, tavern brawls, and shootouts. Killings occurred with monotonous regularity. The fire bell, which tolled the ages of the deceased when they were buried, rang often and long.

The town became known more for its wild living than for its big gold resources. Every other building on the mile long main street was a saloon. Seven breweries were working day and night. The whiskey was brought in by horse carriages, one hundred barrels at a time.

Bodie became a boom town in 1877 and by 1879 boasted a population of about ten thousand with two thousand buildings, and was second to none for wickedness, bad men, and the worst climate out-of-doors. One little girl, whose family was taking her to the remote and infamous town, wrote in her diary: "Good-bye God, I'm going to Bodie."

Bodie is located at the end of a twenty-five-mile unimproved road, so rough and rutted we would call it a "jeep trail." The road was left that way through the years to discourage visitors. When we visited, the buildings were mostly intact. It looked like the people had just left, taking their possessions but leaving their trash. It has been a State Historic Park since 1962, managed in a state of "arrested decay"!

This fabulous trip would be the last for Porter and me with our father. But automobiles have become a part of our lives, as you will see in later Scenes.

**With Porter on our visit to June Lake, 1928**

# SCENE 6

## THE GREAT DEPRESSION—1928-1930

The global economic depression is dated from the crash of the stock and bond market and bank failures in 1929, and lasted until the beginning of World War II. It was the worst depression ever, and the government was not prepared to handle it. It was a failure of our capitalistic system. Plutocrats saw their investment portfolios wiped out. Wageworkers lost their hard earned savings. In desperation, people would follow any man who promised change—the communist, the socialist, the fascist, or the dictator. When faced with starvation, Security takes priority over Freedom in many nations. Not so in America. Our Constitution guarantees us Freedom, and we will fight for it even at the expense of Security.

Those of you who did not live through the hardships of the Great Depression are tired of hearing about it, for it seems unreal in our land of plenty. It affected everyone from rich to poor, some so severely they were uprooted from their homes in search of means of survival. Others, like ourselves, had only to be thrifty and live frugally. We always had food on the table, although the only income source I know of was my grandmother's Civil War pension and my aunt Grace's salary as Principal of Bakersfield High School and Dean of the Junior College. We learned to repair things. It was not a throw-away society like now. Porter and I had a "growing up" agenda through Scouting which kept us busy and happy. But the morale of our nation was shattered. The radio music-makers used the newly available loudspeakers to cheer us with uplifting songs such as:

> I can't give you anything but love, Baby.
> That's the only thing I've plenty of, Baby!
> Oh, I ain't got plenty of money
> but we'll travel along, singing this song,

Side by side!

Keep your sunny side up, up!
Hide the side that gets blue.
Be like two fried eggs—keep your sunny side up!

I've got plenty of nuthin', and nuthin's plenty for me.
I got no car, got no mule, got no misery.
Once I built a railroad. Made it run,
Brother can you spare a dime?

President Herbert Hoover took the rap because he was so conservative and didn't take federal relief action fast or extensively enough. This song was sung about his approach to stimulating the economy:

Mr. Herbert Hoover
Says that now's the time to buy,
So let's have another cup of coffee,
And let's have another piece of pie!

A hobo, by definition, is a wandering worker or tramp. During the Great Depression, thousands of men, young and old, left home seeking work in the fields or the cities. They were not bad men but they were desperate. They went to backdoors of village homes asking for food. They established a code of marks to let the next hobo know if the house was good for a handout. We had hobo marks on the back of our fence in the alley. Sure enough, my mom gave handouts of any food we had left over from a meal.

**My mother during her long battle with breast cancer**

When my cousin Scott lived in Oregon, he met a young man his age who planned to run away from home. Not believing him, Scott told him he was headed with the Sterling family to Santa Monica to stay with the Sinclairs. One day, the young man showed up at our house. He was a hobo! My aunt Fannie took him in with my mother's permission, fed him, had him bathe, and washed his clothes. She asked why he was running away. His answer was that he was adopted and didn't want to be a burden to the family as they had too many mouths of their own to feed. He left. We never heard of him again.

Porter graduated from high school in 1928. He was a good student and accepted into UCLA immediately. UCLA was located in downtown Los Angeles at the time. Porter would need a car to commute. He found an old **Model T Ford** (the car that made Henry Ford and his assembly line famous. At peak production, Ford could turn out, sans body, a Model T in ninety-three minutes!). Porter paid $25 for an old, well worn one. Two years later, UCLA moved to its new campus in West Los Angeles. Wheat fields were converted into a planned college complex that included duplex fraternity houses scattered to the west of campus and lovely single sorority houses for the women, all in a row on one side of a nice curved street to the east. By this time, Porter had saved money from a variety of jobs and upgraded from the Model T to the much better **Model A Ford**…just what he needed for the summer job described below. This was a pretty good car. I have no idea how much he paid or how he afforded it. Right away, he equipped it with "balloon tires." He gave the Model T to me. I'll report on that later.

Dust Bowl was the name applied to a part of the Great Plains region of the southwestern United States including about half of Kansas and half of Oklahoma. Severe dust storms in the early 1930s blew away topsoil making farming impossible. Many families were forced to leave. California sounded very inviting. They loaded everything they could on dilapidated cars and trucks and headed west. Single men "rode the rails" in empty railroad box cars and even lying on rods under the cars. The migrants became known as the Okies and the Arkies. They were more numerous than California could handle, so the government set up refugee camps in Arizona to remove them from the trains. Porter got a summer job as supply officer in a camp in Nogales. He asked me to come and help him drive home. I would get there by Greyhound bus. I jumped at the chance to see Arizona.

**With Porter, dressed for Easter in my first suit**

I went to the Greyhound bus terminal to buy my one-way ticket. The woman clerk was rude and insulting. I don't remember what she said, but it hinged on me being a child. *I told her off.* She had no right treating me that way just because I was young. I stormed out of her office. But as I hit the street, I remembered I still didn't have the ticket! I had to go back, "eating crow" as they say, and buy the ticket.

There is a saying that applies: "Never insult an alligator until you've crossed the river."

I was amazed how different the terrain was from our Sierra Madre range. The mountains looked like the rocky spines of old worn out mountains and the desert floor like flooded sand spilling out of the canyons to form alluvial plains.

The bus ride was also interesting with its numerous stops in little villages and a mixed class of travelers.

Porter was assigned to a **refugee camp** for male blacks. I had seen a few "colored people" (as we called them in those days) before, but these had quite different features—very black, heavy skull formation. It was an eye-opener.

The drive back home was uneventful. We drove straight through, mostly at night. That was my first open-road cross-country trip on which I got to drive. Quite a thrill!

Many volumes have been written about the Great Depression, so I don't have to, except to point out that it did affect my life. I sought government employment for financial security by seeking a career in the Coast Guard. I sought a "free" college education at the Coast Guard Academy. And you might say I have been a "tightwad" as a result of those frugal years.

We were slow coming out of the Great Depression, but we did, as the following Scenes will show.

# SCENE 7

# BOY SCOUTS, SEA SCOUTS, EAGLE SCOUTS—1927-1932

Porter joined Troop 2 when he was twelve years old. There was no Cub Scout program in those days. The Troop met in the basement of the Baptist church where they seemed to spend most of their time shooting baskets at the single hoop. I loved to go and watch them, wishing I would soon be old enough to join Scouts too. Little did we know how many of the summer camp staff would come from that Troop.

**Camp Emerald Bay** is located in the westernmost cove on Santa Catalina Island. There were eight tents (originally old World War I army tents, later modern wall tents) each to accommodate eight Scouts and a Patrol Leader. There were senior staff tents or cabins for four, a mess hall, recreation hall, and handicraft hut. And outside toilet facilities.

The Scouts came individually or with friends, not as a troop unit, and not with a Scoutmaster. The Patrol Leader knitted his charges into a team and kept order.

The camping and skill programs were conducted by the senior staff.

The summer camp had four periods of ten days each, with a three-day break for the staff between the second and third periods. The staff members also attended a Spring

**Scouting played an important role in my life, from childhood through adult years**

Work Camp of one week for preparing the camp for summer occupancy.

The senior staff members were paid $1 per day. The Patrol Leaders were not paid. The attending Scouts paid $10 per period. Transportation to camp was provided. Porter served on the camp staff for several years, finally running the Handicraft Lodge.

**Troop 1**. As soon as I could, I joined Troop 1, the biggest and the best at that time. We had a Scoutmaster we all liked. His name was Ray Burdick. He said he was a retired Army Drill Sergeant. He was short, barrel-chested, and tough looking. He was a bachelor. Every Monday night, he drove down from Los Angeles in his open touring car to attend our meetings. He taught us military infantry drill using the fancy little steps that the rear rank of a squad uses to stay in line with the front rank. We always took first place at inter-troop pow-wows. We also excelled at wall scaling. Our big guys almost tossed the little ones clear over the wall. I was neither big nor small so I didn't make that team.

The semaphore contest called for sending a short message from A to B to C. Each station had a sender and scribe. The course went around a building, so C could not see A. A-scribe read the message letter by letter to the A-sender who sent it letter by letter to B where the B-sender read the message as received to his scribe. His scribe read it back to him to send to C-sender who read it out loud for his scribe to write down. When the C-scribe had put the message together the team's time A to C was recorded. The fastest team wins.

Troop 1 had a better idea—as A sent the message, the B-scribe called it out letter-by-letter and the B-sender sent it letter-by-letter to C, thus eliminating recording and read-back time at station B. As might be expected, all the other troops called, "FOUL." The judges agreed and we were disqualified.

**Me, Bob Ruby, and Dickie Braun (of the cooler incident)**

Ray took us to a camp in Topanga Canyon for weekends during the winter. There were small and very old cabins there. He played the ukulele and sang funny songs around the campfire. One of his favorites was "I Wish I Was Single Again." Our Troop had a lot of fun, thanks to Ray.

BUT, several years later, I learned that Ray tried to kiss two of the Scouts. They told their fathers, who in turn told the Council Scout Executive. The next day, Ray Burdick was history. He vanished, never to be heard from again.

**Ercell Hart, Bob Ruby, me, and Chuck Elmendorf**

I went to Camp Emerald Bay in 1927 at age twelve. When the Scout Council started staff training for the 1928 sessions, they announced a course for junior staff members age fourteen to be Patrol Leaders. Porter suggested I take the course. "But I'll just be turning thirteen," I said. He thought it would be good training even if I didn't qualify to be selected. So I took the course. By the end of the course, attrition left the Council one short, and I was made a Patrol Leader. I served in that capacity for three years and apprenticed to Porter for one year, at the end of which I relieved him of the Handicraft Lodge and became a member of the senior staff.

We bought raw materials in Los Angeles for the crafts we taught (*i.e.*, cow hides for belts to be tooled, calf hides for wallets, orange wood staves for bows, sugar pine for wood carving, etc.). Our wages were the profit from the Lodge. I was doing this when the appointment to the Coast Guard Academy came through.

I loved the merit badge challenges of the Boy Scout program which led me to Eagle Scout. I loved even more the Sea Scout challenges that led me to the highest rank of Quartermaster, the first in the Council and the inspiration that resulted in my Coast Guard career.

**Ercell Hart, me, Bob Ruby, and Chuck Elmendorf**

We were truly a Scouting family. My brother achieved the rank of **Eagle Scout**. So did I, as mentioned. My sons, Terry and Scott, and Terry's son Andrew also achieved that highly respected rank. As an adult, I served as Cub Master, Scoutmaster, and on several Scout committees. My wife, Mary, served as Girl Scout Leader and my two daughters enjoyed both the Brownies and Girl Scouts.

**Fish Stories**. One summer between the second and third periods, when we had a staff break, a school of mackerel entered the south end of our cove and sped to the north, apparently being chased. They were so crowded that many ran right up on the beach.

We ran along collecting them, before the gulls did, and had a big luau for dinner that night.

But here is the strange part of the story. The next year, <u>at break time again</u>, the same thing happened except the fish were yellowtail tuna! We launched rowboats and those with fish spears brought them. We jabbed away at those beautiful fish, but I don't recall that we caught even a single one.

**Diving**. A zoologist from UCLA had permission to work our reef for a scientific study. He wanted to stay down for up to thirty minutes at a depth as deep as thirty feet…and in that cold, cold water. He built a wooden raft on which he mounted a professional air pump turned by two eighteen-inch cranked wheels. This was connected by air hose to a hard hat helmet like those used by deep sea divers who wear complete dry suits. He only wore the helmet. Wet suits also were not invented. To conserve body heat, he wore a couple of sweatshirts to hold the water next to his body.

He needed someone to turn the wheels and pump the air to him. <u>If we would pump, we could dive</u>! What a thrill! In the water, holding onto the raft, a helper puts the helmet over your head (which you turn sideways, so it will go on). It rests on your shoulders. You have a heavy lead belt on to help you sink. Down you go! *How beautiful! The seaweed swaying with the current. Fish swimming by. A golden Garibaldi! The silence. Weightlessness.* But kind of scary at first, with water in the helmet up to your chin. Pull on the lifeline when you are ready to go up. Duck out of the helmet when your helper is ready. Remember to turn your head sideways. Wasn't that wonderful? How many in this world get that experience? Well, yes, they do now with scuba gear.

**PeeWee Wise, me, Bob Ruby, and Ercell Hart**

Emerald Bay was a waterfront camp with rowboats, canoes, and sailboats. I learned to row (feather the oars), paddle a canoe (J-stroke), sail a canoe (tricky), and develop all around sailing skills in a Snipe.

**Sailing**. One day, I was sailing in a little day-sailer about sixteen feet long, sloop rigged, with two other senior staff members, Ercell Hart and PeeWee Wise. PeeWee was the chef's assistant. He infected his thumb using steel wool to wash pots and had it wrapped in a big wad of gauze. He announced that he had to urinate real soon. What to do? It would take time to get to the dock. I was a pretty good sailor and offered a plan. I would sail close hauled and heel us over so he could eliminate between the boom and the gunwale. The plan was agreed upon and put into action. He got ready and, by hauling off the wind, I heeled us way over. But when he shifted his weight for a better "window of opportunity," the gunwale went under and we went over! Two of us thought it was hilarious to see our friend treading water with his thumb pointing at the moon. A commercial fisherman saw us go over, weighed his anchor, and rescued us before we stopped laughing.

**Thieves**. At the end of the 1934 Boy Scout summer camp session, I was chosen to stay over at the camp and run the supply boat (an outboard-powered canoe) between the camp and the Isthmus, for the Long Beach Boys Choir that chartered the camp. I was assigned a helper named Dickie Braun, the son of a donor to the camp. I was nineteen. He was about fifteen. A nice boy. We got along just fine.

On one trip, the steamer to the Isthmus was late, and we ran late. The camp cook set out plates of dinner for us but did not include our ration of fresh milk, which we had just delivered. While we cleaned up and put away the boat, the cook stored the supplies in the kitchen. When we discovered <u>no milk</u>, we felt gypped. So we decided to go to the closed kitchen and get our milk rations.

We found the chill box unlocked so we entered. Since we had neither matches nor a flashlight, we left the door ajar. Suddenly we heard heavy footsteps enter and, as the cook crossed the floor, he saw the door ajar and slammed it shut!! We didn't know what to do. We hadn't looked to see if there was an inside opening handle. Do we yell, pound, or stay silent and get out after he leaves? Maybe we will suffocate! *Or Freeze!!*

Before we knew what to do, the cook opened the door and turned his flashlight right into our faces. He nearly had a heart attack! He summoned the Choirmaster and a few others, and they held kangaroo court right there at the chill box! We plea-bargained that we weren't stealing; we were only after our fair share of fresh milk, a coveted commodity. The initial decision to send us home by the next boat was modified because "how else were they going to get supplies?" We showed abundant remorse and the case was dismissed.

Dickie Braun will show up on a later Scene under circumstances rare enough to qualify for Ripley's "Believe It Or Not!"

**High Sierra Staff Camp**. When the summer camp sessions were over at Catalina, we had the privilege of attending the mountain camp in the Sequoia National Park. Included in the group with which I attended were Otto Metzler, an excitable German chef, and the donor of a staff cabin and father of one of the Scouts. His name was Warburton. He was fat, flat footed, with a businessman's sunburn. Inviting him was a show of thanks for his contribution. He and Otto were assigned a tent to share for the night.

We all went to a place to see the feeding of the black bears. The Park Rangers dumped garbage hoping the bears would stop begging off visitors. But the food Otto served to us campers that night gave everyone the trots about 2 a.m.! There were long lines at the privies waiting one's turn. Otto, used to his own food, was sleeping soundly, but Warburton received the call. Relieved, he returned to his tent, sans flashlight, and groped in the dark for his cot. In so doing, he placed his hand squarely on Otto's face! Otto leaped up, ran out into the night and assembled campers screaming, "Der BEARS, der Bears, der God Damn Bears!!!"

One new experience for me was the use of pack animals. We had two donkeys to carry our packs on an overnight to Twin Lakes. We learned to tie a diamond hitch to hold the load without slipping off. At the camp site, we hobbled them to keep them from straying overnight. We were above "tree line" altitude, which was news to me that there was such a thing.

Another experience, but this one with a tragic ending, was bathing at the swimming water hole. It was a beautiful pool in the icy mountain stream, surrounded by huge boulders. The top of one boulder was about ten feet above the deepest water, which was about ten feet deep. One Scout challenged a show-off Scout to dive from the top of the big boulder. The showoff accepted the challenge and went to the top. The challenger could see the danger and cancelled his bet. The challenged Scout said he was going to dive anyway, took one step backwards, and dove in headfirst. His dive would have been a good one, but a rock ledge projected under water, and he hit it with his forehead and nose.

**Ship 16**

He floated up, bleeding profusely. Two big Scouts jumped in and pulled him to the bank shouting to get help. I took off running and yelling and found an adult camp staffer. There was more action than I can recount, but a litter was sent to the pool, and when it was carried to camp, a pickup truck was waiting to take the injured Scout to the village first aid room.

Another Scout and I were each given a semaphore flag and assigned to lie on the front fenders and wave frantically while the driver drove as fast as he dared, tooting the horn. We got attention all right! Traffic cleared the road for our safe passage.

We learned days later that his nose was badly broken but his eyes and skull were okay.

**Sea Scout Ship *Islander*.** During this time, Troop 2 was transformed into the first Sea Scout "Ship" in the Council and named "**Ship 87**." Its members came largely from the camp staff. When they became college men, they sponsored my group of high-school-aged boys. We were designated as "**Ship 16**." We also were formed mainly from members of the camp staff. There was a big brother/little brother bond between our two Sea Scout Ships which lasted the remainder of our lives. We called ourselves "The Islanders." But what good is a Sea Scout Ship without a boat?

The Council checked with the Navy to see what surveyed boats were available and picked out a twenty-four-foot motor-sailer for us. It was of the style used by the Navy to run their liberty parties ashore where the fleets were at anchor, but a miniature as compared with the forty-five-footers in general use. The hull was in terrible shape. We spent the whole winter caulking it. But the engine was an antique. It was a four-cylinder two-cycle World War I engine. To start it, you wrapped a line around the flywheel and pulled it through. There was no crank case, so an oil drip system was used to keep the bearings lubricated. We put hundreds of miles on that engine and it never let us down.

Same as on the bigger boats, the coxswain stood on a little deck at gunwale level inside a heavy brass railing, steering with a long brass tiller connected to a transom rudder. The engineman was just below and forward of the coxswain's feet. Instead of using bells, we just called to the engineman for "Ahead Slow," "Stop," "Fast Forward," etc.

The *Islander* became a workhorse (or should I say seahorse?) for the Council in transporting supplies, and at Catalina taking Scouts to different bays for overnights.

Our skipper was Al Miller, a small and modest man who knew how to take charge, but who also knew how to delegate and when to trust us. He started a confidential session known as "Lights." Our meeting place was an empty city-owned cottage we called the "Castle" (short for "forecastle"). There was a fireplace at the end of the living room and on each side of the hearth were side lights. Red to left or port. Green to right or starboard. Anyone wanting to discuss a problem could ask for a "Session of Lights." All other

**As of this writing, the friendship of the Sea Scouts of Ship 16 has lasted for over seventy years. In 2006, five shipmates are still living**

room lights would be turned off, and Skipper Al would monitor the questions and answers and help steer the discussion. Many teenage problems were put to rest during these sessions. And the discussions were not to leave the room!

I don't know how good a rag-sailor Al was, but he was great in power boats and knew how to keep engines running. He later became a Field Executive and professional skipper of the Emerald Bay supply boat.

Now let's flash back to Camp Emerald Bay for the **Campfire Closing Ceremony**.

You can be the Campfire Leader (you might enjoy this more if you read it out loud).

And consider how well you have complied.

Leader: "Scouts form a single file circle around the dying fire; hold hands and sway as we sing the Scout Vesper Song.

> Softly falls the light of day,
> While our campfire fades away.
> Silently each Scout should ask,
> 'Have I done my daily task?
> Have I kept my honor bright?
> Can I guiltless sleep tonight?
> Have I done and have I dared
> Everything to Be Prepared?'"

Leader: "Attention! Scout sign. Scout Oath:

> On my honor I will do my best
> To do my duty to God and my country
> And to obey the Scout Law;
> To help other people at all times;
> To keep myself physically strong,
> Mentally awake and morally straight."

Leader: "Repeat after me the Scout Law:

> A Scout is Trustworthy, Loyal, Helpful, Friendly,
> Courteous, Kind, Cheerful, Thrifty, Brave,
> Clean, and Reverent."

Leader: "Remember the Scout Motto: Be Prepared!"

Leader: "And the Scout Slogan: Do a Good Turn Daily"

Leader: "And now the Scoutmaster's Benediction:

> May the Great Scoutmaster
> Of all good Scouts
> Be with you
> Until we meet again."

Leader: "Have a Good Night! Dismissed!"

**My cap in this photo signifies the Quartermaster rank—the Sea Scout equivalent of the Eagle Scout rank in the Boy Scouts**

# SCENE 8

## JALOPIES—1932-1935

By definition a "jalopy" is an old ramshackle automobile. The Model T Ford that Porter bought to commute to college certainly qualified. He should have been paid to haul it away. Instead, he paid $25. During the next two years, he got it in good mechanical condition before he gave it to me.

Before leaving for his camp job, he said to me (age twelve and a half) that I would be the only man left at home and as a matter of safety should know how to drive. And I did. Yes, I learned to drive around the neighborhood at age twelve-and-a-half. I have no recollection of licensing, minimum age, tests, car registration, or any regulations. But now I will try to tell you how to drive a Model T Ford:

1. Set the hand brake. It locks the two rear wheels. (No four wheel brakes back then.) There are three foot pedals. When the hand brake is set, it puts the left foot pedal halfway to the floor and the engine in neutral.

2. Retard the spark to avoid a backfire by moving with your left hand the rod that extends to the rim under the left side of the steering wheel. Move it to delay the spark, the amount you need to assure the engine fires past dead-center.

3. A similar rod under the wheel to the right is the throttle. Adjust it to a little above idle.

4. Pull out from the dashboard the manual choke rod to enrich the fuel-air mixture.

5. Go to the front of the car and insert the hand crank to engage the flywheel for turning over the engine (no starter). Crank with your thumb alongside your index finger so if there is a backfire it won't take off your thumb or break your arm. If the engine doesn't start, crank harder and faster. You are turning a magneto that is creating an electric charge for the spark plugs. The car has no battery.

6. When the engine starts, rush to the left side, mount the running board, hurdle the false door (driver's side only), and adjust the throttle (the engine is either throbbing or screaming) and spark (to eliminate clouds of smoke) and choke (to stop the coughing). You are now ready to go for a pleasant (?) ride.

*The engine is now running (RIGHT?)*

7. There are three pedals for your two feet. They have bands that grab wheels when pressed. The left pedal halfway pressed is in neutral. It also goes halfway down to neutral if you pull on the hand brake. In this halfway position, it grabs nothing. All the way down, it becomes a low forward gear. Let all the way out, it becomes high forward gear. Remember what those do as we look at the right pedal.

8. The right pedal is the brake. Press it to slow down, but to stop get the left pedal down into neutral. What about the middle pedal?

9. The middle pedal is for backing. Come to a stop with the left pedal halfway down and the right pedal pressed to stop. Holding the left pedal in the halfway position, exert pressure on the middle pedal, and LO you start backing! If you are held up at a long red light, set the hand brake to relieve your left foot.

10. Don't forget your hands. The left one is free because the spark will not need adjusting and you will need your left arm to signal turns. Your right hand will be busy on the throttle and working the hand brake.

11. Here I go for my driving test with Porter the examiner. I did all the right things and started us down Eleventh Street. Porter demonstrated how you could get more power out of the engine by relieving the back pressure caused by the muffler. To do this you pulled on a ring on the floor. He opened a gate that let the exhaust bypass the muffler and the engine ROARED. But when we came to Montana Avenue, there was a car coming down and I had to stop in a hurry. In my excitement, I went down hard with both feet and stalled the car right there. (Get out the crank, quick!)

"**Tin Lizzy**" was the name for a Model T Ford. They were turned out of the factory plain black. Mine was showing rust, and since I would soon be entering UCLA, I thought I should spruce it up. I found a can of oil-based enamel (water-based paints were not yet invented). The color happened to be a medium-green. I thought it was pretty nice until a know-it-all friend said it looked like "bile." After that, Lizzy was sometimes called "**Miss Bile**."

Porter had the engine in good working order, but there were other defects showing up. One was a front tire worn through the tread and well into the inner lining. To get some more miles out of the tire, this condition was fixed by installing a "boot." You found a discarded tire and cut out a section of the inner lining about eight inches long. This you placed inside the tire over the worn spot and held it in place with the inner tube. This, of course, unbalanced the wheel and when you got up to top speed of 35 mph, the front end of the car bounced a bit. This led to another name: "**Leaping Lena**."

I only drove my car to UCLA for a few months when a breakdown was the last straw. The bands would wear and eventually start slipping. It was an easy matter to take off the covering plate and tighten the band with a wrench. I had done this at home, and kept the necessary tools in the car.

UCLA was built on a small mesa. The west side dropped to the men and women gyms, a practice athletic field, and a large parking lot. As I approached the entrance to the parking lot, the bands started slipping so badly I didn't think I could make it in. Where the approach roads came together, there was a good-sized off-road clearing. I managed to get well off the road and into it. There, right at the bottom of the eighty-seven steps to the campus, I tightened the bands and went home determined to sell Miss Bile, aka Leaping Lena.

I found a nice **Chevy coupe**. I was moving up! For it, I gave the salvage yard the Tin Lizzy and $35. It was painted black but in good shape. To add my touch, I painted the disc wheels bright RED.

Talk about being up-to-date. In this car, we installed <u>seat belts</u>! This was a new idea and kits were available. I bought two. They worked like a man's belt with a similar buckle. It just went across your waist and was bolted by drilling a hole in the floorboard.

To help with the fuel cost, which was nine cents a gallon (yes, 9¢!), I found a girl taking the bus from near my Santa Monica home which cost her 15¢ each way.

**My first car. This Chevy was my pride and joy. I customized it by painting the disk wheels bright red**

With our different schedules I could only take her <u>to</u> school, but it was convenient for her, and she didn't mind that I charged her 15¢. I made money!

I drove this car until I left home for the Coast Guard Academy in 1935. The poor car never acquired a name other than "The Chevy."

**Mount Whitney**. It must have been the summer of 1933 when, after summer camp, two Ship 16 shipmates and I decided we should climb the tallest mountain in the United States (only forty-eight states then. Remember?). PeeWee Wise borrowed his father's Chevy roadster. Ercell Hart and I bought the gas.

**PeeWee Wise and me at the top of Mount Whitney**

A roadster in those days had only a front bench type seat with a little storage space behind the seat and a small trunk. A canvas top was held in place by overhead ribs of curved wood. There were isinglass panels that could be attached at the sides in case of rain or snow.

It is about 250 miles between Santa Monica and the Portal to Mount Whitney. In a small town about fifty miles short of our destination, the engine "threw a rod." We found a garage with a sympathetic mechanic who went to the salvage yard for a part. He worked all night and had it ready for us in the morning. We had our sleeping bags and camping gear, so we just slept it off in his garage. We gave him all the money we had minus the gas money we calculated we would need to get us home after the climb.

The climb was *wonderful*. We camped the first night at Mirror Lake. The assault to the summit the next day was on a good trail but the altitude reaching 14,496 feet made one breathless very easily. The vistas were spectacular! The wind at the top was cold and brisk.

After reaching the summit, we made it down all the way to the car in one day and hit the road for home. We soon noticed the fuel was getting low. We pooled our gas money and concluded we weren't going to make it home the way we were guzzling fuel. It was dark now and we'd better get to a gas station before they close. To save fuel, we turned the engine off at every down slope.

It had been a long and exhausting day. We three sat in the front seat and agreed two could sleep on each other's shoulders while the third one was driving, provided he kept turning the engine off going down hill. And we also found that, better than a shoulder, we could thread our neckerchiefs over the overhead rib, tie it in a loop, then rest our chins in the loop. Sort of hanging there.

We pulled into a service station while two were sleeping that way. The old lady attendant came to the car to wait on us and darn near fainted when she saw two bodies <u>hanging</u>!

We made it home and PeeWee found a dime in his pocket. Shucks, we could have bought another gallon and made it easily.

# SCENE 9

## UCLA (FRATERNITY, BASKETBALL, UPLIFTERS CLUB)

By now, you must have surmised that Porter was not only my brother but also my best friend and sometimes served me as a surrogate father. His influence was especially strong during my teen years. He encouraged me to stay on the straight and narrow and study hard to qualify for college. He said that, without a college education, I would likely wind up driving service vehicles or doing menial or manual jobs for low pay and be unable to enjoy some of the finer things in life. I heeded his advice and am glad I did so.

But now, our lives are not so closely bound as we start setting our career courses.

The four years that separated us meant I entered high school just after he graduated. I entered UCLA just after he graduated. The opportunities to seek his counsel were decreasing.

Porter did make two suggestions for my college experience: 1. Join a fraternity. He recommended Theta Chi, which he enjoyed and in his senior year lived in as House Manager. 2. Join a staff of managers for an athletic team. He was senior manager for the Bruins Ice Hockey Team, of all things.

I pledged **Theta Chi** and went through the hazing and other antics. The final test was to be dumped in the middle of the night way out on undeveloped Mulholland Drive, and left to my own resources to find my way home. I flagged down a milk delivery wagon about halfway to town and thumbed (hitchhiked) the rest of the way.

Monday night was meeting night and attendance was required. We pledges had to wait tables. Then trumped-up charges were raised which demanded punishment in the form of swats with a two-foot paddle. On the order to "assume the angle," you stood bent over at the waist, hauling your "family jewels" safely to the front, as the ordered number of swats was administered. (The paddles were made with two blades an eighth of an inch apart, so that they clapped when the swat was delivered and made lots of noise but didn't hurt much.)

The cost of lunch was over my Depression budget so I brought a sandwich from home and ate in the frat house library with about six others. I became a junior manager for UCLA's basketball team, which had night duties, so for those days I brought two brown bags from home.

For a few months, one of the brothers had a contract to provide breakfast to a businessmen's breakfast club that met at 7 a.m. in the clubhouse of a country club just a few miles south of Westwood. After the fraternity meeting ended, those of us hired by our fraternity brother squeezed oranges and cracked eggs until about 11 p.m. We took naps and then made it to the country club by 6 a.m. to set up and cook and serve the breakfast. Then, we cleaned up the clubhouse and raced back to classes. I had a physics class at 1 p.m. I couldn't stay awake and slept through every lecture. The professor asked me why I didn't pay attention in class, and when I told him about the job he said he understood. I crammed for the final exam and got a B!

The Theta Chi fraternity didn't mean a great deal to me, but it did give me a place to go between classes and to have "an anchor to windward," so to speak. There were no drinking parties, and I did learn a few social graces.

My volunteer **junior basketball manager** job was interesting and fun. My duties before games and practice sessions was to tape the ankles of those so requesting, issue half pints of milk to each player before the games (having one myself), and referee practice scrimmages. And we were each issued six tickets for the big games, which we ducked out to the ticket line to scalp.

Also I was issued a sweatshirt with **BRUINS** across the chest, which gave me access to the locker room. That was a fun experience. Imagine little me at 5-foot 8-inches among those 6-foot 4-inch bean poles! And the jesting, pep talks, and, yes, the odors! They say we have a remarkable memory for odors, associating them with time and place. I'm sure UCLA's locker room will come to mind if I get the right combination liniment, essence of socks, shower room humidity, and body fragrance.

For refereeing practice games, I drew on my high school experience on the junior varsity team. I was pretty good on floor work, down under the tall guys. I could dribble, pivot, pass, and press, but I could never sink a basket. At inter-school games, we JVs played first followed by the varsity. Before the game started, we had a few minutes to warm up with rebound shots and long shots. I was determined to at least reach the basket. I gave that ball my all. It sailed clear over the backboard and landed in the balcony! The rival rooters cheered and booed. Our loyalists roared with laughter. I blushed.

We did a lot more ball jumps in those days, like when there was a foul. I would be surrounded by those tall guys, some complaining of a bum call. I would remind them that I was the referee and it was only a practice game, after all. My challenge was to toss the ball straight up to eight or ten feet.

I accompanied the team to Stanford University for a big game. We went by train. Some of us didn't have train tickets. No matter. We had a system. When the conductor entered the car to punch ticket, someone yelled "MILL." Everyone would mill about, crowding the conductor unmercifully until he gave up and left.

At the end of the basketball season, the head coach had us all to his home for a buffet dinner. It was a strange place for me to learn a lesson about drinking hard liquor. The 1919 National Prohibition Law had just been repealed in 1933. Liquor was available everywhere. The coach offered martinis all around. I was seated on a low couch with three others. We politely sipped our drinks. Then, a second and last round was offered. I accepted. Supper was announced. We all stood up. I came up about thirty degrees off the vertical. I learned this lesson, which I passed on to my children who sooner or later would have a hard liquor drink—gin acts fast. You will feel the effects right away, and you will be warned not to drink any more. Some other liquors like bourbon and rum act slowly. That sounds safer, but is it? NO. Without the early warning one might consume an amount that will sneak up and result in unexpected intoxication!

Working my way through college with part time jobs at the **Uplifters Club** gave me more varied experiences off campus than on.

It was in the 1920s that a group of men from the Los Angeles Athletic Club were looking for a spot to build a summer retreat. They decided there was no place as magical or as dedicated to enjoyment of the good life as Rustic Canyon. At the old 1914 Forestry station, they founded the Uplifters Club (known during Prohibition as the "Cuplifters Club"). They became known for musical and dramatic presentations, for their equestrian and polo fields, and, most raucously, their annual all-male summer excursions.

The assistant manager was Bernard Jackson, who was a member of Ship 87. He found in our Ship 16 a group of responsible sixteen-to-nineteen-year-old young men to draw upon for odd jobs around the club. We all needed money and twenty-five cents an hour, which was the going rate, was a blessing to us. I seemed to be favored with long hours and some great perquisites (perks) which I will try to relate.

My principal job was **evening office boy**, a white-collar position requiring coat and tie. As I recall, I was only there Friday, Saturday, and Sunday nights. My evening's duties started with a *big perk...dinner in the Executive Dining Room*. I sometimes ate with Bernard or alone but at the same time as the manager and his wife. Of all the Ship 16 members hired by the club, I was the only one with the dining privilege. The others had access to the kitchen for the same food, but had to enter through the backdoor. And they never had shrimp cocktail on chipped ice to start them off! They had blue-collar jobs like assistant stage hand, gate guard, and swimming instructor.

The Uplifters Club was famous for their Sunday-night dinner theater. There were talented Hollywood actors and musicians who were honorary members but in return were expected to display their talents on special occasions. From the back of the theater room, I could also keep an eye on the office front desk, and it was okay with Bernard if I did so. One evening, they had a Las Vegas-type pageant of famous Black Beauties! Another time, there was a comedy, with the leading actor wearing what looked like an old-fashioned cork lifejacket. But it was suppose to be dynamite. He had the trigger in his hand while looking for a place to blast off!! That wouldn't seem funny now (year 2005) in this time of international terrorism with its suicide bombers.

My job was to answer the telephone which usually was a member making a dinner reservation. I wasn't awed by the Hollywood celebrities so their names didn't impress me. "Hello? This is Cary Grant." "Cary who?" "Would you spell it, please?" That didn't go over very well. I also sold cigars and cigarettes and guarded the vault of bootleg liquor in the back of the office.

When I was not in college or at camp, I made myself available for other jobs. One was **pumping gasoline** at the club. The pump was an antique even for those days. On top sat a glass cylinder that would hold five gallons. The customer would say the number of gallons he wanted and I would hand pump to fill the tank to that mark. Then I'd put the hose to the car's tank, which was commonly under the hood with the filler just forward of the dashboard. Gravity drained the gasoline into the car's tank and gravity fed the engine. No need for a fuel pump.

On holiday banquet nights, the ballroom would be full of highly decorated tables celebrating the theme. Many times the guests wore costumes. I had never seen such a party. The bar room was crowded as you would expect. Men hovered over the bar and carried drinks to the ladies. (No "lady" would sit at the bar.) My job was to be **bar cashier**, taking the money for the drinks, thus freeing the bartender and saving him time. I witnessed prominent men starting off looking great and deteriorating before my eyes on consuming too many drinks. (I promised myself never to become a barfly.)

There were about half a dozen privately owned cottages on the property. One of my now-and-again jobs was **reading the electric meter**. They were usually located on the screened-in service porch. I would enter quietly, read the meter, and leave. I would have been smarter if I made some noise because sometimes I alarmed the resident. A popular white-hat cowboy hero named Jack Holt was shaken when he wandered out in his skivvies to find me there. He didn't look very bold without his six-shooter!

At the end of summer, the Uplifters Club gates were closed for a week except for members and male employees. Women were strictly forbidden. Even those whose homes were on the property had to leave. The news media (newspaper and radio; there was no such thing as TV) were not allowed. Even the police and sheriffs were convinced to stay away.

The first five days were "Low Jinks." I never saw any "naughty" action except the member's freedom to get drunk without it being reported. We rehearsed during that week for the closing **pageant** called "High Jinks." I don't recall the story, but I was one of a troop of soldiers that shooed away a tribe of Indians (Hollywood Filipinos).

Another unusual experience was to **usher** at the Uplifters Club's polo field located on the floor of Santa Monica Canyon. The grandstand consisted of about a dozen private boxes, owned by members. When the owner and his party, or the owner's guests, arrived, we would show them to the proper box. This was a high society event. The ladies, in particular, would dress high fashion, and arrive in top-down touring cars. They kept smiling for the press.

In the 1930s, there were over twenty-five polo fields in the Los Angeles area. **Will Rogers**, the famed humorist, newspaper columnist, (real) cowboy, author, movie star, and polo player built his own polo field a short distance further up the canyon. During this time, he and his friends (*i.e.*, David Niven, Spencer Tracy, Hal Roach, Walt Disney, and Clark Gable) played on his field on weekend mornings and would then ride over to the Uplifters to watch the "high goal" games.

Attending the Uplifters games, Rogers, who owned a box, preferred to sit on the grass in front of the grandstand with the stable hands. During one game, a player was injured and needed to withdraw from play. Rogers was invited to take his place.

He jumped up, peeled off his suit coat, revealing a blue shirt and bright red suspenders. He took the rider's helmet, which sat comically high atop his head, mounted the uninjured steed, and galloped to join the game. Almost immediately, he gained possession of the ball and scored a goal!

We ushers were also privileged to go into the tack room where the horses were brushed and "tacked up" in their special saddles, bridles, and leg protective wraps. And the players were dressing in their white jodhpurs, team shirts, boots, knee guards, and riding spurs.

**And we got paid!**

One last story about the Uplifters Club and a lesson I will *never* forget. Friday night was **poker night**. Two or three tables of men only would meet in the back bar room. The bar was kept open until 9 p.m., and the games were to quit promptly at 10 p.m. My duty was to see that the doors were locked and all lights extinguished. Then I could go home.

I flicked their light a couple of times, but they had already quit the games and were just visiting. They left for their cars except one man who had consumed too many drinks and he wanted to talk. The others avoided him and left him alone with me! I nicely urged him to leave and got him headed for the door when he remembered his hat. He went back to the counter where he had left it. He held it in his hand as I gently nudged him again toward the door. But he kept talking and slowly came to a halt. In exasperation, I took his hat out of his hand, placed it on his head, and led him with extra encouragement towards the door. He sobered up immediately. He lectured me for the next five or ten minutes that one NEVER places a man's hat on his head. With that he put his hat on and left. GOOD NIGHT.

That is enough for my *College Daze.* My career starts with Scene 10.

**Long Beach Earthquake of 1933**

# SCENE 10

## COAST GUARD ACADEMY—1935 (SWAB SUMMER)

The Tehachapi Mountain range forms a natural boundary separating Southern California from Central California. The range runs from southwest to northeast and rises to eight thousand feet with the Tejon Pass at four thousand feet. The climb from the Los Angeles basin at four hundred feet to the pass was a challenge for the automobiles of the '30s, but easy compared to the ascent from the San Joaquin Valley. That route was so steep it was necessary to wind the road all around from which it has been given the name "Grapevine."

That climb is even a challenge to cars and trucks today. Pullouts are provided for stopping to rest engines and add provided water to radiators. Motorists are advised to turn off air conditioners.

It was spring 1934 that we received a long distance telephone call from my aunt Grace, Dean of the Bakersfield Junior College. (Long distance calls usually meant an emergency. Whenever we made such a call, the points to be covered were written down to get the message across without visiting, and thus staying within the minimum three-minute charge.) She wanted to drive down to escape the awful summer heat, but she would have to drive her stick-shift car over the Grapevine.

That would require pumping the clutch numerous times. She wasn't sure she had the strength to do so, and asked if I could come to help.

I was turning nineteen and thought it would be a great experience. I went by bus, and on arrival she informed me we were going to the Spring Prom at the college. I was not into dancing, but I had to attend anyway. I was standing around like a wallflower when a college man approached me and said he recognized me from a Sea Scout event in Santa Monica. Conversation led to "what are your college plans, etc." He said he was going to the **Coast Guard Academy**. I had never heard of it. I had been interested in Annapolis but that needed a congressman's appointment. I had considered the California Merchant Marine Academy but wasn't sure I wanted that life. The Coast Guard sounded good. "How do I apply?" I asked. He said to write to the Navy, Bureau of Navigation, for an application. His directions were all wet, but somehow my letter got kicked around until it found the right place and I received an application to take the competitive entrance exam, which I did at Los Angeles City Hall, administered by a Civil Service man who knew nothing about the Coast Guard. I had read up, which I guess impressed him. It was just a matter of waiting to see what would happen. In fact, I waited almost a year.

I went back to Camp Emerald Bay in 1935 for another summer on the senior staff, in charge of the Handicraft Lodge. At the break between camp sessions 2 and 3, when we on the staff were free to do our own "thing," my closest friend, Bob Ruby, and I took a canoe to circumnavigate the west end of the island. We portaged across the Isthmus, and had supper at a snack bar there, and I telephoned home. There was no phone in camp and it was a perfect opportunity to telephone home, as we were within a day or so of my mother's birthday.

She was surprised and pleased at the call but could hardly wait to tell me that I had received a **Western Union telegram from the Coast Guard**. She read it to me: I had been accepted and would be made a cadet if I reported on a certain day in late August and passed the entrance physical exam. If appointed, I would be reimbursed for my travel expense. If I failed the physical, I would have to return home at my own expense!

Bob and I then continued on our voyage, and, as we entered Emerald Bay, put in at Sandy Beach, built a little fire, each drank a can of beer that Bob had somehow acquired, and we contemplated our futures!

I don't remember how I got rid of the Lodge, but I do remember I got a ride back to the mainland on one of the yachts that often participated in Sea Scout events. It belonged to a retired Chicago banker. Sailing with him were his beautiful twin daughters in their upper teens. *But,* sadly, both of these girls were *cross-eyed!*

**Cross-country** by train was another all new experience! I had ridden the rails on that trip to Seattle in 1928, but I was older now, halfway to an engineering degree, and would see things in a different light.

I would ride the **Santa Fe "Chief"** from Los Angeles to Chicago, change trains from Chicago to New York City, and take a local to New London, Connecticut, home of the Coast Guard Academy.

Steam engines exhaust their water supply powering the train, so watering stations are required. These consisted of elevated tanks located where water is available and alongside the tracks where gravity can feed the water to the engine. Rather than have a dining carriage on the train, the Santa Fe route had eating houses at the watering places. These were built to accommodate the railroad passengers. They were known as **Harvey Houses**. From the *Slaton Slatonite*:

"Harvey placed ads in eastern and midwestern newspapers that read: 'Wanted, young women of good character, attractive and intelligent, 18 to 30.' Harvey Girls were trained to high standards of prompt and courteous service. They were the key to serving hundreds of passengers in about twenty minutes...the average length of time a train would need for servicing every four hours.

"Harvey Girls all wore the same uniform, a long-sleeved black dress with a stiff 'Elsie' collar, black shoes, and stockings. The company furnished a full, white, wrap-around apron that was so stiffly starched that it had to be pinned to a corset, longtime Slaton resident and former Harvey Girl Cleo Wolf remembers. The girls were closely supervised by their manager (or manager's wife), and curfews were strictly enforced in the early years. They worked very hard and their eight-hour-a-day shifts were often split to conform to train schedules. In the late 1800s, Harvey Girls earned $17.50 per month plus tips, room, board, and train passes. When the Harvey Girls were recruited in the early years, they were asked not to marry for at least a year. It has been estimated that more than five thousand women married and settled in the west, as a result of Harvey Houses.

"The combination of good food served in a fine dining atmosphere with imported linen, china, and silver created a distinctive contrast to the typical eating establishments in turn-of-the-century small-town Texas. And the hope of catching the eye of one of the Harvey Girls no doubt kept many a poor farmer, rancher, and railroader coming back to dine again and again."

The Harvey Houses were a little expensive for me, so I followed the trainmen around the corner to the cheaper coffee house they patronized.

Boy! One thing you learned going from "sea to shining sea" is that we have one huge country! And it is truly "beautiful for spacious skies, for amber waves of grain, for purple mountain majesties, above the fruited plain!"

I was thoroughly enjoying the trip, but I had one worry as to whether or not I might fail the final physical exam. I didn't have enough money for the trip home, should that happen. My worry? A big carbuncle on the back of my left hand. It was tight as a drum and paining a little. In the Chicago train station, I sought relief at the first aid station. The doctor said it would have to be lanced to relieve the pressure. I said, "Okay." He grubbed around his medicine cabinet and announced he didn't have any anesthetic, and could I stand it if he lanced without it? I saw no alternative, so said, "Yes." I bit the bullet. He lanced. *I felt no pain!* The pressure was so great there was no sensitivity to pain, I guess.

The train out of Chicago was first class, as contrasted to the tourist class I had been on. It had a diner. A nice experience. I transferred at the Pennsylvania Station in downtown

New York City to a local that would complete the trip to New London. As we emerged from the city, I was very impressed by the fresh green foliage of the Connecticut countryside. It was in such stark contrast to our western conifers and arid lands.

In the same car with me were three others on their way to the Academy. We "bonded" immediately, needless to say, and wound up spending the night at the Crocker House hotel, ready to report in on schedule the next day. We walked the final mile or so lugging our suitcases (wheels on bags were unknown). We found the Academy reservation at the north boundary of New London on high ground and sloping eastward down to the Thames River where six twenty-six-foot knockabouts lay at their moorings in a nice little cove.

The buildings were red-brick-colonial-style, appropriate to the northeast and just two years old. The Academy had previously been at Fort Trumble at the downtown docks. The buildings lacked the warm look and lush landscaping of our southwestern college campuses but looked very "military." Not missed in our first look around was the Connecticut College for Women, directly across the street from the Academy!

**First Day**. There were eighty-two of us reporting in! We were assigned rooms in the barracks to locate and then report to the sickbay for our final physical exam. I sweated it out when the doctor said he thought he heard a heart murmur. A second doctor said I was okay—and so I got in. (Phew!) When through with the physical, we were to report to the gym to be issued our uniforms: Navy Undress Whites with black neckerchiefs. White underwear, black shoes, and socks. Navy white hats, except ours had a blue band around the brim. And a black wool jersey to be worn under the jumper in cold weather. We were to put our civilian clothes in our suitcases and stow them in the attic. Civilian clothes were allowed to be worn only on leave, not even on liberty.

The Academy was ghostly quiet. The First and Third Classes were on a foreign cruise. The Second Class was on summer home leave. (Remember the military rating system? The seniors are First Class, freshmen are Fourth Class, etc.)

The swearing-in ceremony was the next day, and a small number of Second Class cadets showed up to begin our "indoctrination" immediately. The first order was to form a straight line. "Suck up your guts! Throw out your chests. Chin in. Hands relaxed at your side. Square up those hats." (Those hats, square on top of your head certainly made you look stupid. But wait 'til you get the visor caps and square them up with just two fingers between the visor and nose. Now you look like a nerd!)

The **Swab Summer** is a time to screen out those misfits who shouldn't become cadets. Many were obviously unsuitable. It made one wonder about the entrance exams and the interview that gave such weight to adaptability. And there were several who said "no thanks" to the obvious coming regimentation. They wanted to go home. "Granted."

Our principal activity was a treat. A local cruise with our new Fourth Class divided between some 75-foot patrol boats and a 145-foot Bluenose Schooner. We visited favorite yachting ports, and in New Bedford we went to the movie *Captains Courageous* starring Spencer Tracy and Mickey Rooney! The movie was staged on a sister ship to ours.

There was one other treat, or was it? A Tea Dance! We were all fitted out now in our ill-fitting Undress Whites. We were required to attend. Local girls were invited to meet the new crop, and we new cadets might meet a local girl to help us avoid being homesick.

The girls surely looked young. I believe they were still in high school. I was an "older man" at twenty. Hadn't dated a high school girl in three years. I wasn't a good dancer but felt I had to push someone around. I took a good look at the wallflowers and found one looking a little older. She was a good dancer and we carried on a pleasant conversation. When the music stopped, she led me over to meet her friends. *Egads! They were wives of the officers assigned to the Academy as instructors! She was a junior officer's bride of just a few weeks!*

Swab Summer was drawing to a close. What had we learned? A LOT:

1. The **Coast Guard Motto**: Semper Paratus = Always Ready.

2. The **Coast Guard Academy mission** goes well beyond academics. It is: "To graduate young men and women with sound bodies, stout hearts and alert minds, with a liking for the sea and its lore, with that high sense of honor, loyalty, and obedience which goes with trained initiative and leadership; well grounded in seamanship, the sciences and amenities, and strong in the resolve to be worthy of the traditions of commissioned officers in the United States Coast Guard in the service of their country and humanity."

3. The **Coast Guard Marching Song**:

    > So here's the Coast Guard marching song,
    > We sing on land or sea.
    > Through surf and storm and howling gale,
    > High shall our purpose be.
    > "Semper Paratus" is our guide,
    > Our fame, our glory too.
    > To fight to save or fight to die,
    > Aye! Coast Guard, we are for you!

4. The **Coast Guard Academy Anthem**:

    > Men, we are Kaydets, Proud of our Corps.
    > Proud of our heroes brave who guard every shore.
    > Men, ours is courage, Service our fame.
    > So, hearts stout and minds alert
    > As we sing—Honor to thy Name.
    >
    > *Chorus:*
    > Coast Guard fore'er Aye! Coast Guard fore'er!

> Always we'll honor thee, Pride of our Nation.
> Academy and Corps. Feel thy mighty lore.
> We the Corps uphold thee, our Coast Guard fore'er.

When I refer to Classes, remember the military system of the higher the rank the lower the number. Thus, the seniors are First Class cadets and the freshmen are Fourth Class cadets. But stripes for designating rank go up with rank. An Ensign has one gold stripe. A Captain four gold stripes. That is enough for here.

Another tradition: you may address an officer by his rank from Admiral down to Commander, and, as a courtesy, a Lieutenant Commander may be addressed simply as Commander. Lieutenants and below down to Fourth Class cadets and Warrant officers are addressed as, "Mister."

In saluting, the junior recognizes the senior by his uniform, not the person, and initiates the salute. The senior returns the salute. This also applies to commissioned warships as they pass. They salute by dipping their nation's flag.

When in uniform out-of-doors, the hat or cap must be worn, this is known as being "covered." When indoors "uncovered," except for ceremonial occasions such as Color Guards and certain affairs where protocol calls for being covered.

Salutes, therefore, are normally not exchanged indoors for salutes are only exchanged when covered.

When in uniform, any equipment being carried should be in the left hand or over the left arm so as to leave the right hand available to render a salute.

One *No-No*: Don't try to make out with an officer's wife!!

---

I will end this Scene with my audacious request to check out one of those beautiful day-sailers still sitting lonesome at its mooring.

The other classes would soon be returning. This would likely be my only chance. We Fourth Classmen were not given liberty, but we were given the afternoon off to take care of personal affairs. I went to the office of the Officer-of-the-Day. He was seated at his desk. I knocked and asked permission to enter. "Granted," he said, without rising. "Sir, I would like to check out a knockabout for the afternoon." His eyes dilated as he gave me his most disdainful stare and said, "Mister, when you are a Second Classman, you can take out a boat, and, when you are a First Classman, you can take a date out with you. Dismissed!"

Coast Guard Academy—1935

**All Swabs scrub down fore-and-aft!**

# SCENE 11

## COAST GUARD ACADEMY—1935-1936 (FOURTH CLASS YEAR)

### Cadet Life

The end of Swab Summer marks the beginning of my first academic year. The number of Swabs remaining to form my new Fourth Class had been reduced in size by the traditionally high attrition of the summer screening process. The returning upper classes also have some members withdrawing by choice and some being "bilgers."

(Perhaps I should explain what is meant by "bilger." When you bail water out of a leaking boat, you dump the bilge water back over the side. When a cadet fails to meet the minimum standards of the Academy, in other words "flunks out," he is discharged "like bilge water" and sent home. Some voluntarily quit. Some take the entrance exams again and re-enter. These are known as "bilgers.")

To illustrate how great the attrition is at the Academy (viewed by cadets as how hard it is to make it through the Academy), let's look at my Class of 1939:

> Number sworn in as Fourth Class cadets (beginning of Swab Summer) = 87
> Number sworn in as Third Class cadets = 45
> Number sworn in as Second Class cadets = 37
> Number sworn in as First Class cadets = 24
> Number that graduated and were commissioned Ensigns = 23

(One developed tuberculosis in his First Class year and did not receive a commission but did receive a diploma.)

**Company A in Parade Formation—"All present or accounted for"!**

**Getting Organized.** With the corps shaken down in size for the year, now was a good time to get further organized. The first step was to get the Battalion looking its best in Parade formation. To get a straight line of caps, no hills and dales, we were all put in a single line and rearranged so that the tallest were at the north end and the shortest at the south end. First Classmen were pulled out of line to be the staff officers. They were assigned corner rooms in the barracks and charged with keeping order. The tallest of the other cadets were assigned to the north wing and the shortest to the south wing. Some system, huh?

Now was the time to get our other uniforms (to be paid for out of our monthly cadet pay, as there was no clothing allowance). We received one-half of an Ensign's pay which was $125.00 a month. Our $62.50 went into our accounts which the administration controlled. We used it to pay for laundry, dry cleaning, and various sundry items, as well as to pay for new uniforms. Our weekend liberty allowance was $7 in our Fourth Class year, increasing to $11 in our First Class year. We had to submit a voucher for Christmas and summer leave money.

We were not granted liberty during Swab Summer as we had no liberty uniforms. That would change now. We were issued Blue Service, White Service, white shoes and socks, visor caps, gray gloves, pea coat, white leggings, drill belt, and white shirts with stud-fastened collars.

Our blue uniforms (which actually were black) were tailored to us individually. They fit beautifully and made the Annapolis midshipmen's off-the-rack uniforms look seedy!

**Vignettes**. I think you might get a better feel for the life of a cadet through some memories that come to mind. I will put them in somewhat of an order by my class standing at the time (*i.e.*, Fourth Class year, Second Class year, etc.).

At the end of Swab Summer, I began to experience for the first time the seasonal changes of the weather. Newcomers to the West Coast often said they missed not having **seasons** like Back East. I was anxious to experience them. The first weather change was not a season but was a hot and humid week or two called Indian Summer. It led into autumn when the leaves changed color and dropped from the trees. It all happened fast and mostly while we were confined to the reservation and in class. Before we knew it, a freezing nor'easter whipped through and denuded all the deciduous trees. I thought they were dead! Closely following the short autumn came not only the long cold winter of Connecticut but a record breaking extra cold one. Spring arrived at last and the "dead" trees came back to life with beautiful light green foliage and blossoms on the fruit trees. Summer was a welcome relief with generally comfortable weather.

Our cadet view of the environment was very limited. The two-year-old reservation was sparsely landscaped. No color changes there. Our opportunities to "go ashore" were limited to being granted liberty, and without transportation there was no way of going to the countryside.

Liberty was granted from 1-4 p.m. on Wednesday afternoons, from 1-8 p.m. on Saturdays, and from 10-12 a.m. on Sundays (for those wishing to go to a church in town rather than to the chapel service).

To call the times we could leave the reservation **liberty** is a distortion of the word which means "free to do as one pleases." We were cadets at all times and subject to Academy regulations and orders. For example: no smoking in public. No loitering on street corners. (No watching all the girls go by!) No hands in pockets. No drinking hard liquor. Be attired in the designated uniform of the day. (The uniform might be simply Blue Service, or Blue Service with gray gloves carried (in left hand to keep right hand free for saluting), or Blue Service with top coats and gray gloves carried. )

Liberty granted? Or parole granted?

A cadet could lose the liberty privilege if he received too many demerits or fell below passing in his study courses. He received demerits if his room did not pass inspection, or his uniform was dirty, or if late to formation, and for many other things. Cadets were taught that a sailor must learn, for the safety of his ship, to have a place for everything and keep everything in its place. This discipline started with room inspection. Even in the drawers of his dresser every item (socks, underwear, shirts, etc.) had to be folded and in the designated place within the drawer!

For full liberty privileges, a cadet had to be passing in all subjects. A grade of sixty-five was required. If he fell below that level, he would be placed on an Academic "Tree" and lose liberty days according to some kind of a scale. By the time Christmas leave rolled around, the autumn leaves were gone. So much for **fall colors.**

Until the weather turned from fall to winter, the cadet corps jogged before breakfast to the cove where we manned ten-oared lifeboats coxswained by First Classmen, for a row across the Thames River. Sometimes in thick fog, we would row only into the "soup" and rest there for an appropriate period of time before returning. One officer was on to that and required we bring back a rock from the other shore.

When the river began to ice over, the morning row was cancelled and instead we went jogging before breakfast around the Connecticut College for Women, loudly counting cadence.

**Flashback! Football** was a favorite sport when I was a lad in Santa Monica. We would follow the college games on the radio, and at halftime we would run out and toss the ball. I was just under 145 pounds and eligible for the junior varsity team. I was made a tackle, a good spot for a heavyweight that wasn't any good elsewhere. On the opening game of the season, and on the starting kick-off play, as defensive tackle I rushed down the field and made the tackle! I was so proud, I raised my head to be recognized just as the pile-on started. My face was bashed into the victim's thigh pad and my nose smashed. That ended my football career. Cotton was stuffed up my nose, and I stopped by our family doctor's office on the walk home. He pushed on one side of my nose and straightened it quite a bit. I smelled dried blood for a month.

When I was in college, I loved to go to football games in the Los Angeles Coliseum and sit in the rooting section. We were required to wear white shirts which would give a background for the colored card displays. We basked in the sun until after halftime when it started to cool off, and then we could put on our sweaters. If the game turned dull, we could always admire the antics of the beautiful cheerleaders.

Attending an Academy game was entirely different and we were required to attend. There was either rain or snow or sleet, and a freezing wind. We always lost, as we were playing against small colleges that could offer incentives like football scholarships. And we Fourth Classmen were required by our Second Class tormentors to yell <u>constantly</u>, whether winning or losing a play. And there were <u>no</u> female cheerleaders to ogle. I haven't enjoyed football since.

That is enough about fall in New England. Now for **winter**. I had no idea it got so cold anywhere. It brought out some strange behavior in the easterners. I was used to lots of fresh air in classrooms. At the Academy, if a window was ajar, someone would rush over and close it. The room would get stuffy. The Californians, Texans, and Floridians would fall asleep in class.

One way to haze Fourth Classmen went like this: a designated Swab would have to get up thirty minutes before reveille, run to the First Classmen's rooms, close the windows, and turn up the heat. Go back to bed.

My first winter was extra cold. The river was frozen so solid the town people drove a light pickup truck all the way across, which was unusual. Never mind the cold—some days we were mustered on the cement road in front of the barracks in "Undress Whites with jersey worn," dressed for infantry drill (*i.e.*, rifles, belts, and leggings). One Officer-of-the-Day came out to inspect the troops and their rifles. He wore his heavy bridge coat and gray gloves (turned down so we could see the rabbit fur lining). Cadet McDowell, from southern Texas stood next to me. He was shivering from the cold. He found that by lifting the rifle about one-eighth inch off the pavement he could make it chatter loud and clear. OOD: "Mr. McDowell, stop that noise." Mac: "Sorry, sir. I can't stop shaking." With that, the OOD proceeded with infantry drill.

The only good thing about a New London winter was the ice skating. Several little mill ponds froze solid enough. One was right across the women's campus and made for a convenient rendezvous. Another reward, if you could get in with a group that included a local girl, would be the hot toddy offered in front of a roaring fire in the open hearth!

What can I say about **spring**? These young men's hearts turned to thoughts of the summer training cruise to far off places and the summer leave that follows. But I also had two other things on my mind.

In the mess hall, we ate at tables for ten. In the center of one side, there was a single table for the Officer-of-the-Day. We would enter all at once from being mustered outside, and when all were at their places the OOD would command, "Be seated." When he thought we were through eating, he either commanded, "RISE. PASS OUT." Or, "LEAVE AT WILL."

At the table, we were made to do things like saluting the catsup as it passed by down the table, announcing the contents of a fresh pitcher as "muddy bottom" for coffee, "shallow water" for cocoa, "rocks and shoals" for lemonade on ice cubes, etc. If ordered to "eat a square meal, mister," we would raise a loaded fork vertically from the plate to mouth level, execute a square corner, and direct the fork and food horizontally into the mouth.

I have always been a slow eater, so I would often be cheated out of dessert if the OOD commanded, "RISE AND PASS OUT." I thought that unfair. I got my dander up and went to the Commandant of Cadets and complained. He agreed and told the OODs to only use "LEAVE AT WILL."

Still on my mind was the desire to take one of those knockabout sloops out for a sail. The chance came! I learned that, every year during Graduation Week, there was an inter-class race. I talked my class into letting me skipper. I picked three to crew, and we got permission to practice during our regular liberty hours!! I beat the system!

It was a dumb racecourse. We simply started at a line between two buoys, sailed up stream to round a buoy off the Navy submarine base, and return to the starting line to finish. We were first across the starting line, so we were first to finish. I skippered the next three years and we won every time!!

With graduation of the First Class cadets, we became Third Class cadets, and started that year off excited about the forthcoming cruise to Europe. I will report on that in the next Scene.

# SCENE 12

## COAST GUARD ACADEMY—1936-1937 (THIRD CLASS YEAR)

### Cruise to Europe, Home Leave by Train/Air

It was a great day for the First Classmen who filed up onto the platform to receive their Diplomas, their Bachelor of Science Degrees in Marine Engineering, and their Commissions as Ensigns in the Coast Guard. It was a great day for my Class too, because we were automatically advanced to Third Class.

We were no longer subject to hazing and harassing. We were pretty much left alone, which made studying easier and life in general more pleasant. We could smugly watch the new Second Class work on "indoctrinating" the Swabs.

The 250-foot **Coast Guard cutter *Cayuga*** was waiting at the Academy dock to receive us. The regular crew had been reduced to a minimum number of key officers and enlisted personnel. The new First Classmen would understudy the officers while my class of new Third Classmen would fill enlisted billets. Some billets would require supervision by senior rated men.

We had readied our "sea bags" of uniforms, including work and service dress whites, toilet articles, and everything we would need for a two-month-long cruise. Our first seagoing act was to shoulder them like old salts as we toted them aboard. The gangway was shipped, and we were underway before we knew it. The first order of business was to secure (*i.e.*, fasten down everything so that nothing went adrift or rolled about with the cutter's rolling and pitching). By the time we crossed Block Island Sound and took departure straight for Scotland, everything was stowed away, wardroom chairs bolted to the deck, hatches dogged down, lifeboats rigged out, cruising ensign streaming, and all was unusually quiet on deck. Why?

The *Cayuga*'s course took us straight into the Gulfstream. The weather was fair but a gentle swell from our starboard and a confused sea from an earlier blow gave the ship a corkscrew motion that gave many of us that uneasy feeling. I felt a tinge myself, although I claimed I never got seasick. I took a look around at how hard some were taking it and, believe it or not, I immediately felt fine. (I have ever since felt that there is a psychological factor in seasickness.)

**This is the 250-foot CGC *Cayuga*, which we took on our Third Class year cruise to Europe. Before our return home, the decision was made to keep the *Cayuga* in Spain to serve the Ambassador, and we returned home on the Navy battleship USS *Wyoming***

**Scotland**. Edinburgh was our first port of call. Our sightseeing coaches took us into the highlands for views of a beautiful landscape complete with "lochs" and old castles. Nessy, the famous Loch Ness Monster, had not yet been "invented"! At pull-outs along the way, there were pipers droning and cantering to entertain the tourist buses.

We cadets and our officers were invited to tea in Edinburgh Castle. We were told to form a line so that Lord So-and-So could greet each of us. We were to give our names. (I think now that he must have been intrigued by the ethnic origins of our American family names.) When I gave my name as "Cadet Sin'clair" he chuckled and said, "Ah,

Scottish eh? Sink'ler, Sink'ler." We were then offered a "nice cup o' tea." With it came a little cookie and a choice of lemon or milk. I chose the lemon, but the tea was too hot to drink, so I added milk...which curdled! I discretely deposited my awful looking tea on a convenient shelf, and went for a stroll around the castle. There in the pavement was the burial stone of Lord Sinclair!

**Denmark** was our next port of call and the best by far. We moored at the guest dock at Langelinie Park, the gateway to Copenhagen. Just a few boat lengths ahead was the famous "Little Mermaid," known to the Danes a "Havfrau," meaning half woman! A beautiful young female seated demurely on a bolder surrounded by bay water (to keep children from climbing on her and photographers from using her for a photo prop).

We set port and starboard watches in port. On the first watch, I was assigned as Messenger, under the direction of the First Classman who was assigned as Officer-of-the-Deck. We were hardly oriented to our posts when a Dane approached by water in his single scow, getting his morning exercise, I suppose. We watched and admired his adeptness on the oars. Suddenly, he boated his oars and crawled aft to where his Danish flag was flying and he dipped his flag! The cadet OD called to me, "Hurry! Return the salute!" I dashed to our stern and lowered our ensign and immediately "two-blocked" it again. Salute returned. The Dane was pleased (and so were we).

One of our treats was hosted by the Danish Navy—the biggest, best, and most artistic smorgasbord I have ever seen, before or since!

Another special treat was a night visit to **Tivoli Gardens**. It was ablaze with lights and an extra large crowd. We soon found out why: it was the night of the Summer Solstice, which the Danes called "Mid-Summer Night"—cause for celebration! Like we might expect at Halloween, a witch came out of nowhere (on a wire) and streaked across the sky, tail of fire, fireworks, and all! (The Danish beer wasn't bad either!)

One more treat I will mention was a tour of the **Tuborg Brewery**. It started off as usual looking at the vats and uninteresting equipment which we had to tolerate before we got to the tasting room. While huge trays of draft brew were brought endlessly into the room, the lights were lowered so we could see a movie of Tuborg Beer being shipped around the world. Well, after the first round of drinks, matters got out of hand. We picked up on the movie's theme song: "It's Tuborg Makes the World Go 'Round." At about the third time 'round, beautiful four-part harmony filled the room. What gives? When the lights came on, we found we were in company with the Yale Glee Club on concert tour.

The story doesn't end there. At our tables were ceramic ashtrays about six inches in diameter and two inches thick with TUBORG in bold letters. I'm sure they were meant to be swiped, but who was asking? I got one. So did our heavyweight boxer nicknamed McGuff. I don't recall how I carried mine, but he tucked his under his belt and topcoat. Outside, waiting for traffic to pass, his fell out and smashed on the pavement. A Dane equal in size said, "Ve doan do dat. Pick it op!" McGuff did. We helped. I had mine at home for many years...advertising TUBORG, the beer that makes the world go 'round.

**Germany**. Hamburg was our port of call. Before we were granted liberty for a tour of Berlin, we were thoroughly briefed on the political situation. Note these dates: Hitler was the leader of Germany from 1933 to 1945. The Summer Olympics were held in Germany in 1936. The Holocaust, or mass murder of Jews, was from 1939 to 1945. Our cruise visit was in summer 1936. We were not to discuss politics with anyone, not even among ourselves. Quislings were everywhere. Storm Troopers were to be avoided.

While Hitler was brainwashing the people into believing they were a superior race, he was preparing for war. We would not see any evidence of this. What we saw on our city tour of Berlin was a clean city, with old historic buildings scrubbed and painted. No beggars or homeless.

We toured in a big open bus. It was a lovely, clear day with a warm sun. It was sooo relaxing after scrubbing the *Cayuga's* decks and standing watches that we couldn't stay awake. The poor tour director was at wit's end, shouting, "Gentlemen! You are supposed to be sightseeing Berlin...not sleeping through it!"

We were ordered not to leave the main streets and to always be in a group. And so a small group of us visited a nightclub. It was not unlike ours at home except for the table arrangements. Spaced around the dance floor, each table had a number clearly displayed above it and a telephone on it. If you saw an attractive girl at a table across the room you could break the ice by telephoning that table and visiting awhile, or send over a drink and play cool until you stirred up interest and got an invitation to join forces.

**France**. We moored portside to a quay in Le Havre. It was made of cold hard granite, which was covered with slimy algae kept wet by a fifteen-foot tidal range. We rigged four mooring lines: bow, forward spring, after spring, and stern. They had to be adjusted every watch. No fun.

I don't remember the tourist sights of Paris except for going up the Eiffel Tower. What I do remember is seeing the Red Light District! We had been thoroughly briefed on the hazards of romancing a local girl or woman. Incurable sexual diseases were rampant. Becoming infected would lead to dismissal from the Academy. We would be physically examined (called short-arm inspection) after sailing. When ashore, stay in groups. Avoid "ladies of the night" and their pimps. If in close encounter, "looky but no touchy."

With a group of cadets, I walked the Red Light District streets past the cribs of prostitutes beckoning for your trade. They were licensed and regulated. They stayed in their cribs and did not come out to harass or touch us. Really, a very pathetic sight. So much for France.

**Spain**. En route to the Madeira Islands, we were diverted to Bilbao, a port on the north coast of Spain. The Spanish Civil War (1936-1939) was raging, and was being won by the rebels. Francisco Franco later became dictator. Our orders were to evacuate U.S. citizens, transporting them around the corner to Saint-Jean-de-Luz.

The Naval Academy midshipmen's cruise, consisting of two old battleships, was also sent to Bilbao. Those ships were too large for evacuating Americans locally, so the decision was reached to transfer us cadets to the battleship *Wyoming* for the return to Norfolk and leave the Coast Guard cutter *Cayuga* in Spain to serve the Ambassador.

**USS *Wyoming*.** This cruise would provide an interesting comparison of the training opportunities for the small number of cadets as compared with the problem of training the large number of midshipmen.

For example: at sea, we were on watch four hours and off eight. Our Third Class stations were helmsman, messenger, and lookout. We would steer almost every watch. A midshipman got one hour on the helm during the entire cruise, with a quartermaster at his side. When assigned to engineering duty, we traced pipes and cables for our notebooks, helped change and adjust burners in the boiler room, kept the areas clean, etc. I drew engineering duty with the midshipmen assigned to the boiler room (130 degrees and under pressure). Our duty was to sit four hours in the entrance way to keep cool in the forced draft. No work of any kind. Just an endurance test.

At the end of the engineering watch, we went to the head and drew a bucket of water, which we poured over our heads to cool off.

The head had a trough of sea water running all the time out the stern. Mounted over the trough were toilet seats. A favorite stunt was to wait until several seats were occupied, then gather a big handful of toilet paper, light it off, and send it downstream. Need I describe the action that followed?

When on a day-shift without watch-standing duties, our whole class was assigned to the starboard air castle, a shelter in the superstructure, to keep it clean. We were to chip away the rust and slap on fresh paint. That took about two days. After that, we spent our days in a watertight compartment down in the bilges, where no officer would find us! (It was kinda scary.)

Some higher authority thought it would be fun to have a little competition between the midshipmen and the cadets. There must have been about one thousand of them to one hundred of us. Anyway, we were game.

Their first mistake was boxing matches. That was one event in which we excelled because our trainer was once a national lightweight champ. We easily took that challenge.

Their second mistake was to have a race launching the lifeboats for a man-overboard drill. This we did regularly on our cutter, completely handled by cadets with the First Class in charge. The "Now Hear This" speaker came on announcing, "Man overboard. This is a drill." Our designated First Classman took charge with a First Classman on the boat falls fore and aft, and a First Classman ready to man the steering oar and take charge as coxswain. Members of my class were assigned to the oars.

We rushed to our boat and were ordered by our Cadet-in-Charge to "take your stations." When all aboard, he ordered us to "lower away fore and aft." The naval officer in charge of the drill about had a fit. "What are you doing?" "I'm launching the boat, sir." "You have no permission to launch." "I'm in charge, sir." "You must have a Warrant Officer on each fall." "We don't have any Warrant Officers, sir." "Stop lowering. I will get you one." The Navy won this contest.

Back at Norfolk, we joined the Midshipmen in gunnery practice, firing a few rounds. I don't remember the details but am told we scored better than they did.

That is enough about my year as a Third Class cadet. On return to New London from our training cruise, we were granted our month long summer leave. It was a long way to my Santa Monica home, an adventure in itself. I went west by tourist coach, sitting up all the way. I returned hitchhiking on the Navy Secretary's plane to Montgomery, Alabama, an Air Corps' Flying Fortress to Wright Patterson Field in Ohio, and lastly by train to the Academy just before my leave was up! That leave was tremendously important to me. It was the last time I was to see my mother.

# SCENE 13

# COAST GUARD ACADEMY—1937-1938 (SECOND CLASS YEAR / ACADEMICS)

### Academics, Local Cruising in Schooner *Chase*, Home Leave by Car

In June each year, there is a special formal ball known as the Ring Dance. A replica of the First Class ring (but large enough to walk through) is fashioned and mounted on a raised platform. A rite of passage will honor the Third Class as it ascends to Second Class status, and honor the Second Class on becoming First Class cadets. The Third Classmen have designed and purchased miniature rings sized to fit their little fingers, but they have not yet been allowed to wear them. The Second Class purchased their miniatures last year and now have their full-sized rings ready for the ceremony. (These rings are, by design, a standard tradition of all the service academies. It is one way to spot an academy grad.)

When his name is announced, the Cadet Third Class and his date mount the platform and stand inside the ring. He takes out the miniature, and she places it on the little finger of his left hand. She most likely will give him a kiss. If they are, or intend to become engaged, the cadet may place the ring on his girl's ring finger. (Not usually the case with a Cadet Second Class.)

A similar ceremony takes place for the Cadet Second Class ascending to First Class, except he already has the miniature on his little finger. His lady removes it and hands it to him. If they wish to signal an engagement, he places the miniature on her ring finger. Otherwise he simply pockets the miniature. Then, he hands her the full-sized ring for her to place on his ring finger. (And surely he will get a kiss!)

The miniature is often used instead of a diamond solitaire along with the wedding ring. My wife, Mary, chose to do that.

**Academics**. The curriculum is structured to meet the requirements for a Bachelor of Science degree in Marine Engineering. To qualify, the Academy must be "accredited" by the New England Association of Schools. To meet their goals, we followed closely the M.I.T. curriculum. But in addition to their courses in science, mathematics, mechanical, electrical, electronic and chemistry, we had superimposed professional subjects including seamanship, navigation, ordnance, military law, leadership, infantry drill, and physical education.

**The *Tide Rips* yearbook staff**

The spring and fall terms lasted about seventeen weeks, with one week devoted to examinations. Each cadet had to pass all subjects in the prescribed course of study. A grade of at least sixty-five was required to pass. Cadets attended seven class periods a day of fifty-five minutes each. Those who scored below sixty-five in the final exam would be given a re-exam. Failing that exam led to dismissal.

However, there was room for manipulation by the teaching staff when it was in the service's interest to retain a cadet with high adaptability. Without bragging, I believe I twice fell into that category. The two-and-a-half years of pre-engineering courses at UCLA made the first two years at the Academy relatively easy, and the physics lab a bore. My classmates would crowd around the instructor when he was demonstrating something. I would let them do the crowding while I stood back.

Some wise-guy found out our academic records were kept in the Commandant of Cadets' office, and if we asked his yeoman he would give us a peek. I found that the physics instructor (a Lieutenant) had given me a low mark in adaptability and the Commandant of Cadets (a Commander) gave me a high mark, quite obviously as a counter-balance.

Spanish was my elective foreign language. I took beginning Spanish in high school, beginning Spanish in college, and beginning Spanish yet again at the Academy. Still, I failed the course and had to take the re-exam! My re-exam grade was sixty-five! (They obviously were not going to send me, with high adaptability marks, home for failing Spanish.)

Our navigation instructor challenged our class to do a little research before the next class to explain the difference between a watch and a chronometer and why the precision was essential for accurate navigation. After the "ATTENTION" and "BE SEATED," the instructor asked, "Who can tell me about the chronometer?" (Silence! What he didn't know was that we were having an exam in physics later in the morning, which was of higher priority and to which we gave all our study time to the exclusion of the little chronometer question.) He asked the question again. Again silence! Finally, in an exasperated voice he said, "Doesn't anyone know anything about chronometers?" To which a voice from the back row exclaimed, "NO, SIR. YOU CAN SPEAK FREELY!"

When the Connecticut winter sets in, it is a lot easier to attend chapel in the Academy auditorium than to walk down to town for church. Quite a few officers and some with their wives attended the chapel too. Hymns were belted out accompanied by selected instruments from the official Coast Guard Band. The Coast Guard did not have a chaplain so one from the Navy submarine base came over to conduct our service. One Sunday, the chaplain was a hellfire and brimstone preacher. He was laying it on pretty thick. Directly below the improvised pulpit was the clarinet player who was hung over from the night before. He listened patiently as long as he could, but finally he had to comment. He leaned

**Local sailing on Bluenose Schooner** *Chase*

way back in his chair and looked straight up at the chaplain and said in a loud gravely voice, "You tell 'em, chaplain!"

Our formal uniform jacket was short-waisted with two rows of buttons to a built-in high collar. It was nicknamed the monkey jacket because it resembled the uniform worn by an organ grinder's monkey. A group of us wore them during one Christmas leave to crash debutante coming-out balls in New York City. It worked! We were never thrown out or asked to depart.

But one night, I was waiting in the lobby of the Pennsylvania Hotel in that uniform when a dowager came up to me and asked for a light. I didn't smoke and had no matches anyway, but I was put out that she thought I was a bellhop. I simply said, "I'm sorry ma'am. I am not a bellhop." To which she replied, "Well! I thought at least you were a gentleman!" and walked away. (I was so embarrassed that I remember that put-down to this day.)

I owned an auto the last two years at the Academy. It was against regulations to own a car in New London, so I kept mine just across the city line, in a farmer's old barn a short walk from our North Gate. My winter project was to put it in good condition for a drive to California during summer leave. But, returning from liberty, the engine threw a piston, and I had to leave it on the street outside. Together with three other cadets who were planning the cross-country journey, we laid detailed plans to repair the engine in the Academy's garage.

We talked a classmate into going to a wrecker for the necessary part and driving the car onto the reservation and into the garage. This he did and on a Saturday afternoon, in the garage, we pulled the pan and replaced the piston. We worked late into the evening, a time there would be no officers around. We tuned the engine and had it running beautifully. Now part of our plan was based on the garage being directly across from the auditorium where chapel services are held. We had just one chance to pull this off or we were in deep trouble.

The band struck up a good Baptist hymn and everyone present burst into song with loud, clear voices. We swung open the garage door, revved up the engine, and the same classmate drove the car off the reservation and to my barn garage, without missing a beat.

We were getting the car in as good shape as we could because three classmates joined me in a plan to drive to the West Coast on summer leave. One had a mother in Oakland. One a mother in Coronado. My family was in Santa Monica. The fourth's family was in New Jersey, and he had been visiting home regularly, but had never been far from New England. He grabbed at this chance to see the West Coast.

The car was a two-door Ford, which I bought off the salvage yard lot. (Back to Jalopies.) It was a drab olive color, which was nice because it didn't show the dirt. There was a running board on each side and a rack on the back bumper on which we tied everything we could. We pooled our resources for a new set of tires. We bought the cheapest we could find, guaranteed to last four thousand miles. We named the car "Fukalo," although I never did know the meaning. It sounded nice.

One fine spring day, I followed the practice we cadets had of checking our mail boxes en route to the next class. I found this in mine: "WESTERN UNION 1937 MAY 10 COMMANDING OFFICER…USCG ACADEMY…NOTIFY CADET SINCLAIR HIS MOTHER PASSED ON PEACEFULLY AT SIX THIRTY THIS MORNING= FRED W SINCLAIR." Yes, I was notified, but in what a cold way…left standing alone with the telegram in my hand.

This was shattering news, but with the support of the others we decided to go ahead with the trip.

There were no Interstate Highways in those days. There were U.S. highways, but these were not Freeways. They were numbered by routes. For instance, the northernmost east-west route was Route 10. The southernmost was 90. North and south were odd numbers like 1, 17, and 101. In the Plain states, squatters were granted land in parcels often in squares. The U.S. highways honored those property rights and made square corners (tricky driving at night). And we drove day and night. We slept in Fukalo anyway, so it didn't matter much if we were underway or pulled off to a side road.

Top driving speed was 45 miles per hour. It took us five days each way. We used public and service station toilets, but we didn't have a bath or shave the whole way from sea to shining sea. We ate at diners and car-hops. It was about six thousand miles round trip, and, as we reached the final stretch back to New London, we had blow-outs one by one! We replaced them with re-treads.

My time at home was bittersweet. It was _so_ sad that my mom was not there, but so wonderful to see many family members and Sea Scout friends. And to sail to Catalina with my brother on his boat.

# SCENE 14

# COAST GUARD ACADEMY—1938-1939 (FIRST CLASS YEAR)

## Cruise to South America, Gunnery & Small Arms, Hurricane

The new uniform insignias showed our new status. Fourth Classmen had only the Coast Guard shield on their sleeves and shoulder boards. Third Classmen had a single narrow gold diagonal stripe. First Classmen had one narrow horizontal stripe with extra stripes for Battalion Officer status. I was a Company Adjutant with two stripes. The Company Commander rated three and the Battalion Commander four.

We were feeling pretty important now, sporting the class ring and feeling we were sure to make it to graduation and its rewards.

Yes, I was sailing the sloops quite often now and enjoying the privilege of taking dates along. On one occasion, a funny thing happened. Two of my classmates were very good friends, but they complained about everything. We called that "bitching." Their term of endearment each for the other was shortened to simply "bitch." One day, they were sailing in a brisk breeze with their dates when they accidentally jibed, which meant the boom changed sides violently. The cadet on the tiller saw it coming and the other one didn't, so he yelled, "Duck, bitch!"—and both girls "hit the deck"!

It is time now to start our First Class cruise aboard the **Coast Guard cutter *Bibb***, one of our six largest cutters known as the Secretary Class, length 327 feet. Beautiful lines. White hull with buff colored stack and trim. A long teak quarter deck was designed to carry a single float aircraft on board. (There were no helicopters in those days.) Our courses will take us to the east coast of South America. The *Bibb* is moored at the Academy now. The First Class and Third Class cadets are aboard.

We First Classmen will fill officers' billets under the eyes of the skeleton crew of regular ship's officers, such as Officer-of-the-Day, Officer-of-the-Deck, Navigator, Engineer, Quartermaster, First Lieutenant, and Chief Boatswains' Mate.

Listen in on the bridge and this is what you might hear as the Captain takes the conn. The Executive Officer is reporting to him: "Sir, the chronometer has been wound. The siren and whistle have been tested. The crew has been mustered and all hands are accounted for. The anchor detail has been posted (safety precaution) and a Quartermaster is on the helm. Second Class cadets are on the dock to handle mooring lines. The Chief Engineer reports steam up and ready to answer bells."

Captain: "Very well, single-up all mooring lines and take in the gangway."

"Sir, the gangway is on board."

"Very well, take in all lines. Shift the ensign to the gaff for cruising. Quartermaster, sound one long blast (on the whistle to announce to other ships we are leaving the dock). All engines astern one-third. Quartermaster, sound three short blasts (to announce our engines are in reverse)."

(*Bibb* clears the dock and enters the channel.)

"All engines stop. Left full rudder. All engines ahead two-thirds. Rudder amidships. Steady as you go. Mr. Sinclair, take the conn. We are leaving port, so keep the green channel buoys to starboard."

"Aye, aye, Captain. I relieve you, sir."

Our ports of call will be:
- St. Thomas, Virgin Islands
- Port-of-Spain, Trinidad
- (Crossing the Equator)
- Rio de Janeiro, Brazil
- Buenos Aires, Argentina
- Bahia, Brazil
- Norfolk, Virginia
- New London, Connecticut

Let us see what I can remember of each?

**St. Thomas**. We anchored in St. Thomas Harbor, and the anchor was hardly wet when we were surrounded by bum boats. This was my first experience with this type of trade that takes place in little foreign ports.

Native fruits are the favorite offering along with native crafts. The natives like money best but will settle for clothing or candy or food or pens and will practically give you their boat for American cigarettes.

Diving for coins tossed into the water is fun to watch. The coin flutters like a falling leaf as it descends, giving the diver a chance to intercept it.

A popular song was "Rum and Coca Cola" and so was the drink. We saw old sugar plantations, and men harvesting sugar cane with their machetes. We learned about rum punch at Blue Beard's Castle.

The United States purchased the Virgin Islands from Denmark in 1917. Although we have always driven to the right side of the road, here they did not make the change from the European system. They still drive on the left. The explanation is: we could train the stubborn Danes, but we could never train the burros!

In St. Thomas harbor, we experienced bum boat commerce

**Port-of-Spain.** It was a short cruise but a busy one. We held a field day. The first order was to "air all bedding." That meant to bring your bedding to the main deck and trice it up to the lifelines. One big chore was to rig the awning which sheltered the whole quarterdeck. Another detail was assigned to look for rust spots and to chip away the rust and paint. (The saying was, "If it don't move, paint it!") Holy-stoning that huge teak deck was reserved for another day.

It was hot and sweaty work. The Trade Winds were light and following. The heat was getting to us as we came to anchor. Suddenly, and I don't know from whence it came, but *ice cold grapefruit* appeared with a half for each of us. It is my fondest memory of Trinidad.

On liberty, we visited the ANGOSTURA aromatic bitters plant where the world's supply is made. I use it to this day for making a good manhattan into an excellent manhattan.

**Crossing the Equator.** The age of exploration of oceans began when Christopher Columbus demonstrated by his journeys to the New World that sailing uncharted waters need not be become voyages of no return. Astronomers and navigators working together plotted on charts the newly acquired knowledge of the earth and sun movements. It became a challenge and honor to cross those lines. The Equator was known to the ancients, but now there were several new lines, like the Arctic Circle, Antarctic Circle, Tropic of Cancer, Prime Meridian, and Date Line. Several of them have ceremonies and recognition for crossing.

The planners of our cruise knew, of course, that we would cross "the line" between Port-of-Spain and Rio de Janeiro, and we came prepared for the traditional high jinks with costumes and other contraptions.

King Neptune holds court to pass judgment on the pollywogs, those who have not crossed the equator. He initiates them into the *Ancient Order of Shellbacks.* The Queen, Davy Jones, and the Royal Babies help carry out his orders. Traditional antics include lathering with goop and shaving with a rusty piece of barrel stave, wearing a wig of unbraided rope, kissing a Royal Baby's belly, dunkings, etc.

Many buckets of water were dumped on the unexpected. It felt good since we were in the tropics. A portable pool was rigged on deck. A special chair was mounted on the edge of the pool, backside to. It was reserved for special candidates, namely the Captain and Commodore and other pollywog officers. At King Neptune's command, the chair was tilted backwards and the victim slid head first and face up into the pool. The Captain and Commodore were good sports, and everyone had a good time. We were all awarded certificates for our transformation from Pollywogs to Shellbacks!!

**King Neptune and his court. Crossing the equator on our cadet cruise, 1936, we advanced from "Pollywogs" to "Shellbacks"**

**Rio de Janeiro**, the "Gem of Brazil," was our next port of call. Brazil is the fifth largest country in the world, larger than all of Europe. But how come they speak Portuguese when most of the other South American countries speak Spanish? Here is how come:

Following the discovery of America by Columbus there was a rush by ships claiming new territories under the Spanish flag. While they were doing this the Portuguese were working their way around Africa and to the east seeking the Spice Islands and a route to the Orient. When the Portuguese woke up to what the Spanish were claiming, they cried, "Foul," and appealed to the Pope saying the new found islands should be theirs as they already had islands nearby (nearby? some four thousand miles away!). Since both Spain and Portugal were Catholic, Pope Alexander VI would rule. It led to the 1494 Treaty of Tordesillas, where a north-south line was established 370 leagues west of the Cape Verde Islands. This turned out to be the 46-degree-west meridian. The Portuguese would claim lands east of that line and the Spanish west. Most of Brazil was east of the line. That is how come the Brazilians speak Portuguese.

That imaginary line became known as the "Line of Demarcation" and was to have far reaching effect. Unlike the other lines mentioned, this was unrelated to the antics of the sun, moon, or stars. When the longitude line is followed down to the South Pole and up the other side, it puts the Pacific Ocean and its islands in the Spanish sector. It reached to the Philippine Islands. Magellan complied with this ruling although he was a Portuguese navigator sailing on a Spanish mission. When he reached the Spice Islands, he found the Portuguese were already there. He was killed there in a local war.

RIO DE JANEIRO at last. The famous Sugar Loaf Mountain at the entrance to the bay rises to 1,299 feet. As the bay opens to full view, the statue of Christ the Redeemer is seen standing on top of Corcovado (Hunchback Mountain) rising to 2,300 feet above the city. The *Bibb* was assigned a berth alongside the landscaped park at Avenida Rio Branco, one of the city's main thoroughfares.

We cadets were invited to a reception at the Brazilian Naval Academy. As soon as we were settled in, Brazilian cadets appeared with trays of rum punch. We were dumbfounded and didn't know what to do, as our Academy regulations forbid drinking alcohol. With the speed of lightning, the word was passed that the Flotilla Commander said one or two drinks would be okay. (We mustn't offend our hosts.)

I'm foggy about what that night's activities were all about, but clear on what went on. We assembled at the bottom of a trail leading up an undeveloped hill. We were joined by a group of college age Brazilian youth. The girls carried bamboo poles with little paper lanterns dangling from the end with a lighted candle inside. The boys carried roman candle fireworks, which they shot off unannounced with reckless abandon. We threaded our way like a torchlight parade to the top without causing a firestorm or incinerating anyone and groped our way back down and out of harm's way! (I'll never know what we were celebrating.)

It was customary in Brazil, as in most tropical countries, to have the major meal midday. A special meal had been arranged for us in a very nice restaurant, elegantly served. After a small salad came a little fried fillet of fish. (We thought that was it! They call this "dinner?") We were insulted. Just as we were about to storm out, lo', the main course appeared. It was a big chunk of beef, and there was a delicious big dessert to follow! (A culinary lesson learned.)

Three of us cadets were sightseeing (yes, girl watching) along Copacabana Beach when a middle-aged woman approached us. She was an American lady whose husband was with IBM and stationed in Rio. She said her home was across the bay, and if we would bring our bathing suits, we could change in her house and walk to a much nicer beach than here. She gave us her address and bus directions. We took her up on the invitation. Her home was middle-class U.S. except that in the bathroom where we changed there was a strange porcelain plumbing fixture we couldn't make out. Was it a drinking fountain for a pet? Was it for a foot bath? What use could it possibly have? (It was my first look at a bidet.)

**Buenos Aires** at last, the southernmost port of our cruise. We were out of the tropics, which was a relief. Buenos Aires is at about the same latitude south of the Equator as San Diego is north of the Equator. It felt very much like Southern California.

We were treated to a wonderful "asado" or Argentina barbecue. I have never seen so many beef steaks in my life. It was delicious and we gorged ourselves. Then, the gauchos put on demonstrations of their special skills. One was walking on hot coals from the barbecue pit. Another riding horses at breakneck speed while bringing down calves with their bolas. They demonstrated use of the bullwhip to control herded cattle. And, of course, there was some native music and dance. A great day!

That night, three of us went ashore for a night on the town. At a night club, which seemed to be closing for the night, we met the director of a little combo who said he was an American and would show us around. Well, after a couple of rum punch drinks, he did steer us to another night club which was open but almost empty. LO and BEHOLD, there across the room sat our Commodore with a sexy looking babe! We had ordered another drink, but one look at the clock reminded us that liberty was almost up. We gulped the drinks and got out of there.

I don't remember any trouble getting back to the ship and hitting the sack, but come morning, that was another thing. I am told my classmates tried but couldn't stir me. I missed first muster, was allowed to sleep it off, and was awarded fifty (50 that is!) demerits. (I had failed to apply the knowledge I had learned back at UCLA when the basketball coach served us martinis, about how rum can act slowly and sneak up on you in contrast to how gin right away tells you if you are getting a buzz on.)

**Bahia**, over halfway up the coast from Buenos Aires, was our last foreign port. It was an anti-climax. About all I remember (and, yes I was sober) was the big spread of souvenirs, fruits, and native crafts laid on the dock around our gangway. The harbor scene was tropical beauty—lush foliage and a little fishing harbor of gaff-rigged sailing craft with masts made of crooked tree trunks. Off now for good old U.S.A.

**Norfolk** for live gunnery drill. (I will probably do a poor job describing the required teamwork.) Arrangements had been made with the Navy for a towed target at which we would fire our five-inch gun. There was a fire control team that calculated entries for the gun sights. An ammo team to bring the projectiles and powder charges from the magazine in the bilges to the ready boxes on deck. Spotters to report the hits and misses. The gun crew consisted of the gun captain, the pointer, the trainer, the sight setter, the loader, and the swabber.

The gun captain opens the breach. The swabber looks through the bore to make sure there is no residue from a previous firing and swabs it out if in doubt. An ammo man inserts a projectile through the open breach (breach-loading gun). Another ammo man inserts a package of explosive powder. The gun captain closes and locks the breach and inserts a fuse. The trainer and pointer get on target. The gun captain reports ready for firing. Fire control gives permission to fire at will.

An announcement alerts all hands. Those on deck cover their ears and open their mouth to ease pressure of the gun blast, the loudest you have ever heard. The gun recoils about two feet. Fire control tries to fire a little long and next a little short, thus bracketing the target. The third round is expected to hit the target. I have conveniently forgotten our results!

**New London**, at last, ended our cruise unceremoniously as we had to shift gears for the Marine Corps Firing Range at Cape May and instruction in the Springfield 30-caliber bolt-action rifle and the Colt 45 pistol. I did pretty well there, earning the Expert Rifleman Medal and the Expert Pistol Medal. (Not surprising, as I was on the Rifle Team at the Academy.)

**This picture was taken on the Thames River in New London, Connecticut, in the aftermath of the hurricane of 1938**

With the cruise and the small arms instruction behind us, we were granted summer leave. On our return we had to face one more academic year, now as First Classmen, and we had just settled in when the infamous hurricane of 1938 hit New England. The Academy buildings were not hurt, but the training Schooner *Dobin* was sunk at her dock. A small colony of houseboats up the Thames River was wrecked. As a member of a search party, I discovered an old woman, dead and curled up in a corner of her little houseboat home.

My First Class year was a long and eventful year finally culminating in graduation and the beginning of a lifetime career as a Commissioned Officer in the United States Coast Guard.

# SCENE 15

## COAST GUARD ACADEMY—1939 (GRADUATION)

### Drive Home for Leave and on to First Duty Station

Graduation Week is a joyful one for almost everybody. The final exams are history. The Formal Ball is glamorous with cadets in formal uniforms and their dates in formal gowns. The Inter-Class Sailing Race was exciting and my class entry, which I skippered, won for the fourth year in a row. A Coast Guard single float aircraft was giving rides to First Classmen and demonstrating water takeoffs and landings for our guests. The Baccalaureate Service was well attended. The many parents and siblings of the cadets present added a festive mood to Grad Week. My father and brother Porter had driven all the way from California to honor me. That certainly added to my pleasure that week.

My classmates and I could hardly wait for the Graduation Ceremony where we received our Diplomas, Bachelor of Science Degrees in Marine Engineering, and to my great surprise I was awarded the Charles S. Root prize for the highest grade in Mechanical Drawing. As a class, we took the Oath of Office and we were commissioned Ensigns in the United States Coast Guard.

Immediately after dismissal, we removed our cadet shoulder boards and had them replaced with Ensign boards. They are traditionally pinned on by one's mother, if present, or best girlfriend, if you have one. I had neither, so I gave the honor to my dad and my brother simultaneously, one on each shoulder.

There were some tears as the reality of leaving the Academy sank in. But for most of us, it was exciting to be leaving the confines of the reservation for the world outside. But there were some girlfriends, if not betrothed, who could see their handsome cadets slipping away.

**My father came to my graduation from the Coast Guard Academy in 1939. We then drove together across the United States to my first duty station on the West Coast**

**Permanent Change of Station (PCS) Orders.** We were given the privilege of selecting our first duty station from a list of those available. But the order of granting the request was based on the class standing. I was tenth out of eighty-seven when I entered the Academy and I graduated tenth out of twenty-four. The choice was limited to large cutters. I requested a ship based in San Diego, but a classmate outranked me. However, I got my second choice which was the **Coast Guard cutter *Duane***. It was one of our largest and newest cutters. It was based in Oakland. *California here I come—right back where I started from!*

**PCS Orders** could come with short notice to execute. If they arrived by radio and were classed as **Dispatch Orders**, the recipient must be underway within twenty-four hours. This would mean leaving without time to wrap up personal affairs. Dispatch Orders were only issued in an emergency.

**Proceed Orders** allowed four days to arrange personal affairs and get underway. In addition, there was an allowance for travel time. Flying was unheard of, so driving time was based on mileage at four hundred fifty miles per day. And between stations might be a good time to take some earned leave.

This worked great for me. I usually had plenty of leave "on the books." Since most of my transfers were all the way across the United States, I usually put four days proceed plus six days travel plus thirty days leave together and had a nice long break of forty days!

To ease the pressure upon getting orders, there was a Friday Night Gazette which listed forthcoming orders that would permanently change stations. If you were expecting orders, this advance notice helped a lot.

**My first PCS Orders** were hand delivered to me and read something like this:

From: Commandant U.S. Coast Guard

To: Ensign David W. Sinclair, USCG

Subj: Orders. Permanent Change of Station

1. When so ordered by the Superintendent, proceed and report to the Commander, San Francisco District for further orders to the USCGC *Duane* stationed in Oakland, California.

2. You are granted 4 days proceed time, mileage calculated at 450 miles a day by the most direct automobile route, and leave not to exceed 30 days.

3. Submit a travel claim upon reporting to the CGC *Duane*.

And so it came to pass that it was time to depart the Academy and drive with my father and brother to California, a new adventure contributing to this Great Life. The scenery of the most northern cross-country route was beautiful and different from the other areas I had visited and three stops en route were especially educational.

New York World's Fair, 1939

First, the **New York World's Fair**. It had just opened in April. Sixty-two nations took part. Its theme was "the world of tomorrow." The fair was symbolized by the Trylon (triangular obelisk seven hundred feet high) and Perisphere (great ball two hundred feet in diameter). Both snow-white. The buildings and exhibits were designed to point out how man's accomplishments could improve world living conditions. Over twenty-five million attended the first year and another nineteen million the second year. It was really great.

My father wanted to visit the **Niagara Falls** because they had become a favorite tourist center and known throughout America as a "honeymooner's paradise." They are truly a sight to see. The river plunges <u>five hundred thousand tons of water a minute</u> into a

**Niagara Falls, at the beginning of our westward journey**

steep-walled gorge. We took a ride on the *Maid of the Mist* excursion boat that takes passengers as close under the falls as safe. Yes, under pretty heavy spray, but we were all fitted out with rain gear—sou'westers and all.

Our next big stop on our Westward Ho drive was the **Mount Rushmore National Memorial** in the Black Hills of South Dakota. It was built to embody the spirit of the foundation, preservation, and expansion of the United States. Four presidents were chosen to have their faces carved in the solid granite out cropping of Mount Rushmore.

The birth of our nation was guided by the vision and courage of George Washington. Thomas Jefferson always had dreams of something bigger, first in the words of the Declaration of Independence and later in the expansion of our nation through the Louisiana Purchase. Preservation of the union was paramount to Abraham Lincoln but a nation where all men were free and equal. At the turn of the twentieth century, Theodore Roosevelt saw that in our nation was the possibility of greatness. Our nation was changing from a rural republic to a world power. The ideals of these presidents laid a foundation for our nation as solid as the rock from which their figures are carved.

We visited the work studio to learn more. Sculptor Gutzon Borglum made models scaled one inch to one foot. These the workmen used in the studio and hauled up the mountain to take measurements and compute how much rock to cut away to form the faces and heads, which were each as high as a five story building. The workmen cut the figures from the granite with drills and dynamite. The project was started in 1927 and took fourteen years to complete.

**Scale model of Mount Rushmore used to take measurements for the carving of the actual monument, which was nearly completed at the time of our trip**

It was a beautiful drive out where the tall corn grows, across the prairie grasslands, up and over the Continental Divide, through big tree forests, and on miles of endless desert roads with their beautiful sunsets. At last we were on our final leg to Santa Monica and **638 Eleventh Street.**

What a difference four years can make! It was sad to see my home was no longer family packed and vibrant with activities. Where had everybody gone?

Cousin Scott Sterling was first to leave. After graduating from Santa Monica Junior College, he signed on with the Civilian Conservation Corps, which was a government service to help us recover from the Great Depression. They built and improved mountain trails. Scott was kicked in the head by a horse and wound up in the hospital. When released, he got a job with the Interior Department working on civil engineering projects.

I was next to leave, to serve my country as an officer in the U.S. Coast Guard.

My mother died of cancer in 1937, as I have previously reported.

Cousin Virginia Sterling had earned enough money to return to the University of Oregon to complete her education. She fell in love with Professor Charles Easton Rothwell. Even before we entered World War II, Easton was called to the State Department to help formulate post-war plans. He became the Executive Secretary in drafting the charter for the United Nations. Later, he was president of the prestigious Mills College for Women.

My aunt Fanny Sterling, mother of Virginia and Scott, died of meningitis while living at 638. Her husband, my uncle Ed Sterling, lost a leg to diabetes. He could no longer be cared for in Santa Monica, so Virginia and Easton took him in for the remainder of his life.

Who was left at 638?—Porter.

War was on in Europe and the draft was on here. Porter volunteered to join the Coast Guard, but he was classified 4-F because of poor eyesight and physically unfit for duty. He gave up his stockbroker job and found war-related work at the South Coast Company in Newport Beach, in construction of small craft. He met and fell in love with Margaret "Jill" Jillson, who lived in Pasadena. (That was too long a commute for dating, so he said they would have to get married, and they did.) They sold dear old **638** and bought a small house in the Bay Shores Estates. They added to our Sinclair Clan a son—Roy Porter Sinclair.

But what about our "extended 638 family"? What happened to my father's sisters, Aunt Lill and Aunt Kathryn? And Uncle Bill Gray? And my dog, Bobbie?

The Great Depression left Uncle Bill and his wife Lill destitute. Porter got them a job with the Boy Scout Council as caretakers at the Scout Weekend Camp in nearby Topanga Canyon. It didn't pay much but gave them a quiet place to live. They took Bobbie with them. Unfortunately, Bobbie, age about thirteen, jumped from the camp truck and broke a hip. He had to be put down. I don't know where or when Bill and Lill died, but they were heavy cigarette smokers, and I don't suppose lived for long.

When the Grays went to the camp job, my aunt Kathryn rented a room in Costa Mesa to be near Porter and Jill. She bought her meals at the corner drug store. One day she failed to show up, and they found she had died of a heart attack in her room.

Where did all those nice people go? Now you know! Virginia and I are, in 2004, the only 638 survivors. She is 97. I am pushing 89.

Continuing now with my **leave** en route, I enjoyed a couple of weeks with Porter, which included a sail from Santa Barbara to Newport Beach in his twenty-nine-foot Norwegian-built gaff-rigged **Dagge**, and a reunion with the few longtime friends still in the area. Then, and I don't remember how, I made my way to San Francisco, where I reported for further assignment to my first ship, the **Duane**. The trouble was, she was at sea enforcing the new twenty-mile fisheries limit. Since she would be out for another two weeks, the District Commander decided to send me to the **Coast Guard cutter Hamilton**, a sister ship on a local district patrol. Her duties were to follow into port the cargo vessels coming from the Orient to make sure they didn't drop bales of opium to be picked up by drug running speedboats for transfer ashore.

The *Hamilton*, like the *Duane*, was a 327-foot cutter with beautiful lines. These cutters, of which the Coast Guard had six, maintained strict adherence to military traditions, and kept the crews smartly uniformed, unlike several classes known as the Hooligan Navy for their dungaree uniforms for servicing buoys, ice breaking, lightship duties, etc.

When I reported to the *Hamilton,* she was anchored off the Marina District of San Francisco and undergoing an annual inspection by a special team of inspectors. Captain Romer, with forty years of sea duty, was Commanding Officer. I think it was satirical (or maybe sadistic) humor that he chose me to coxswain one lifeboat for man-overboard drill, and an Ensign one year my senior and on engineering duty to man the other lifeboat.

Before World War II, if you were in distress at sea, you tried to save yourself by sending out a distress message by wireless telegraph and heading for the nearest land. Consequently, the lifeboats were equipped with mountable masts and sails, and rations of water and hardtack (biscuits). And the officer wore a belt with a pistol, known as side-arms. (But since World War II, the procedure has been to stay put and let Search-and-Rescue find you.)

The instructions by the inspector was to launch the boat, row clear of the ship, set sails, and await the signal to return to the ship.

I knew there was a swift current plus wind coming at us from under the Golden Gate Bridge, so my plan was to sail close hauled as best I could to try and stay upwind of the *Hamilton*. It worked!

By the time of the recall signal, I had gained confidence in the control of the sails and the response of the crew. I asked them if they wanted to row back to the ship, as the "engineer" and his boat were doing from way downwind, or should we try sailing under the falls? They said, "Let's Sail!" And so we did by coming in up-current, dropping the sails, and boating the mast as we drifted in the falls. Boy was I proud!

The crew hooked on and we were raised to deck level. The inspector leaned over to me and said, "Mister, where is your first aid kit?" Well, I didn't have the slightest idea. I had to be honest and said I didn't know. He pointed out to me that it was on the back of my belt! I heard from the Captain. But he thought it was a good joke.

**From the 1939 *Tide Rips*—the Coast Guard Academy Yearbook**

## DAVID WILLIAM SINCLAIR

*Santa Monica, California*

■ Folks, meet "Soupy" Sinclair, the bonny Scot. You should have seen him swell with pride when we stumbled on those weathered headstones in Holyrood Castle that marked the place where some of his ancestors lay. A chip off the old block, he is thrifty to the Corps. His good business sense has carried TIDE RIPS through a stormy year and without his well-thought-out ideas the staff would have been in a bad way. He's as handy with a shovel as with a sail; we've heard many a regaling tale of the virtues of his sunny California. Be it weather, water, or women, she's got the best. Soupy's energy was not quite equal to his thriftiness, however, and during his last three years at the Academy his walking was confined to that necessary to carry him to and from class. In the past, the art of sailing in small boats has been somewhat neglected, and his work in making sailing a minor sport will always be appreciated. If there's work to be done, Soupy is the man who will "gripe" the most and get the most done. His ability to work hard at anything he undertakes will stand him in good stead always.

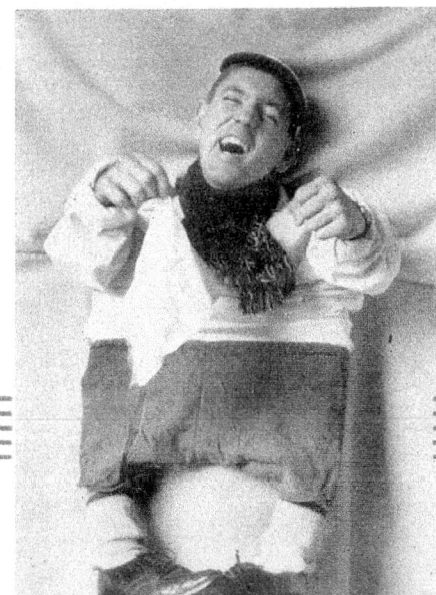

Business Manager, TIDE RIPS; Company Adjutant; Expert Rifleman; Rifle Team 3, 2, 1; Fifty Club; Commodore of Sailing 1.

*Coast Guard Academy—1939*

Graduation Parade

# SCENE 16

## CG CUTTER *DUANE*—1939-1940 (NEUTRALITY PATROL / WEATHER PATROL / GREENLAND VISITATION)

I reported to the *Duane* on her return to her Oakland, California, home port, and just in time for my August twentieth birthday. I turned twenty-four years old. Commander Grogan was the Captain. He assigned me to deck watches in port and the mid-watch underway (12-4 a.m. and 12-4 p.m.). My stateroom was the aftermost on the port side in officers' country. By ancient nautical custom, the starboard side of the ship is the senior side. A battleship at anchor would have a gangway on each side for liberty boats. The officers used the starboard side, the enlisted men the port.

On the *Duane*, the staterooms for officers lined the starboard and port sides with a passageway down the centerline. The Captain had a two-stateroom "cabin" under the bridge; the Executive Officer the forward stateroom on the starboard side; the Chief Engineer the forward stateroom on the port side. Other officers were assigned going aft with lowering rank until there was yours truly, most junior officer in the most junior stateroom! That put me directly above the port propeller (swish-swish-swish-swish, not to mention the rise-and-fall when pitching).

After about a week in Oakland, we relieved the *Hamilton* and anchored off the Marina District. The **Golden Gate International Exposition** was underway at Treasure Island, the landfill expanding Yerba Buena Island to the north. It was a beautiful sight at night—like a golden city of ancient lore!

On the third of September, while at anchor there, the radioman received an ALCOAST dispatch which read "A STATE OF WAR NOW EXISTS BETWEEN ENGLAND FRANCE AND GERMANY X JUDGE YOUR ACTIONS ACCORDINGLY."

On September 5, the messenger, with clipboard in hand, let officers read the dispatch just received as he made his way looking for the Exec in the wardroom. It read "DIRECT DUANE PROCEED TO EASTCOAST IMMEDIATELY X PERMANENT EASTCOAST STATION WILL FOLLOW." The time was 2020. At 2150, we were moored in Oakland and word was being spread like wildfire! It was tough on family men and their families. Easy for me. All I had to do was get rid of my jalopy.

On September 6, we went to the Mare Island Naval Shipyard for fuel and our wartime allocation of ammunition. On September 7, we passed under the beautiful Golden Gate Bridge at the start of our 5,450-mile cruise to the East Coast, still not knowing our destination!

On September 9, excitement so soon! I woke up after a short nap following the mid-watch to find everybody busy dogging down hatches and lashing things in place. The ship was being readied for a **hurricane**.

I am now going to quote from a notebook I kept. Bear in mind that we didn't have electronics like today with satellite navigation, or radar, or LORAN, or weather reports, or GPS. But we were more attuned to reading the weather as ancient mariners did through the ages.

*"We were about 400 miles south of San Diego and the storm was well ahead but heading our way. A large swell was coming from the south. The barometer was dropping with unsteady fluctuations. The clouds overhead were cirrus. Ahead on the horizon they were alto-stratus with some stratocumulus, much as should be expected. By mid-afternoon the wind hauled around indicating the storm had passed. Winds never exceeded 48 knots. The preparations were for naught, and I missed an experience which, while perhaps not pleasant, would be interesting to have while on a safe ship like this."*

It may have seemed like an anticlimax to us, but it was the only Mexican hurricane to strike Southern California in the twentieth century. And it hit during the Labor Day weekend, the traditional end of the summer sailing season. Hundreds of yachts were caught at sea in the Catalina Channel and many had serious storm damage.

Porter and two male friends, Onnie and Marty, with their dates were anchored in Emerald Bay when the storm hit. Porter feared *Dagge* would drag anchor and be washed ashore. A plan was decided: Porter and Marty would sail to Fisherman's Cove at the Isthmus, which had complete shelter. Onnie and the girls would hike to Fisherman's Cove and meet there.

The plan failed. *Dagge* was a slow, low-performance cruising boat. Try as they did, they couldn't beat against the strong wind to make it to the cove. There wasn't enough fuel aboard to motor, and it was years before VHF ship-to-shore communications. What to do? Porter decided to set a small storm tri-sail, heave-to, and ride out the storm.

The next morning, a Greek freighter spotted them off Point Hueneme, 60 miles up the coast. They radioed to Coast Guard. The **Coast Guard cutter *Ingham***, a sister ship of the *Duane*, also ordered to the East Coast and two days behind us, took them in tow. Off San Pedro, the tow was taken over by the **Coast Guard cutter *Hermes***, a 165-foot patrol vessel that took them to a safe haven.

Do you think that is the end of the story? Stay with me.

I had a classmate, Lynn Parker, on the *Ingham*, who was assigned to the mid-watch (12-4 a.m.) as was I. After his watch, he took a nap and after breakfast wrote his log. *Dagge* was in tow. The skipper's name was Sinclair. Lynn mused that he had a classmate named Sinclair who often spoke of sailing with his brother when on home leave. Do you suppose??

We cleared the Panama Canal before we received orders to Boston, our new home port. *Oh, No! Not New England again! What happened to that dream of West Coast duty?* And we learned that the *Hamilton* was ordered east too. And the *Ingham* was following us. *What's the big deal? Why the big rush?*

The biggest and newest cutters in 1939 were known as the Secretary Class, being named after Secretaries of the Treasury Department, of which the Coast Guard had been a part since 1790. There were only seven of that class and they were stationed with one in Pearl Harbor, three on the West Coast, and three on the East Coast. They were designed to be compatible with Navy operations and especially equipped for convoy escort duty. This class would join Navy destroyers in the **Neutrality Patrol** being established. They lacked the speed and fire power of a destroyer but had better sea-keeping qualities, could stay at sea more than a month without logistic support, and could cruise twelve thousand miles without refueling. The armament consisted of a five-inch gun, two twenty-millimeter machine guns, two fifty-caliber machine guns, two K-Guns, and depth charges. They had sonar and primitive radar. They had turbines with double-reduction gears and a top speed of twenty knots. They were beautiful ships, 327 feet in length and equipped to carry a single float seaplane.

Yes, but why the rush? We weren't at war! Maybe not, but the **Battle of the Atlantic** had started. German U-boats were sinking merchant ships of our allies close along our Atlantic coast. The U-boat operation they called "Drum Beat" sank three hundred sixty ships totaling 2,250,000 tons! And Germany lost only eight U-boats.

As I found out later, on September 5, 1938, President Roosevelt ordered the Navy to organize the Neutrality Patrol. By September 10, the plan was in place. By October, it was established for

Grumman J2F Duck scout plane used to search for potential airfield sites in Greenland, being lowered off the *Duane* for takeoff. Upon landing, the amphibious biplane was caught with a net and pulled to a crane to lift it back on board

continuous patrolling of an area about two hundred miles offshore, extending from the Grand Banks to Trinidad. The Coast Guard cutters would cover the easternmost areas and the Navy destroyers the coastal waters.

Lots of actions were taking place, including assignments of senior officers. Commander Grogan was relieved by Commander von Paulson. He was one of the Coast Guard's earliest aviators, who were known to be a daring and non-conforming bunch.

**Giving "sideboys" to the Governor of Greenland on board the *Duane***

He took command in Boston. The military etiquette we were taught at the Academy said that we officers must call on the Commanding Officer at his home and leave a calling card. The hours of 8 to 9 p.m. were specified. I tried to find his home in Chelsea, but by the time I got there it was after 9 p.m., so I tried again the next night. Right on time I found his apartment with a bare light bulb lit and hanging by its cord from the ceiling. I rang the door bell. No answer. I rang it twice more. Finally, his gruff voice came through the speaking tube, which old apartments often had in those days. He asked, "Who is there?" I said, "Ensign Sinclair calling, sir." He said, "I'm not at home!" (Click, voice tube shut.) I left my cards, one for him and one for his wife, as proper, and got the heck out of there.

*"One day on Neutrality Patrol we were hove-to but unable to maintain steerage-way at slow speed so needed to use the twin screws to keep us hove-to. The starboard lifeboat worked loose, but was on the lee side, so the crew secured it. Later the port lifeboat broke its gripe and we had to wait and hope until we were able to give it a lee. The anemometer exceeded its 90 knot limit and took off like a helicopter. The* Hamilton *stood by the ocean liner* President Harding *who reported numerous fractures among the passengers. An SOS from the* Blainby*, a Scottish freighter, said the steering cable broke. It was 300 miles from us. We started that way but soon they said assistance was no longer needed. The MV* Selve *reported loss of a propeller. We found her 21 miles southeast of St. Pierre but a commercial tug was en route from Halifax. We stood by while the* Selve *was taken in tow."*

Such was the life on Neutrality Patrol.

We were assigned a sixty-mile square to patrol for our month on station, unless we were needed on a rescue case. We did have some boring days. One day, after a series of days steaming upwind and drifting back down, I had the afternoon watch as Officer-of-the-Deck. The Commanding Officer (von Paulson) came to me and ordered me to "get underway for Boston and make twenty knots!"

What does a poor Ensign do with such an order? I said, "Aye, aye, sir," and walked over to the messenger and told him to find Commander Littlefield, the Executive Officer, and tell him the OD wants him to the bridge immediately.

He showed up immediately and out of breath. I was waiting out on the wing of the bridge, where I could tell him quietly of the Captain's order. He calmly approached the CO, who obviously had been drinking, and suggested they retire to the cabin, which they did. (End of incident.)

On January 27, 1940, we received orders from the Commander, Boston District, to the *Duane* and the *Bibb* to prepare to establish and "OCCUPY TWO WEATHER STATIONS BETWEEN BERMUDA AND THE AZORES X DURATION WEATHER STATION PATROLS AND SCHEDULES TO BE DETERMINED LATER X DUANE AND BIBB PREPARE TO SAIL THIS DUTY 31 JANUARY PREPARED TO KEEP TO SEA FOR A PERIOD OF AT LEAST ONE MONTH X DEFINITE INSTRUCTIONS RELATIVE THIS DUTY WILL BE ISSUED LATER X THIS IS TEMPORARY ARRANGEMENT PENDING REFITTING AND FURNISHING FOUR MARITIME SERVICE VESSELS TO BE PERMANENTLY ENGAGED THIS DUTY MANNED BY COAST GUARD PERSONNEL."

On January 31, we arrived in New York, where we picked up two Weather Bureau men and special weather recording instruments. Then, on to Norfolk for fuel and liberty. On February 5 we left, bound for our assigned weather station between Bermuda and the Azores, 1,760-miles distant.

Our sister ship, the cutter *Bibb*, was assigned to Weather Station #1, one third the distance from Bermuda to the Azores. We, in the *Duane*, to Weather Station #2, two-thirds the distance. We inaugurated an expanding **Weather Patrol** program that included weather stations in the Pacific. The program lasted from 1940 to 1960, by which time technical advances in aircraft capability, satellite communication, weather tracking, and new technology made weather stations obsolete.

There was an urgent need for the services provided by the North Atlantic weather ships. The war was raging in Europe, and American civilians were fleeing. Most were leaving by ocean liners, but many diplomats and wealthy American were being evacuated by **Pan Am Clippers** (seaplanes) flying from Lisbon to New York via the Azores and Bermuda.

The weather patrol cutters were already along the flight route should search-and-rescue become necessary. Radio contact tracked their positions and flight conditions. A radio beacon from the cutter served as an aid to navigation.

Although we were unaware of it, we also had a military mission—to provide to allied commanders on the battlefields of Europe accurate weather data from its source of origin. This gave allied forces lead time for planning maneuvers. That explains why we had Weather Bureau personnel with us. Anyone can read a thermometer, a barometer, and an anemometer and estimate the direction and force of the wind, but the weathermen could do more.

Six times a day, they sent surface weather conditions to their bureau for analysis and forwarding encoded to the Army. Twice a day, they released a pilot balloon filled with helium. These were about five feet in diameter and colored red, white, or black. The color was selected for best contrast with the type of sky. The rate of ascent was known. Our gyro repeaters were used to obtain the azimuth and an astrolabe measured the altitude. The cloud ceiling is determined by the time the balloon disappears in the cloud cover. These reading were corrected for the ship's course and speed.

At midnight, a pilot balloon with a radio device that measures temperature, pressure, and humidity was launched. This balloon penetrates the overcast and continues sending data until it bursts. Our first try was almost a record. It went well into the stratosphere and reached the troposphere with the temperature a minus seventy-two degrees Centigrade.

We also had a **Public Health Service Doctor** assigned for the cruise. And we were happy to have him when one of our enlisted men had an appendicitis attack.

He determined that the man needed to be hospitalized as soon as possible. Ponta Delgada on São Miguel Island was the nearest hospital. We steamed there at twenty knots. The man's appendix was close to bursting. The operation was difficult and the man required continued hospitalization. We left him there for the next Weather Patrol vessel to bring him home.

We returned to our #2 Station just in time to face a HURRICANE!! *"We were tossing, rolling from 20-30 degrees. There was a choice mixture of rain and spin-drift driven by a 50 knot wind with seas running 50-60 feet high, confused by a cross swell. In one hour the barometer had dropped over 1 inch down to 28.86 inches. At noon the wind shifted to NNW and reached 80 knots. The seas couldn't increase for their tops were shaved off by the wind. Plenty of green water hit the bridge as we sliced and knifed through the on-coming combers. As the eye of the storm passed over us, we made our way into the Halifax outer harbor where we rode out the remainder of the storm at anchor."*

July 5, 1940. My notes are incomplete and confusing, but we received a message stating that on relief by the *Ingham*, we were off Weather Patrol for awhile. We would go to Norfolk for battle practice and back to Boston for a six-week in-port period of regular district patrols (one week out, two weeks in). Not another Weather Patrol until November for the *Duane*!

July 26, 1940. Our rejoicing was short-lived. Halfway through the battle practice came this message from headquarters to COMEASTPRACFOR: "DIRECT DUANE PREPARE FOR THREE MONTH SPECIAL EXTENDED DUTY TO DEPART 22 JULY." That is all we had to go on.

Our Captain telephoned headquarters and found out our destination would be Greenland. I call it a **Greenland Visitation**. Our battle practice was cut short. Hectic days followed loading ammo, fuel, dry stores, Arctic clothing, etc. Also a **J2F Duck** single-float seaplane with spare parts, two pilots (Coast Guard Lieutenant Shields, Army Air Corps Captain Lacy), and a Coast Guard Aviation Radioman (Johnny Merada).

Our mission would be diplomatic and exploratory, as the Greenland Patrol would not be officially established for another year.

July 22, 1940, was an unrealistic target date. We did very well to depart on July 28. And on that very day near the end of my 1200-1600 watch, while steaming east just south of Sable Island, in a thin fog, the bow lookout called the bridge reporting something in the water about a mile off our starboard bow. Through binoculars it looked like a lifeboat. I slowed the ship, headed in that direction, and notified the Captain who appeared immediately and took the conn.

It was a lifeboat with twenty men aboard who had survived a convoy attack the night before. We rigged a cargo net over the side for them to scramble aboard. We assigned them Chief's Quarters, and, of course, fed them. I was too junior to be privy to the debriefing, but I know they asked where we were bound. They were told Greenland. Although we had just "saved their lives," they complained bitterly. They wanted to go to St. John's, Newfoundland. Well, that's where we went, as it was on our way and was an interesting port. We stayed two nights. About 200 locals lined the docks to see us off.

Between Newfoundland and our landfall on Greenland's southwest shore, we saw beautiful Northern Lights and our first icebergs. On nights with good visibility and clear skies, the illumination from Northern Lights makes night navigation quite safe. The piloting problem is to gain entrance to the fjords that lead to the villages. The fjords were deep and clean cut by glaciers, many over one hundred fathoms deep, but the debris was pushed and dumped at the entrance—and there was not a single aid to navigation in all of Greenland except for cairns (piles of rocks) that are marked on Icelandic charts.

Greenland had been a colony of Denmark for several hundred years. The larger villages are governed by Danes, accompanied by their families. The Eskimos prefer to be called Greenlanders because they have acquired European blood lines through the years, and look different.

When the Nazis moved into Denmark, the lifeline to Greenland was severed. Our Army and Navy moved immediately into Iceland along with the British, and our Coast Guard moved into Greenland.

Another cutter brought the first U.S. Consular Officer to Greenland slightly ahead of us. We (on the *Duane*) gave the Governor of Greenland full dress honors. (My Academy Class was the last required to purchase frock coat, fore-and-aft hat, epaulets, white gloves, and sword. World War II ended that degree of formality.)

We visited native villages to establish friendships and ascertain the loyalty to the Allied Forces and denial to the Axis. And to establish means of logistical support. Also to find alternate colleges for the Danish students visiting on summer break. The Sears Roebuck catalog was the book everyone wanted. We entertained the Danes with on board movies and American meals, and they treated us to Danish fare in their homes. The Danish ladies were especially proud of their home brew!

To conclude this lengthy Scene, I must describe **Storis** ice. The North Sea freezes solid, but then storms and currents break it into leads and rafts and sets some free to follow ocean currents. Ice floes, called Storis, leave the North Sea drifting southward down the east coast of Greenland to Cape Farewell. It then goes west around the Cape and starts drifting north up the southwest coast. By then, warmer climate and water melts most of it and the floe doesn't normally get above Ivigtut. But this year, the Storis drifted farther north and caught us at anchor. I watched in horror as a big hunk of ice slid down our starboard side going forward and reversed its direction and slid aft catching our starboard propeller. As it left, drifting away, I saw floating on it a one-by-three-foot tip of our starboard propeller.

We were immediately relieved to return to Boston and yard availability. We limped and thumped our way straight into the path of another **hurricane**. We were just south of Halifax, and with our maneuverability hampered by the damaged propeller and the vulnerability of the seaplane on deck, a wise decision was made to duck into Halifax harbor and ride out the storm at anchor. Ahhh, what a comfortable night's sleep!

The storm passed about forty miles west of us and the winds only reached fifty-five knots, but there was over a million dollars in damage around Halifax with yachts washed ashore, fires from power lines down, an apple crop of one-and-a-half million dollars destroyed (largest ever).

When the weather cleared the next morning, there was a sight to see—over three-dozen loaded ships at anchor waiting to form a convoy to Europe. We saw twenty-three stand out to sea. And ten of the fifty four-stack destroyers we were trading to England for Atlantic island bases were still at anchor.

We made Boston on September 21. It was hard to believe that we were not yet at war. Preparations were evident everywhere. On September 28, I was off to **Optical and Fire Control School** at the Naval Gun Factory, Washington, D.C. This was an enjoyable change of pace. I lived at the Theta Chi fraternity house for the four-week course. And that enabled me to visit the Capitol with Congress in session, the Smithsonian Institute museums, and the many famous memorials.

Before that assignment was over, I had orders to the Army Fort Tilden at Rockaway Beach, Long Island. There we would learn more about our machine guns and fire live ammo at <u>towed sleeves</u>!

Life back on the *Duane* wasn't too great. Arming her meant shipyard workers everywhere with their electric drills and welding torches making a mess, reports and paperwork piled up, and on top of it all I had to take written promotion exams given service-wide on a designated day! (In those days, a new officer had to serve for three years as an Ensign and under two or more Commanding Officers, then pass promotion exams to become a Lieutenant Junior Grade.)

The holidays were a lonesome time for me. Being a bachelor with no strings attached led the married watch standers to expect me to take the duty on holidays so they could be with their wives and children…and I usually did.

January 1941 was a quiet month moored in Boston. I managed liberty to New York City where I met my dad, who was on a business trip. We saw many of the tourist sights. I bought a little eight-millimeter movie camera which led me into a long-lasting hobby.

There is nothing like a North Atlantic winter cruise to make one yearn for inshore duty. Ours came in February with orders to escort the Army troop transport SS *Edmund B. Alexander* with twelve hundred troops from New York to the newly established base at St. John's, Newfoundland. Our coastal waters were now quite safe from U-boats, they having been driven away by our Neutrality Patrols and the effective little aircraft carriers affectionately known as "Jeep Carriers." We had good weather for a change, so it was a pleasant cruise.

Back in Boston, someone couldn't stand to see us idle so they sent us on a two-week district patrol. Mainly, we guarded the fishing fleet on George's Bank and the Grand Banks. I don't recall any calls for help.

I became an orphan while out on patrol. **My father died** of a heart attack in the Portland hotel where he was staying while employed as the Northwest Sales Director for the Pepsi-Cola Company.

On May 7, 1941, I was transferred to the **Coast Guard cutter *North Star***, a veteran of both Arctic and Antarctic waters. Could that mean back to Greenland? Well, "Good bye, *Duane*. Thanks for a GREAT two years!"

P.S. Where is the *Duane* now (2004)? She and the *Bibb* are keeping company in Davy Jones' Locker at the bottom of the sea just off the Florida Keys. They are part of an artificial reef formed to give shelter to fish and recreation for scuba divers.

**In full dress uniform with fore-and-aft hat**

# SCENE 17

## CG CUTTER *NORTH STAR*—1941-1942 (GREENLAND PATROL / SLEDGE PATROL / WORLD WAR II)

My transfer orders to the *North Star*, also based in Boston, directed that I report "...on commissioning of that vessel," but gave no date. I wanted to visit home, so I applied for three weeks of leave en route. My leave request came through approved about 11:30 p.m. I worked all night packing, stowing gear in Navy Yard facilities, parking my Studebaker "double-date" coupe in the long-term lot, and on May 8 I caught the first train out for Los Angeles. The train to Chicago was smooth and comfortable but west of there it was slow and dirty. The traveling companions were a jolly bunch, however, and by the time we reached Los Angeles we were all "cousins."

The next two weeks were filled with activities, including Catalina in my brother's boat *Dagge*, outdoor ice skating in the sun in Westwood, the Sea Scout mountain cabin which my group had built in one weekend, yacht racing, and visiting with the few old friends still around Santa Monica.

In conversations with other military men on the train, I learned that I qualified for space available on military aircraft. Maybe I could find one going my way. I didn't know how to find a ride, but by phoning around to military airfields I lucked out. There was a flight leaving for Pensacola in a couple of days out of Burbank. I met the schedule and it was great—a commercial Navy transport, plush seats and all!

The chances of getting out of Pensacola looked bleak, so I took an ancient southern train to Air Force Maxwell Field, Alabama, where I caught an Army transport plane to Patterson Field in Ohio (not exactly on course to Boston). With the Memorial Day weekend coming up, I decided to take trains the rest of the way. All in all, it was a *great* experience and saved a little money.

I found the *North Star* in the Boston Navy Yard and in a state of chaos. The Commanding Officer, Lieutenant Commander Frank Meals, a "mustang," had orders to prepare for sailing to Greenland on June 1. That was *clearly* impossible, but he stubbornly held to that date. I was to be assigned as Commissary Officer, but since I had not yet reported aboard, he gave the initial provisioning chore to the Navigator, who was loaded with his own preparations. He turned to the Navy Cookbook, where he found an inventory list giving the amounts of provisions per man for thirty days. He multiplied those figures to cover ninety days and one hundred thirty men! I went to bed just as the crew was starting to unload canned tomatoes from a railway boxcar. When I woke up the next morning there were cases of tomatoes all over the main deck. They had run out of space below. We returned most of those tomatoes, but we were stuck with tons of produce. To explain I must first describe this unusual ship.

**CGC *North Star*, supply ship to Greenland Patrol vessels**

The *North Star* was a 240-foot wooden-hull little freighter. She was not an icebreaker but was ice-protected with an ironwood band at the waterline. She had a well-deck forward with cargo booms to the hold. The 'tween-deck spaces were converted to the crew's living quarters. The officers' quarters were in the deck house. Mine was a nice little cabin furthest aft on the starboard side, with a large view window. The built-in bunk had a curtain around the open two sides to keep out the midnight sun. The *North Star* was single screw, powered by a diesel engine.

She had served in Alaskan waters for many years for the Bureau of Indian Affairs. More recently, she made two expeditions as a supply ship for Admiral Byrd to the Antarctic.

We missed the sailing date of June first by almost a month, leaving just before the Fourth of July celebrations. During this time, the Boston weather remained steamy hot and sultry. An alert engineer feared the fresh produce would suffer, so he turned on the cooling system. It *worked...too well!!* Heavy ice formed on the tubes. Now afraid the produce would freeze, the engineer turned off the system. The ice thawed and drenched everything!!

A strange feeling of relief rippled through the ship as we left the tensions of the long preparation days behind us. The sea breeze smelled sweet. All was quiet except for the monotonous hum of the engine. No workmen drilling holes. No welders. *And* I no longer was the boot Ensign. I was now a Lieutenant Junior Grade! And I had a little stature, having recently been to Greenland and learned a lot I could share. I was assigned the 8-12 a.m. and 8-12 p.m. underway watches.

On the second morning out, the Captain had the crew assembled for a briefing. We knew we were headed for Greenland, the largest island in the world, but did not know what an important role we would play in the war now raging in Europe. He made it clear.

Germany, under Hitler, was conquering Europe in all directions. His western front had just taken Denmark, the motherland of the Greenland colony. President Roosevelt knew he must act fast to confine the Axis powers to Europe. Our Army and Navy together with British forces moved the Allied defense to Iceland. We needed Greenland to build airfields for ferrying fighters and bombers. We needed to keep the Axis forces from establishing U-boat bases in Greenland. And, very important, we needed the cryolite (used in making aluminum) from the world's largest mine in Ivigtut for our aircraft factories that were building thousands of warplanes. *And* to prevent the Axis forces from having weather stations in Greenland. The weather generated in Greenland would be extremely important to General Eisenhower for planning to attack the Nazis.

The fjords of northeast Greenland are the most beautiful in the world. They are deep, long, and navigable with towering cliffs of colorful treeless rocks. It is isolated from the world by the barrier of Storis ice, previously mentioned. There are no villages in the region. It was not "occupied" by the Danes. A few Norwegians lived in the area for trapping polar bears and white fox. They claimed it was their land. In 1931, Denmark filed a suit in the Permanent Court of International Justice (World Court) countering claims by Norway for eastern Greenland. The court ruled that Denmark must "occupy" the territory to maintain their claim. To do that, the Danes establish outposts at about two-hundred-mile intervals.

Our mission was to give support to those stations and provision them for two years (some years supply ships cannot get through the ice). We were to inspect fishing camps to ascertain their real mission, and to destroy weather reporting facilities.

As we rounded Cape Farewell and headed north up the Denmark Strait, we began a whole new experience for me in polar navigation. As we entered the Greenland Sea, we encountered scattered ice floes and a few icebergs. About halfway up the east coast the ice began to pack too heavy for us to penetrate. We skirted to the east by heading north when possible. We needed to reach latitude seventy-four degrees north before heading west back to land. When we did, our longitude was twelve degrees west, and we were one hundred eighty miles off the coast. We turned west and entered the ice pack.

Remember, *North Star* is not an icebreaker. All we could do was follow leads in the ice and push aside ice in our way, or redirect our course around the big chunks. We were in twenty-four hours of daylight now, but fog and icebergs obscured our vision much of the time. One way to find a lead in the ice was to look for a dark line on the underside of the overcast.

On July 23, we moored to a large ice floe. In its center was a fresh water pond made by thawing snow (not saltwater ice). With our portable pumps, we skimmed off some five thousand gallons of fresh water into our ship's tanks.

LAND-HO!! Our Navigator allowed for the southward drift of the Storis that we had been working in for six days, and we made a perfect landfall on Cape Hold-With-Hope!

Almost coincidental with our landfall, the American naval forces congregating around Greenland were organized officially into the **Greenland Patrol.** The mission was outlined as follows:

> ➤ To support the Army in establishing in Greenland airdrome facilities for use in ferrying aircraft to the British Isles.

> ➤ To defend Greenland and specifically to prevent German operations in northeast Greenland.

With the mission firmly in mind, we cruised the beautiful fjord region in unbelievably good clear weather! We visited the Danish weather stations at Ella Island and Eskimonaes. We learned that wintertime, when the coves are frozen, is visiting time by dog sledge, being faster and easier than summer commute by motorboat. Since there are no trees, the dogs are tethered in a fan pattern rather than in tandem. The Greenland breed are smaller than huskies, they pull harder and eat less.

We re-provisioned one Norwegian man-and-wife camp that had operated for years and were allowed to remain. And we found one abandoned camp where we destroyed remaining radio equipment.

One of the Danes stationed at the Ella Island weather station was out working his trap line when he saw a trawler up a narrow fjord. He hurried back and reported to us. We immediately went up that fjord and found that the vessel had left. They had, in fact, steamed right into the hands of the **Coast Guard cutter Northland**. It was a Norwegian trawler named the *Buskoe*. There were twenty-seven persons on board, most of them Danish hunters and Norwegian trappers, and one woman who said she was a nurse. Also found were up-to-date radio transmitting equipment, which may have been used for sending weather reports and information on Allied shipping to German U-boats and Axis-controlled territory.

The *Northland* immediately put a prize crew aboard and directed the old **Coast Guard cutter Bear**, now with all Navy crew, to tow the *Buskoe* to Boston. The most complete book on "The U.S. Coast Guard in World War II," published by the United States Naval Institute, states the "CGC *Northland*, 12 Sept.1941—Seizes *Buskoe* (Nor). First Naval Capture World War II."

**Many of the Officers and crew were permitted to grow beards while on Greenland Patrol**

Here are a couple of Arctic tricks I experienced. The famous quote from the "Rime of the Ancient Mariner" about "water, water everywhere, nor any drop to drink" can be paraphrased for winter in the Arctic to read "frozen water everywhere, nor any drop to drink." But we were there just before the freezing season. This is how we topped off our drinking water tanks: we scrubbed out a lifeboat and towed it under a cataract waterfall until full and used a portable fire pump to transfer the water to our tanks.

And where there was no handy cataract, we towed the scrubbed-out boat to a fresh water stream, pumped water to fill (but not ground) it and towed it back to the ship for transfer. There was one hazard—polar bears! They were seen around the area, and they are not afraid of humans. Our men on the detail were armed and snipers were alert from the ship's bridge.

Anchored off Blomster Bugt (Bay of Flowers), another officer and I got permission to go on a hike. We strapped on side-arms (45s) because we knew there were musk ox nearby. We hiked to a rather flat area and when we came over a small rise we encountered a small herd of six or seven. We didn't need to fire to alert them for they were already in their defense position. That consisted of facing us in a tight shoulder-to-shoulder line with the calves and cows protected by a bull at each end. The procedure, we had been told, was that one bull at a time would charge if threatened, making his thrust and returning to the herd and another would do the same. We wanted none of that, so we each fired one round and watched them saunter off.

My ship, the *North Star*, was the last to leave northeast Greenland. Our patrol mission to clear the territory of unwanted people and silence unwanted radios was completed. The Danish weather stations were re-provisioned. The men were assigned to the newly established **Sledge Patrol** and given military status. The traditional shipping season closes on September 1 due to the consolidation of the Storis and the freezing of the fjord ice. We stayed until October 1, taking a risk but to make sure no Axis ship was planning a late arrival.

We made a final cruise to our northern-most latitude of seventy-eight degrees north, then south to Scoresby Sound at the southern end of the region. There we learned that a German recognizance aircraft had searched the area. After one night, we departed for **Iceland.**

By this time, I had jettisoned all the vegetables and fruit that had been rotting in the chill box, but still had tons of potatoes and dozens of eggs. I thought maybe some Navy ship could use them.

We were greeted upon arrival at **Reykjavik** by a naval patrol craft. The officer said (somewhat disappointed it seemed) that we had just passed over the newly established minefield that guarded the entrance. He thought our wooden hull must have saved us!

I naively called the Army base to see if they would like potatoes and eggs. I was turned down emphatically. So I boarded an American battleship (I've forgotten the name) and offered them six thousand pounds of potatoes and eleven hundred eggs. No dice. I was told I had more potatoes than a battleship. They are happy to rely on their biweekly supply "train." My first act on leaving Iceland was to dump eleven hundred eggs and six thousand pounds of potatoes overboard!

All was not peaceful in the harbor. There were too many ships anchored every which way, and gusty winds and rain arrived at dusk. A trawler dragged anchor and drifted into us. We, in turn, trying to avoid it gently rammed a corvette and one of the old four-stack destroyers we gave to the British. Dawn was breaking as the last squall lifted. We found a safer place to anchor and enjoyed liberty and a restful day awaiting our next orders.

Our Captain returned from making official calls with details of our next assignment. A Navy survey team had selected a site on a small island near the mouth of Tenuglliarlik Fjord for installing a radio direction-finding station. A small number of construction workers and crates of equipment and supplies would arrive by Navy tanker in a few days. Because we were a little freighter with cargo booms, we were selected to take the men and cargo aboard to relieve the tanker for other duties and to assist in getting the station equipment to the site ashore. We were into November now, with long nights and short daylight hours. It was going to be a tough assignment. We named it "**Boxes for Boston**"!

We waited for the tanker to arrive by anchoring in a rockbound cove we had visited before. We named it Nordstjerne Havn. It opened to two channels: one from the west which was too narrow for safe navigation by a ship our size but used by our smaller cutters, and a safe entrance from the south, which we previously had used.

It was a dark moonless night when I came off watch at midnight with a strong breeze from the east. I headed straight to my bunk. About 3 a.m., I awoke to the tune of the engine racing first ahead, then backing. I peaked out my window and my gawd the rock shore was close! But we were pulling away towards the center of the cove. Back to my bunk, but I stayed fully dressed.

There goes the engine again—ahead—now astern. With this engine, it is stopped and started in reverse, then stopped again and started in ahead. Each start is by compressed air. When the engine is running, it recharges the compressed air bottle. If they shift too many times, we may run out of air and be helpless!

I was almost back in bed when five blasts were sounded on the ship's whistle: *Collision/All Hands On Deck!*

Can you believe this: our stern fetched up on the rocky shore and the wind caught the bow and pivoted us around until we were aimed at the south channel. We took it and got the heck out of there, then cruised around in open water for the rest of the night. *Thank you, Lord!*

The next day, we found the tanker anchored near the site selected for the station. We moored alongside and went to work to transfer the cargo. The crew enjoyed the hard labor after being cooped up aboard ship so long. But the boxes kept coming and coming. Our excitable Executive Officer took charge. I soon realized they were sending big items down to the bottom of the forward hold where my commissary provisions were stowed. *That would cut off the food to feed the entire ship's company!*

I pointed this out to the Exec, but he said it would only be for a day or two and we could make do. I objected louder. He said, "If we run out of food we can feed them bread and water!" That did it! I went straight to the Captain, over the Exec's head. (A NO-NO.) Needless to say, the Captain called in the Exec and we discussed the matter calmly and found a way to serve both causes. We would make like an elevator shaft, down which the Jack-of-the-Dust could go for the food items needed, and up which he could pass food items with the help of mess cooks. (The Exec never said a word to me about it.) The job took about three weeks during which something changed our lives.

We were seated in the mess deck for the evening movie. The Captain was in his reserved chair with officers around him, and the enlisted men were seated wherever they could find a space. The messenger came in with clipboard and flashlight in hand. He illuminated the clipboard with the flashlight and thrust it in position for the Captain to read. There must be a reason for this unbecoming conduct. We craned our necks to read over the Captain's shoulder but he quickly took the message off the board, folded it and put it in his cap. When the movie ended, he told the officers to remain and he read to us the message: "**AIR RAID ON PEARL HARBOR X THIS IS NOT A DRILL.**" The date was December 7, 1941.

That job of two or three days turned out to be two or three weeks, but it got done and we got released to head for Boston. We might be there for Christmas after all.

After cruising around outside the entrance torpedo net trying to exchange recognition signals, we were finally admitted and moored at the Navy shipyard at 2230 hrs, 23 December 1941. We had won our prize of Christmas in the States!

All hands were granted forty-eight hours liberty with orders to return sans beards and sans civilian clothes. We were now **AT WAR.**

In the mail, I found an invitation to attend an anti-submarine training course in San Diego. I could visit home, this time transportation at government expense. I, of course, jumped at it and made reservations for the first airplane out of Boston to New York. But come morning, a heavy snowfall cancelled all flights. I took the train to Pennsylvania Station where there was an airline ticket counter. It was so crowded I couldn't get to the front to revise my ticket. Time was short so I went across the lobby to a telephone booth and telephoned the counter, told them my rush and military priority and they saw that I got to the head of the line. Whew! Here is the neat part—I was booked to depart at 11:30 p.m. on a "**skysleeper**." (Who have you ever heard of that has flown coast to coast in a sleeper plane?) It was a **Boeing Model 307 Stratoliner**, the first with a pressurized cabin capable of flying above most weather. The berths were like on a Pullman railroad train. It was also neat to have a pretty stewardess duck under the curtain to wake me up!

My leave was spent much the same as earlier ones, but all too soon I was on a flight back to Boston. Again, it was a **sleeper** but in a **Douglas DC-3**, so a much smaller berth. We landed several times for fuel and bounced around in the clouds, not over them. I had the upper berth. My compartment companion with the lower berth was President Roosevelt's "my son James," Captain USMC. Across the aisle were movie executives. They visited about training films they were making for the military. I sat and quietly listened (I should have given them some sage advice).

My schooling was preparation for the orders that were awaiting my return to Boston assigning me to the **Coast Guard cutter Mohawk** (WPG-78), also based in Boston and preparing to join the Greenland Patrol. I was now a full Lieutenant, having been a junior grade just six months. I would be the Navigator and be leaned on for my "knowledge of the Arctic." See Scene 18.

# SCENE 18

## CG CUTTER *MOHAWK*—1941-1943 (GREENLAND PATROL / CONVOY DUTY)

The assignment to Anti-Submarine Warfare School was a nice relief from the long deployments I had been having. And with the United States now in the war, it felt good to be an active participant in an armed force defending our country.

The training I received qualified me to conn an attack on a submerged U-boat using underwater **sonar** equipment to track the sub and position my ship to drop depth charges that would intercept it at the depth set for the underwater explosion. *No easy task!*

The sonar in the control of a skilled operator sends out a narrow directional beam like a lighthouse. The submarine hull reflects the sound as an echo. The operator can determine the size and depth of the target and its direction and speed. The Conning Officer has to visualize the relative movements of his ship and that of the submarine to judge when to order charges dropped (over the stern) or when to fire K-Guns (that project depth charges off the ship's port and starboard beams).

At school, we practiced on mock-ups and on a real submarine using pop-gun explosives. One day, my student class got to make a dive. Afterwards, when I was on my way back to the barracks, a smart newspaper kid said, "You take a dive today, mister?" I said, "Yes. How did you know?" He said, "I could smell the diesel oil on your clothes!"

When I arrived back in Boston, my immediate problem was to find my new home.

**Coast Guard cutter *Mohawk*.** She was one of six small icebreakers designed to clear winter ice in harbors around the Great Lakes and the East Coast. They were beautiful, stout little ships, only 165 feet in length, but were part of the Coast Guard's "Great White Fleet" with white hulls and buff-colored stacks, davits, and trim. All smaller ships and boats were painted gray. The famous Coast Guard "racing stripe" was not conceived for another forty years. The hull of these icebreakers was steel with a re-enforced bow cut away at the waterline to enable the ship to ride up on the ice to crush it for clearing channels. The thirty-six-foot beam made a wide path for most following ships. These cutters had one screw delivering fifteen hundred horsepower and a draft of fourteen feet to protect the single screw.

**CGC *Mohawk***

The living quarters were very nice until we became crowded with wartime complements. The Captain's cabin adjoined the wardroom aft and had a ready-room off the bridge. Officers' staterooms surrounded the wardroom. I was assigned the second stateroom aft on the starboard side. It was very comfortable but no view.

I knew my ship would be in the Boston Navy Yard, so I went directly to the Officer-of-the-Day to locate the dock. It was hard to find. Everything was a mess with all the wartime conversions taking place. Finally, I spotted a little dark gray vessel that looked like a tugboat nested among huge destroyers. When I read "**78**" on the bow I knew it was **My New Home!**

It seemed logical to send these little icebreakers to join the Greenland Patrol. Four of the six were sent, but there wasn't any winter ice to clear. And these little ships were no match for Storis ice. Maybe the planning staff knew that all along because we were soon organized into convoy escort duty. The whole complexion of Greenland had changed from a sightseeing voyage to a war zone patrol.

That wasn't all that changed. Our innocent little ship was converted into a fierce fighting man-o-war!! She mounted two three-inch fifty-caliber deck cannon, two twenty-millimeter machine guns, two depth charge racks, four K-Guns, and two mouse-traps. Sonar and LORAN. Most staterooms were doubled up. The officers and crew complements were increased about fifty percent. It is not surprising that the crew referred to the *Mohawk* as <u>MIGHTY MO</u>!

The convoy escort ships were in two groups. Two of our little ships joined larger 250-foot cutters. The major North Atlantic convoys sailed to Europe with our biggest and newest cutters and Navy destroyer escorts, with fast ships in the convoys, but we could only make twelve knots, and so we were assigned to escort the dregs, who could not keep up with the sixteen-knot speed of the big convoys. Our routine route was not to Europe but between Sydney, Nova Scotia, and southwest Greenland, crossing the **Davis Strait**. By using the **Strait of Belle Isle**, we saved mileage and time by cutting off Newfoundland and avoiding Cape Race with its usual thick fog. But using the straits was like running a gauntlet of U-boats.

**CGC *Mohawk*, in Arctic blue and white camouflage**

Of course, everything needed to support all operations in Greenland had to get there by ship: building materials, power plants, instruments, fuel, food, trucks, manpower, everything.

The ships forming northbound convoys assembled outside Halifax or Sydney. Southbound, they assembled at anchor in a large, well protected cove called Kungnat Bay near the head of the Tenugliarfik Fjord that led to Bluie One, the principal airport and shore base for the construction projects.

The Baffin Island chain of stations was a whole separate program ongoing at the same time. A number of New England fishing trawlers were pressed into service. Crews were needed. Officers and men were drawn from Greenland Patrol vessels for their Greenland experiences. From Mighty Mo, we transferred two Ensigns and a Chief Quartermaster.

As it so happened, Ensign Oakley, one of those selected, had brought aboard a springer spaniel named **Rickey** to be the ship's mascot. But since the trawler would be too small, I volunteered to see that the dog was well cared for. And he was. We slept together from then until he came to an untimely death. (We anchored each other in our shared bunk with Rickey curled up in the hook of my knees. Let the ship roll! We were firmly secured!)

**As an Ensign in "Cold Weather Service Dress"**

One of the convoy problems was how to keep the ships together in the fog or snow showers. They lacked radar in those days and it was scary knowing there were other ships close by. One of our crew had a solution to keep the ship following us at a safe distance—he made a wooden raft about four-foot square. Down through the center he put a shaft with a scoop at the bottom which had a larger opening than the shaft. When towed at the end of a very long line at convoy speed a "rooster tail" of water was shot up into the air. The following vessel could see the spray and maintain position on it.

We had one terrifying experience when we rounded Cape Race and headed west in deep fog and found ourselves threading our way between lines of a big convoy headed east!

When hit by fog or heavy snow while in the Davis Strait, the masters of the merchant ships were likely to say "to hell with this" and break away from the convoy to go it alone. When the weather cleared, we might collect them again or maybe next see them at the end of the run.

We received radio reports of U-boat positions from the Navy Radio Direction Finder Net that kept us especially alert on our sonar. We had lots of contacts, probably large fish and whales, but one time the echoes fit the pattern of a submarine perfectly. It was **General Quarters** (GQ) as we set up an attack pattern. On our final approach, we were traveling directly up a bright moonbeam when crossing at right angles to our course appeared the unmistakable silhouette of a Navy destroyer!!

We had one real encounter when we, with our sister ship, the **Coast Guard cutter Algonquin** (WPG-75), were escorting four ships through the Strait of Belle Isle on a clear, moonless night.

Personnel in our fire room heard a hissing and whining sound pass under the ship, undoubtedly the sound of a torpedo. A few seconds later, the Navy tanker *Laramie* was struck on the starboard bow. We, together with the *Algonquin* and the *Laramie*, fired star shells in hope of silhouetting the U-boat. No luck. She sank the U.S. Army transport *Chatham* and the freighter *Arlyn* and escaped.

We picked up survivors from the *Arlyn* and put them ashore in Labrador, then we escorted the *Laramie* back to Sydney.

While we were at the southern end of the Greenland convoy run, our sister ship, the **Coast Guard cutter *Escanaba*** (WPG-77), was torpedoed and sunk as she approached Greenland. There were only three survivors. I lost a classmate in that sinking.

As we approached Sydney, we received a coded message from Ensign Oakley's trawler that he was being followed by a submarine with its snorkel showing. That was the only message. We reported it immediately in Sydney seeking follow up information. They had not received the message. We thought that strange. Checking into it showed the encryption took place on a day after the code had changed. We had not updated ours so we got the word and the HQ did not. We learned later that the sub left her alone, probably thinking she was a fishing boat.

One of the real dangers cruising in subfreezing weather is spray forming ice on the superstructure. It simply must be removed or the ship may be in danger of getting top-heavy and capsizing. The trawler *Natsek* was probably lost from icing up because the *Nanok* in the same area worked long hours for three days to prevent a dangerous accumulation of ice on the superstructure.

**The load of ice must go!**

Here are a couple of anecdotes I would like to relate before moving into calmer waters.

Our course put us in the trough of a stormy sea. It was nearly midnight and pitch black outside and red lights only inside. The *Mohawk* was in a deep roll when suddenly there was what sounded like an explosion. We all thought we had taken a torpedo. The ship went dead in the water. The main circuit breaker had kicked out and all was silent. A huge swell had come aboard hopping on top of the Captain's gig, driving the chocks up through the bottom! All we could do was leave the gig's problem until morning, collect our scattered wits and sail on.

It was on a different convoy run, but it sounds like a repeat performance. A young Ensign Butt was Officer-of-the-Deck. He found the sound-powered-telephone to the depth-charge rackman to be unreliable. As a backup, should he need to drop a depth charge, he would use the salvo buzzer. One long buzz would be the signal to drop one depth charge. A second buzz would call for a second drop, etc.

In the constant rolling, something on the flying bridge went adrift and rolled back and forth. Mr. Butt sent the messenger up to find the source and silence it. The messenger found the buzzer plunger adrift, but didn't know what it was. He dutifully coiled it but unknowingly depressed the plunger. The rackman announced, "ONE AWAY." Before the charge had reached its preset depth, he heard another buzz and announced, "NUMBER TWO AWAY!" Those charges nearly blew us out of the water. Again the ship went dead. Everyone headed for GQ. I had to fight Rickey to be first out of that bunk. Keep him in the bed. Put on exposure suit. Grab red flashlight. Lash on side-arm. Dash to the bridge. Up the starboard ladder, where two Ensigns were trying to get out the waterproof door. One would lock the door and the other would unlock it. Finally, one got his sheepskin-lined mitten hopelessly jammed in the door lock. I went up the port side.

We all stood around at our GQ stations in black silence while the engineers worked with flashlights to close the circuit breaker and get us back to normal. But that was an eerie feeling imagining U-boats lurking all around us!

Inspection next day showed <u>no harm done</u>. If ships are female, as sailors seem to think, then the *Mohawk* was a tough old gal!

**Viking church circa 1000 AD**

The next day, on the crew's bulletin board, appeared a cartoon of a grave with a tombstone that read: "Mr. Butt…1920-1942…Died of Embarrassment…World War II" and an

    EPITAPH TO MR. BUTT

    Here lies the body of Baseball Butt, an Ensign of renown.
    He gained his fame by dropping cans, when no subs were around.
    And now he rests beneath this slab, far from the *Mohawk*'s terrors.
    His depth charge score was only fair, No hits. No runs. TWO errors!
        Amen

While waiting for ships to arrive to form a convoy, we would go to the naval base in Argentia, Newfoundland. It was a full-service facility with an all-weather airfield. A destroyer tender was moored there to provide water, fuel, food, movies, and assistance with repairs, medical care, etc. There was an Officers' Club with a good dining room and bar, and separate facilities for the enlisted personnel. On our first visit to Argentia, our ship was completely painted with a white-and-blue Arctic camouflage.

I got a glimpse of how naval aviators live (in contrast to us poor "black shoe" sailors). This experience added to an earlier one I got on approaching the Strait of Belle Isle one stormy day. We were rolling our guts out when two PBY Catalina patrol planes from Argentia circled us to make sure we were safe from U-boats and then went back to their steady bunks in a warm BOQ, and the fresh lobster dinners in the club.

But a sad thing happened as we tied to the dock following our harrowing time at sea. I had the conn as we moored to the guest dock. I ordered the gangway put over and Rickey immediately went ashore and started down the dock. I had the bull horn mike in my hand and ordered, *"RICKEY, RETURN TO THE SHIP!"* And by golly, he put on the brakes and started back. A crewman ran out and grabbed him.

The sad part is that he subsequently went AWOL again in Argentia and was hit and killed by a Navy truck. My bunk never felt the same!

An ALCOAST message arrived stating the next flight training class was being formed and members of my Class of 1939 were among those invited to apply.

That sounded good to me, knowing nothing about flying. I submitted a request for assignment. The Captain forwarded my request "DISAPPROVED," stating I could not be spared. That may have been flattering (and true, as I was a better sailor than that Captain—and we both knew it), but it killed my application. The good luck was that a new Captain was assigned to the *Mohawk* just at that time. I submitted a new application and he forwarded it "APPROVED"! WHEW!

Following another run to Greenland, we had orders to go home to Boston and yard availability. For reasons I have forgotten, we stopped at St. John's, Newfoundland, for the night. Our new Captain said, "Let's have a party!" He went on to say that after that passage we deserved one. He would carve roast beef at the table. We would toast each other's country with wine (the Coast Guard cutters had beer and wine messes), but we needed some ladies to cheer things up. "Mr. Sinclair, you are a bachelor. Go to the hospital and round up about a half-dozen nurses." I did, and they were delighted to get a meal of roast beef and enjoy the friendship of Americans who were sharing "their" war.

And it was my **Farewell to Mighty Mo.**

**Afterlife**. The *Mohawk* returned to Wilmington, Delaware, where she served as the Flagship of the Delaware Harbor Pilots Association and for several years as a floating museum, run by dedicated volunteers. When the city withdrew its support, the *Mohawk* was sold to a Mr. John Azari for testing electrical equipment. He kept her afloat, but the cost was too great. When the Miami-Dade Historical Maritime Museum heard she was available, they became determined to purchase and restore her to her original wartime condition. They placed her in a permanent home as a floating museum at Memorial Park in Key West. (Plans as of 2004.)

Now to a *career change* from a seagoing officer to an aviator!! (if I don't fail Flight Training).

**Greenlander women in Easter finery**

# SCENE 19

## PRIMARY FLIGHT TRAINING—1943 NAAS MEMPHIS

My orders directed me to report to the Commanding Officer of the Naval Auxiliary Air Station by a given date in the middle of June. That was some climate change from the chilly and frozen Greenland to the hot and sweaty Deep South!

**NAAS Memphis** was established to make aviators out of Navy aviation cadets. The Commanding Officer was a high school principal given a wartime Naval Reserve commission with a rank of Lieutenant Commander. The cadets would be eighteen to nineteen years old, an age with which he was used to dealing. I was twenty-seven turning twenty-eight and at the upper limit for entering flight training.

In my class were officers reporting directly from sea duty in war zones. They had four years at the Coast Guard Academy and three years as Ensigns. Some had been promoted to full Lieutenant. Some were accompanied by wives. I don't recall any children.

The married ones received rental allowances and lived ashore. We single ones were billeted in Bachelor Officers' Quarters. The rank of full Lieutenant entitled me to a private room <u>with a portable electric fan</u>!! (There was no air conditioning. I stacked two chairs and positioned the fan to oscillate up and down my spine all night long.)

The first order of business was another physical exam. This one was called a "flight physical." The only test different was a "Snyder." The testee is put in a chair with face down and spun around several times, and then told to stand and walk a straight line. Our fear of this test was that we would get dizzy and flunk out of flight training. Well, we all got dizzy…and later learned that one would flunk the test if he did NOT get dizzy.

Next, we were tested for stamina on the obstacle course. (You know—where you stomp through a line of truck tires, squeeze under the barbed wire fence, scale the six-foot fence, and run to the finish line, if you can.) A Chief was there with stop watch. We asked what that was for. He said we had to beat a certain time. *TIME?* Our question was whether or not we could *make it* from start to finish. Never mind the time.

The next test measured your fighting spirit—boxing. They pitted me against a nice young lad ten years my junior. Fortunately, boxing was taught at the Academy and I had learned how to cover-up for three minutes.

There was one test of bravery or "guts." It was to step off the high-dive platform at the gym pool feet first. Through the clear pool water the tile pool bottom appeared to be at surface level. Yes, it took "guts." It took some several trips up that ladder. I knew that if I hesitated I would freeze. I walked right up and stepped off that platform without looking!

To the **Flight Line** at last. There we met our flight instructors. They were all Ensigns just out of flight training themselves. But now they were the elite and in charge, regardless of rank. And they deserved a little **R.H.I.P.** too. This was performed by the tradition of the student carrying the instructor's parachute out to the plane.

Our **Primary Flight Training** was in the "Yellow Peril," as the **N2S biplane** was affectionately called. The first flight was to acquaint us with the aircraft and the surrounding area. But before we could go flying, we had **Ground School** where we learned the parts of the aircraft and their controls and had to pass a blindfold cockpit test. That was easy, as about all there was were a few instruments like needle/ball, airspeed, and altitude. And control stick, rudder pedals, and throttle.

The plane had tandem controls, with the instructor in the front cockpit and the student to the rear (with limited vision). The instructor could talk and send commands to the student through a voice tube called a gosport. The student could not "talk back." There was no radio. The communication with the control tower was one-way. When in the landing pattern, a green light from the tower was clearance to land. A red light meant to go around for another approach to land.

This "**orientation flight**" was to demonstrate some of the maneuvers we would learn to perform. My instructor took me up to three thousand feet above the ground. It was a thrill, but not scary, to look down at the fields below. It was like hanging from a sky-hook.

Then the fun began. Nice easy wing-overs. A stall and recovery (with the instructor observing my reaction). Now to pep it up—a snap roll. (Was I still smiling?) A loop (and I didn't heave). And the finale—inverted flight hanging from the seat harness. The engine wouldn't run inverted more than about five seconds. When it stopped, the instructor righted the plane, it sputtered back to life, and we completed the flight.

Now I believe the flight was to check on the student adaptability for flying. Did I enjoy the maneuvers or was I pale with fright? Did I quickly recover from vertigo? Did I freeze on the controls? Did I get airsick? etc. I passed!

The flight syllabus eventually led us to perform the maneuvers we had experienced on the "orientation flight" and also included night takeoffs and landings with the only light from a line of pot lights.

**We flew our first training flights to and including our first solo flight in this lightweight biplane. These trainers were painted bright yellow to lessen airborne collisions and were affectionately known as the "Yellow Perils"!**

The emphasis was on **spot landings**. This is where the Navy Wings differ from Air Force Wings. Long, wide, well lighted runways are always available to Air Force cadets. Their flight technique is to fly the aircraft down an imaginary glide path until just a few feet above and in line with the runway. Then use all the runway needed to "squeak" it on.

The Navy must have been thinking about aircraft carrier landings of the future. The chosen landing spot was near the start of the runway. With the Yellow Peril, we slipped or made s-turns to shorten or stretch the approach, and when over the spot we would chop the throttle and drop onto the runway.

With heavier aircraft, including the seaplanes, a "power" approach was made. When all was ready for touchdown, the plane was held in a nose-high attitude. The rate of decent was controlled by the engine power. The higher the power the flatter the glide path. Reduce the power and the glide path was made steeper, but the nose attitude remained constant. When over the desired touchdown point, removing power settled the aircraft onto the runway in a three-point landing. It was bump more than squeak, but you were down and not going to bounce back into the air.

The one flight every pilot remembers is his **first solo flight!** Mine was uneventful, but full of apprehensions. Did I have the *right stuff?* An instructor had always been "riding the controls." Now I was alone, and very lonesome looking at that empty cockpit in front of me. Yellow Perils were swarming about like butterflies. I had to get into the correct flight pattern and stay in it and at the same time fly the plane. I was just starting to feel comfortable when there was the *green light.* My turn to land. The landing was a little wobbly, but I did it ! I passed Primary!

Next, it was off to **NAS Pensacola** for Advanced Flight Training. That is where I earned my **Naval Aviator Wings** and met **Corpsman Mary Evelyn Bond**.

# SCENE 20

## ADVANCED FLIGHT TRAINING—1943-1944 NAS PENSACOLA

There were two parts to the **Advanced Flight Training**. The first was transition from the Yellow Peril to a *real* aircraft. From the fragile fabric-over-wood frame biplane to the all-metal, low-wing monoplane with retractable landing gear, wing flaps, cockpit canopy, and voice radio.

We sometimes flew a Ryan aircraft or the Vultee "Vibrator," but mostly the famous **North American SNJ Texan**. It closely resembled the Japanese Zero and could serve as a dive bomber. We learned the basic flight maneuvers and did a little formation flying in the SNJ. This training took place at Whiting Field, a satellite airport in the Pensacola complex.

During this time we had to select the second and last part of Advanced Flight Training—a choice between seaplanes and fighter planes (including a catapult experience). We in the Coast Guard had seaplanes chosen for us. We used the seadrome around which the Navy training facilities were built.

The **PBY Catalinas** were used in this training. They were the seaplane-only version known as PBY-5, and not the PBY-5A amphibious version with retractable landing gear, which we would fly in our Coast Guard operations. Without the landing gear and all that goes with it, and the absence of machine guns and bombs, these training model were very light and easy to handle. In contrast, when heavily laden they were very heavy on the controls and the high parasol wing added a pendulum motion sometimes requiring cross controls to dampen.

I enjoyed this course with its "boating aspect," and passed.

**Navy Aviator Wings.** I have found among my souvenirs a little folder containing two certificates. One states that, on 7 December 1943, I was appointed **Coast Guard Aviator No. 179!** Signed by Coast Guard Commandant Admiral R.R. Waesche.

The other certificate, dated 25 January 1944, signed by the Commander of the Navy Aviator Training Command, says I "passed the test in Instrument Flying Prescribed for pilots of THE UNITED STATES NAVY and is qualified to proceed on Instruments in Single Engine Type of Plane."

**We were introduced to formation flying (two and three aircraft), instrument flying ("under the hood"), simulated dive bombing, and strafing with the thirty-caliber machine gun firing through the propeller!**

That is enough about my flight training, but I am not through with Pensacola because that is where I met **Mary**, my true love and wife-to-be.

We were in the middle of World War II and both in military service. I was a full Lieutenant in the Coast Guard and Mary a Dental Assistant Corpsman in the Navy Waves. There were certain restrictions and some privileges that went with being in the military. One restriction was that officers and enlisted personnel were not to date. This was ignored, but we couldn't use either the Officers' Club or the Enlisted Club. Consequently, several little night clubs sprung up just off base. One privilege was that military personnel could fly in military aircraft as passengers.

Some of the more daring members of my flight class arranged for a few Waves from Mary's barracks to join us for an evening "ashore." Mary and I, not yet met, joined the group. We rode in a couple of cars, with girls sitting on boys' laps. We breezed through the gate with no questions asked.

The little club had a small dance floor and a jukebox. That made for easy mixing. I had spotted Mary in the car, and liked what I saw, except for the guy on whose lap she was seated. I singled her out for dancing and "rescued her."

We repeated this performance a couple of more times and soon we were a pair. I could see she was smitten by me!

One enterprising member of my group organized a beach party. He "conned" some steaks out of the galley. We brought blankets to lay on the sand around the fire after dinner. I had my arm around Mary and noticed we were fanny-to-fanny against the next couple. My hand was touching the girl. I whispered to Mary, "I'm going to have some fun." I then gently caressed the girl's bottom with a couple of strokes. She cuddled up closer to her date!!

My transfer orders, effective upon completion of Flight Training, assigned me to my first Coast Guard Air Station—St. Petersburg, Florida, thus opening a whole new life for me to pursue. But those orders also meant leaving Mary behind. What could we do about that? You will see.

# SCENE 21

## CGAS ST. PETERSBURG—1944-46 (ANTI-SUBMARINE PATROLS / MARRIAGE)

It is no surprise that seniority plays an important role in military life, both personal and professional, but the unique role it plays in aviation is surprising. For example, in Primary Flight Training we Coast Guard students were senior to our flight instructors by two or three ranks, but the instructor was held responsible for accepting the aircraft (pre-flight), considering the weather safe for the mission, taking command in flight, and safe return of the aircraft at the end of the flight.

When I qualified to fly the **Martin PBM Mariner**, I was assigned a flight crew. My copilots were all experienced pilots whom I could rely on, but I, a greenhorn, was senior in rank and in command by tradition. However, if one of the enlisted pilots was designated by the Air Station Commanding Officer to perform a mission, he would be in Command. This does not designate which pilot takes the pilot's control seat and which the copilot's seat, or such situations as, "Do we try for a landing or shall we take a 'wave off'?" That is when the question must be answered, "Who is in command?" Of course, there usually is agreement and any disagreement can be discussed later in the Ready Room or at the O-Club bar!

I will have more on military protocol in a subsequent Scene.

The Air Station had two primary missions: Search-and-Rescue, and Anti-Sub Coastal Patrols.

**Search-and-Rescue (SAR)** was mostly searching for aircraft of other commands that were lost or ditched. We would locate them, drop message blocks about rescue procedures, and drop lifesaving equipment as indicated.

**Anti-Sub Patrols** covered the entire coastline of Florida searching for German U-boats that were there to attack merchant shipping. Our station was assigned the west coast from Pensacola to Key West. One of our planes made a confirmed hit and sinking. By the time I arrived, World War II was winding down along our coasts and there were no new sightings.

Seaplanes that we used on the Anti-Sub Patrols were **Vought OS2U Kingfishers**, a single-engine observation plane carried on battleships. It had a single float under the fuselage which could be replaced with fixed landing gear. It carried one 500-pound depth-charge bomb and fired a machine gun through the propeller.

To qualify for the Anti-Sub Patrols, I had to qualify in the OS2U. The Air Station had a Yellow Peril (N2S) aircraft just like we had flown in Basic Training except the landing gear had been replaced with a single float. This plane facilitated the transition from a land plane to a seaplane. A qualified pilot took me for a training flight. In the air, the flight characteristics were similar to our training planes, but takeoffs and landings were something else.

Taxiing was weird with one wingtip float dragging, then the other. When the power is applied for takeoff into the wind, engine torque initially takes over and turns the craft to port until rudder control can be gained as the plane accelerates.

A major concern on landing is to keep the wings level to avoid "catching a crab" with a wingtip float and water-looping. We shot several touch-and-goes and I felt confident.

The next day, I took off on a scheduled solo flight. I took along an aviation mechanic, but I don't remember why. (The OS2U had radio and the passenger was taught to signal the Air Station using Morse code every thirty minutes. But the Yellow Peril had no radio.)

It was a beautiful cloudless day...until I got airborne. Then a fog bank rolled in and completely covered the Air Station. My only thought was how to get down. I noticed that just inside the outer keys was a nice clear straight boat channel. I hurried and beat the fog to it and landed. I taxied to a little beach and ran the bow up on it. I shut down the engine, left my passenger in charge, went to the nearest house, and notified the Air Station I was down and alright.

Back to the plane, the fog was dissipating rapidly. I turned the plane around to start the engine and get out of there. The engine has an inertia starter. That means turning a crank to get the flywheel spinning then engaging to pull the engine through. That is done standing on a re-enforced spot on the wing (remember this N2S plane is fabric over wood frame). When the engine starts you leap into the cockpit and take control (kind of like the Model-T Ford!). Everything clicked except, on my rush to the cockpit, I stepped where there was no re-enforced spot and I stepped through the wing! The rest of the flight was uneventful. I was now ready for the OS2U.

The qualifying check-out was much like in the Yellow Peril but with more controls and instruments. On the Anti-Sub Patrols, we trainees flew in the copilot position and maintained radio contact with the Air Station. The flight maneuvers were extended to include dive bombing, dog fighting, and firing at a towed target.

The latter was scary because you had to duck under the sleeve or risk crashing, and the firing approach always closed much faster than expected.

Due to the absence of U-boats, the Coastal Patrols were ended. That gave us time to learn to fly other types of aircraft based in St. Pete—the amphibs: **Grumman JRF Goose, Consolidated PBY-5A Catalina, Grumman J4F Widgeon,** and **North American SNJ Texan**. Cross-country training flights were encouraged to keep our skills sharp and to involve some instrument flying and airways procedures. That gave me the

**Seaplanes that we used on the Anti-Sub Patrols were OS2Us, a single-engine observation plane carried on battleships. It had a single float under the fuselage which could be replaced with fixed landing gear. It carried one five-hundred-pound depth-charge bomb and fired a machine gun through the propeller.**

**To qualify for the Anti-Sub Patrols, I had to qualify in the OS2U. The Air Station had a Yellow Peril (N2S) aircraft just like we had flown in Basic Training except that the landing gear had been replaced with a single float. This plane facilitated the transition from a land plane to a seaplane.**

opportunity to court Mary and **rescue Mary from the Navy.** I usually went by JRF Goose because it was a little seaplane with a comfortable enclosed cabin for pilots and passengers. Mary was in the Navy and therefore could be flown as a passenger. We "courted" by means of these flights across a corner of the Gulf of Mexico.

**I proposed to Mary that we marry** on the condition that she get released from the Navy. I would take leave and we would fly commercially to California to meet my family and be married there. She asked her Commanding Officer for leave and he disapproved. He didn't want *his* "girls running off with the first fly-boy to come along." Mary heard that *marriage* was cause for release. *Not so! Pregnancy, yes, but only when three-months along.* Well, our long-distance commuting by cross-country training flights continued between Pensacola and St. Petersburg until we were married and Mary got pregnant and we waited three months.

Mary arranged for a long weekend off (Friday noon to Monday noon). She would fly down on Continental Airlines, using the priority granted those on military leave. I arranged for a service at **Saint Peters Church** for Friday, and then worried Mary might get bumped off the airline for someone with higher priority. I mentioned this to my Commanding Officer and he said, "Well, if that happens, grab the JRF, get a copilot, and go get her!"

By taking the duty Thursday night, I also would have a long weekend. But on Friday morning at 6 a.m., I received a telephone call. Mary was weeping and announced she had just been bumped from the airline. I asked where she was, and she said still in the barracks. To which I said, "Stay where you are. I am flying up to get you!" And that I did!

The wedding went off as planned. Mary wore a lovely blue mid-length dress and a corsage I gave her. Her brother, a commercial aviator stationed in Miami, drove up with his wife, Mary J, a favorite relative who stood up for Mary.

My best man, Ercell Hart, a friend of many years, was a naval aviator stationed in Jacksonville. He borrowed a Navy plane and flew in for the occasion. He and I wore Service Dress White uniforms. The Air Station officers attending wore Service Dress Khaki.

After the ceremony, we went to the St. Petersburg Yacht Club for a reception. Mary cut the wedding cake with my sword, a service tradition. The date was October 27, 1944.

    David William Sinclair    b. August 20, 1915, Redlands, California
    Mary Evelyn Bond    b. March 25, 1923, Hamilton, Illinois

We ducked out and went to Silver Springs, Florida, for our honeymoon.

Back early Monday morning, we carried out a contingency plan which was in place. Since Mary was bumped coming down, we decided we couldn't rely on the airline to get her back before her liberty expired. So the same copilot and I manned the same JRF and flew Mary back to Pensacola.

**Mary and I were married at Saint Peter's Church in St. Petersburg, Florida, on October 27, 1944**

It didn't take long for Mary to get pregnant, and when the three-month waiting period was up, she came to St. Petersburg to live with me. We rented the downstairs of a large house. Our first born was a boy we named **Terry** (b. September 22, 1945). We were now a *family!* A family that would travel station to station with me for the next twenty-five years.

I was sent to the Naval Air Facility at Banana River, Florida, for transitional training in the PBM-3 Mariner seaplane. I was assigned a permanent crew. CGAS St. Petersburg was our home base, but we made many long-distant flights to points south and west. I would fly the PBM again out of Port Angeles, Elizabeth City, and San Diego.

St. Petersburg was a busy time with lots of flying, a variety of aircraft, and the beginning of a wonderful family. But it wasn't an easy start. When Terry was about three months old, I received orders to Oklahoma for an intensive course in instrument flying. Mary didn't want to be left alone with a little baby so we took Terry with us in our little two-door "double-date" Studebaker coupe. We made the rear seat into an improvised play pen and bassinet. We stayed in an auto court near the airport which previous students had found. It was pretty bad. And poor Mary had to wash all the diapers by hand (disposables unknown). It was a tough introduction for inexperienced Mary with no support on hand. But she did *fine!*

The Civil Aeronautics Administration (CAA) flight instructors were a crafty bunch. We trained in twin-engine Beachcraft airplanes which had a switch for selecting the fuel tanks. The instructor could throw the switch without being seen. This they did without warning and one engine would shut down. The poor student would have to handle this situation remaining under the "hood" which restricted vision to just the cockpit. The solution, of course, was to find the switch and shift to another fuel tank while still dependent on the flight instruments.

On return to St. Petersburg, I found **PCS Orders** assigning me to **CGAS Port Angeles**, Washington, diagonally across the United States. Mary and Terry went by air to my brother Porter's home in Newport Beach, California, to wait there for me. Through a newspaper ad I found a man to share driving with me, and we drove my little car day and night, crossing the United States coast to coast in eighty-seven hours including one stop for repairs while he and I shared a bed in a flea bitten hotel for eight hours of needed sleep.

After a few days of R&R in Newport Beach, Mary, Terry, and I drove to Port Angeles. The weather conditions in which I would fly looked scary. For over a week we didn't see above the foothills of the Olympic Mountains. Locals said we would get used to it...and *love it!* We will see?

**My beautiful bride**

# SCENE 22

## CGAS PORT ANGELES—1946-1949 (SEARCH-AND-RESCUE)

**WOW!!** What a drastic change in environment for flying! The **CGAS Port Angeles** is located on a natural land spit jutting into the Juan de Fuca Strait from the south shore, directly opposite Victoria, B.C. The straits form the border with Canada and a water connection between the Pacific Ocean and Puget Sound.

**Our home in Port Angeles was a little prefab house brought by barge from Seattle, placed on a site, and sold to us. We added the sidewalk, landscaping, and picket fence**

Offshore lies the North Pacific Ocean where storms generate swells making offshore seaplane landing hazardous. Down the coast in Oregon, huge solitary rocks rise to two hundred or more feet above the water surface, making it unsafe to fly under the weather.

Immediately south of the Air Station, Mount Olympus peaks at eight thousand feet. To the east, the Cascades reach even higher elevations, crowned by Mount Rainier and Mount Baker.

Puget Sound is dotted with islands and man-made structures such as bridges, radio towers, and high-rise buildings. Islands cause gusty and shifting winds. Deadheads (ninety-percent-submerged logs) must be missed.

Topping these hazards to flight is the **weather**. The Pacific Northwest is noted for rain. If you can't fly around it, or under it, or over it…what do you do? If you fly into it, you must go IFR (abide by Instrument Flight Rules). That means going under Air Traffic Control (ATC), which will probably put you at some eight thousand feet! And what type aircraft does the Air Station have in which to do this? A little JRF seaplane? Or a lumbering, slow PBY? Where were the helicopters? (They will be there in about five more years!)

On a real emergency search-and-rescue case, we tried hard to get there. If the weather at the Air Station was good enough for takeoff and landing, maybe it would be good enough at the reported location of the emergency. We would take off and find out. If the weather closed in, we would reverse course to go back from where we came and go home. No one not there can criticize or challenge the pilot's judgment.

Now compare all this with the flight conditions out of CGAS St. Petersburg.

If the sun didn't shine before noon you could get a free newspaper! The highest point of land in all of Florida was 345 feet above sea level! You dodge around, not through, thunderstorms. When hurricanes came our way, we flew to Corpus Christi, several hundred miles to the west.

Now back to Port Angeles and cross-country **ferry flights.** The Coast Guard had established its own Aircraft Overhaul Facility at Elizabeth City. Among the aircraft delivered there for overhaul were the PBY-5A Catalinas (amphibians).

Since they had landing gear, those planes on the West Coast were flown straight across country—deserts, mountains, and all. I ferried one from Port Angeles to Elizabeth City and had a weird experience landing in Texas.

As we flew a dead-reckoning course over Texas, we studied our airways charts. Right on schedule, we found the airfield we wanted, identified by it being on the edge of a river, as shown on the chart. I established radio contact and was told to proceed and report when entering the landing pattern. This we did. Using the windsock as our guide, we flew downwind and noticed the runway was marked "16" (meaning 160 degrees by compass). The tower told us to continue our approach and circle to land on runway "32". That didn't jibe. The opposite of 160 would be 160 + 180 = 340. The correct runway should be marked "34". I called this to the attention of my copilot, since I was busy flying the plane, and I thought my math was off, but he also felt something was wrong. However, the tower now gave us permission to land. And we did! We stopped on the runway and waited for a jeep to lead us in when a weak voice said sheepishly, "Coast Guard, where are you now?" To which I replied, "Sitting on your runway." And he said, "You are not at my field. You have landed at the **wrong airport.** You must want the airport five miles to the east." (I have forgotten the name.) Anyway, we taxied around to the active runway and took off for the other field where we landed without incident, but with a lot of kidding. (Note: both airports bordered on the river.)

And now I am going to borrow from a report I wrote for the investigation of one ferry flight that ended in a tragedy:

### A Fatal PBY-5A Crash

The Executive Officer at CGAS Port Angeles was Lieutenant Commander James MacIntosh. (He was senior, of course, to me.) He only flew to get the required four hours a month to receive flight pay. He avoided instrument training flights altogether. I needled him about it and he said he would like to fly more but his job as Exec kept him at his desk. When orders to ferry a PBY-5A Catalina from Port Angeles to Elizabeth City, N.C., for overhaul came through, he accepted the opportunity to not only get in a lot of flight hours but a lot of simulated instrument flight time.

**The Fatal Flight**. MacIntosh selected one of our most skilled pilots whose name I cannot remember. He had come up through the ranks to Lieutenant. He loved instrument flight, but he also took chances, especially on rescue missions. They would have an Aviation Machinist and a Radioman as crew. They were scheduled for a Saturday morning takeoff to land for the night in Medford, Oregon, south of Portland.

I (the Operations Officer) was called at home in the late afternoon with the report the plane had not yet reported its arrival. I went immediately to the station and we began checking with air traffic control and all the airports en route.

I learned that the pilots had decided to maximize instrument time by "flying under the hood" when not flying in real instrument conditions. "Under the hood" means covering the cockpit windows with amber isinglass and having the pilot "on instruments" wearing a blue glass eye shield. The pilot can see the dashboard instruments through the blue film but cannot see outside as that view is blacked out by the combination of blue and amber. The copilot, however, can see everything in the cockpit <u>and</u> outside just as if wearing sunglasses. I had no knowledge of their plan.

Their flight plan began to unravel. They were flying on an instrument clearance (IFR) between Portland and Medford at ten thousand feet at the PBY's cruising airspeed of about one hundred forty knots bucking a forty-knot headwind. It was very turbulent and must have felt like they were never going to get to Medford. They cancelled their instrument clearance and dropped down to fly below the clouds at 6,000 feet using **visual flight rules** (**VFR**). Contact was lost.

**The Search**. I spent a restless night at the station. I convinced the CO it was wishful thinking that they might have found an alternate airport and that I would take the ready PBY and search the route. He didn't object.

The weather had moderated. The winds were still from the south. Most of the turbulence was caused by thermals. I held their altitude of 6,000 feet easily until just in the lee of the ridge when a downdraft hit us and we had to quickly turn and get out of there.

On our second pass, I stayed a little higher and we spotted smoke. We circled and identified it as the crash and, in that pass, we spotted persons at a fire lookout station waving at us. We prepared and dropped them a message block telling them of the sighting west about four hundred yards.

I landed at Medford and joined the land party being organized to go to the wreck to remove the bodies. The crash was a terrible sight. The four man crew was incinerated at their stations. But there was amazing news—two seamen who were getting a ride survived the crash. Riding in the waist section of the plane, they were slammed against the bulkhead but not otherwise hurt. The older of the two reported that he immediately opened the door to go forward to see if he could help and was met by flames. The two jumped out the blisters and ran for their lives to a safe distance, where the rescue party found them.

**The Investigation** concluded that the pilots probably studied the chart and found the highest point on the ridge immediately north of Medford to be 5,050 feet. At 6,000 feet, they would clear the ridge by nearly 1,000 feet. But at the ridge they entered clouds, hit a downdraft losing at least 200 feet, and crashed into the forest of evergreen trees. The plane burst into flames about 200 feet below the crest. That doesn't calculate. What went wrong?

Charts were checked. They had the latest issue. However, an older issue showed the ridge at 5,850 feet. The newer chart showed the eight crudely changed to zero! (Does that calculate? 6,000-foot flight altitude minus 200-foot downdraft equals 5,800 feet. But the ridge crest is at 5,850 feet!!)

The sad fact remains that they violated Visual Flight Rules by entering the clouds thinking they could squeak over the ridge.

End

**Mary and her mother**

Let us leave flying now while I tell you about my family. Mary and I, together with our nine-months-old son Terry, arrived in Port Angeles from my brother's home in Newport Beach, California, in our little car with no idea where we would live. Again we went to an auto court and started our house search. A go-getter realtor just out of jail for embezzlement went searching for us. There were no suitable rentals available but he found us a prefab cottage just brought in by barge from Seattle and erected where the forest trees had just been cleared for a couple more homes. We could get this one on Mary's G.I. Bill with nothing down and $52 per month. It was all-electric. (Electricity was cheap in the Northwest.) Two bedrooms, one bath, room in kitchen for small table to seat six. Cost $8,000. Raw lot—no landscaping. I built a picket fence. Raked thousands of rocks for lawn. We furnished it from the "Monkey" Wards catalog.

Mary was soon pregnant again and decided on her own for a "natural childbirth." Her doctor and a group of other doctors had bought the YMCA building and converted it into a hospital. Mary was one of the first to "deliver" there. I waited in the hall outside. She did it <u>naturally</u>! A girl we named **Christine** (b. July 28, 1948). Our family was growing!

It was past time to replace the little "double-date coupe" with a larger car. We bought an Oldsmobile sedan with an automatic transmission, one of the first to be seen around Port Angeles. When Christmas leave came around, we drove to Newport Beach for the holidays, and we bought a fifteen-foot vacation trailer. In it we, babies and all, would enjoy the Great Outdoors. It was fully screened, had a propane stove, icebox, car battery for lights, and a drinking water tank. We used Forest Service camps and their facilities.

On our trip north, we camped among the giant coastal redwoods. But it froze that night and we worried about the new little baby Chris. I lit the stove and then couldn't sleep for fear of carbon monoxide. But how wonderful it was to enjoy a sunny morning with fresh forest air!

A shock awaited us when we arrived home. A strange big flexible tube entered a bedroom window. It was an aircraft engine heater for freezing weather starts. What is this all about?

In our absence, our water heater, which was located in the attic, froze and burst a pipe. Son Terry's little girl playmate saw water running out of the house and told her parents we were not home. They saw what was happening, called the Air Station, and a work party was sent out to secure the house and try to dry things out. Thanks, Coast Guard, for the rescue!

Mary's parents, Lloyd and Stella Bond, came to visit from Illinois

I will wrap up this Scene with a report about an offshore landing I made. First, some background. The Port Angeles Air Station was assigned a PBM Mariner seaplane about the time I arrived. With my previous PBM qualification in Florida, I was the most experienced in that type of plane. An engineer from some rocket company arrived to show us how to install booster jets for short takeoffs. Each booster was dry chemical in a can about the size of trailer propane cooking gas. One was attached to each side of the fuselage about amidships. The technique was to accelerate on the takeoff run and when the hull rises to running on the "step" (where the bottom has a ledge to break the water suction) to fire both rockets simultaneously. We practiced in our bay just off the Air Station. Each seaplane pilot got a turn. The only trick was to stay low after getting airborne until full climbing airspeed was acquired.

Experiments had been conducted at Air Station San Diego for the safest way to land offshore, where there is sure to be some swell running. We seaplane pilots had studied the reports but none of us really wanted to make an open water landing because even a minor accident might mean taxiing many hours or a difficult tow. (Offshore landings were ruled out when helicopters became available.)

A cargo ship sent an emergency call to "medevac" a seaman who had scalded his eyes and needed immediate hospitalization. I was "elected" to go see if I could land and bring him in.

We rigged the booster rockets and took off with a medical corpsman aboard. We found the ship in light fog. The sea was as calm as offshore seas ever get. We landed quite near the ship, and they came alongside in a lifeboat with the patient. I worried that they might bump my plane and damage it for takeoff. They were careful and didn't.

There was a little swell that I hadn't observed from the air. I would run cross-swell, not into it. I had observed the compass heading I selected and turned to it for the takeoff run. The cargo ship <u>disappeared</u> in the fog dead astern as planned. Oh, God, I hoped I was remembering the heading correctly. <u>She **has** to be behind me</u>. She was. The takeoff was normal. The rockets fired as advertised. We got home and the man got to the hospital on time.

That is it for Port Angeles Air Station. Next, I had another cross-country transfer, this one to Elizabeth City, North Carolina. My assignment was to be in charge of the International Ice Patrol aircraft, flying the **B-17 Flying Fortress**, a famous World War II bomber!

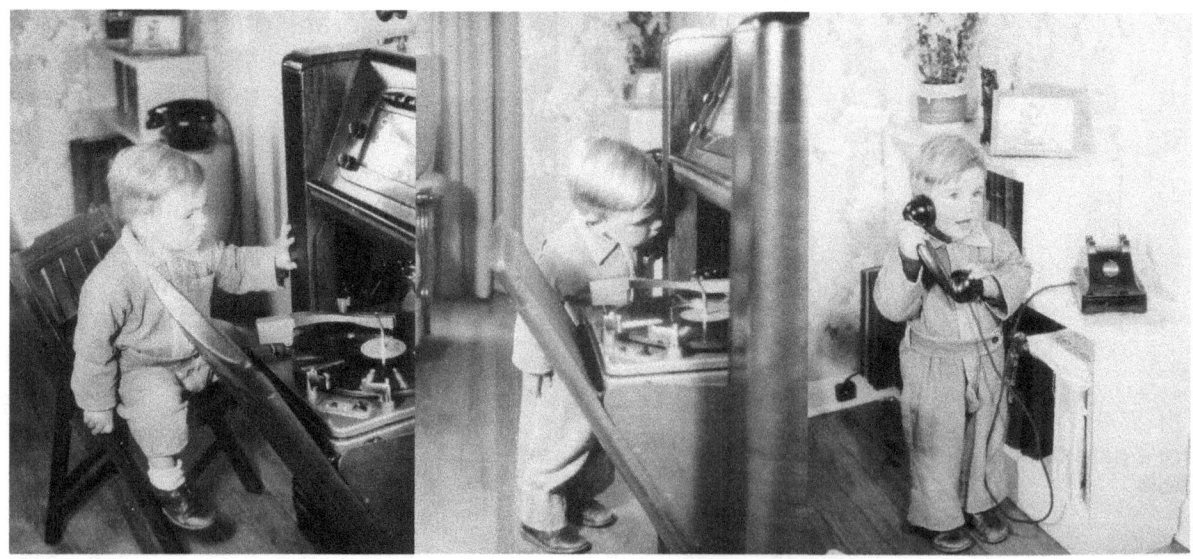

**We settled into family life in Port Angeles, with toddler Terry and new baby Christine**

These Martin PBM Mariner seaplanes were used for long range over water searches and offshore water landings. They were equipped for jet assisted takeoffs from rough water and in restricted areas. Shown above is a takeoff like one I made in the North Pacific Ocean to rescue an injured sailor.

# SCENE 23

## CGAS ELIZABETH CITY—1949-1953 (INTERNATIONAL ICE PATROL)

The three-thousand-mile move from Washington State to North Carolina was far more complicated than the earlier ones. Now, besides Mary and me, we had two children, a newly acquired puppy dachshund we named "Biddie," a house to rent or sell, a house full of furniture to ship, a big new car, and a vacation trailer. Everything fell into place and we started our cross-country journey using the trailer as our mobile home.

I took my allowed proceed time, plus mileage driving time, plus a little accumulated earned leave, and had over a month for the trip. We made it into a great vacation. I had learned how to locate national parks, forest camps, recreation areas, state parks, and highway overlooks.

We spent one night at Mt. Baker in an alpine campground. As the sun went down, the mosquitoes came out. The tenting campers had to break camp and leave, it was so bad. We just went inside our screened trailer and had a good night's sleep.

A nice quiet spot overlooking the Platte River turned out to be Lover's Lane, so there were creepy cars and radio all night. At another stop, we let Biddie out for a run. She followed her nose into tall grass and wouldn't come when called. With two thousand miles yet to go, we darn near left her.

Incidentally, after a pit stop we would count off to make sure all were accounted for. I called: "One," Mary: "Two," Terry: "Three," Chris: "Four," and Biddie we sighted and "barked"!

One night in Yellowstone, we were in a lonely spot, a turn-out with no other cars in sight. It was a cold night, and the moon was peeking out from behind clouds. From afar came the howling of a wolf! Then two!! And finally a chorus!!!! What an *eerie feeling!*

On arrival in Elizabeth City, we didn't know where to stay, but somehow we found a woman who would rent us space in her backyard. We could use her water and electricity and a bathroom just inside the back porch. The Air Station Supply Officer was leaving and his house was for sale for $9,000. We grabbed it. It was on William's Circle where most of the aviators lived. It served us well for four years and when we left we rented it for several years to other officers, then sold it for $16,000.

My orders directed me to report to the Commanding Officer of the Coast Guard Air Station, Elizabeth City, North Carolina, for assignment in charge of a detachment consisting of three B-17 Flying Fortresses and crews for seasonal searching for

**My little detachment of International Ice Patrol aircraft consisted of three B-17 Flying Fortresses, heavy bombers stripped of armament. One was in reserve at Elizabeth City and two were on the line with me, operating out of Naval Station Argentia, Newfoundland.**

**We usually flew at eight thousand feet, above the overcast. Upon picking up a likely radar target, we would drop down to identify it as an iceberg or friendly vessel. Berg positions went through my boss to an international commission that ordered insured shipping to take a safe southerly route.**

**It was a thrill to fly these bombers of World War II fame. The pilot had power in his hands as he pressed the four throttles forward with his right hand and turned on the superchargers! Experiments were conducted with fully equipped lifeboats droppable over water on a cluster of huge parachutes. It worked, but was never implemented.**

icebergs as directed by the Commanding Officer of the **International Ice Patrol**.

The primary objective of these patrols was to observe ice floating in the vicinity of the Grand Banks, so that shipping in that well traveled area can be advised of current conditions throughout the iceberg season. This was, and still is, an international treaty program established in 1914 as a result of the sinking of the **RMS *Titanic*** caused by collision with an iceberg. The patrolling has been a Coast Guard responsibility from the beginning.

The largest bergs calf off glaciers of northwest Greenland and travel first north and west then south with the Labrador Current. The majority melt or are trapped along the Labrador and Newfoundland coasts but some make it into the commercial shipping lanes that traverse between America and Europe. Our aircraft patrols made visual sightings (necessary to distinguish bergs from fishing vessels). The Ice Patrol Commander kept running plots and warned shipping through radio reports.

The season for search patrols was from the first of the year until about the first of June, depending on whether it was a heavy or light ice year. There was plenty of bad weather, but we had several alternate airfields with some sure to be open when others closed. We could normally climb to eight thousand feet and fly in beautiful sunny conditions, but we would have to descend to verify a sighting. That was scary in fog with bergs towering a hundred feet or more.

Our base of operation was at the Coast Guard Air Station located on the Naval Base Argentia, Newfoundland. It was a full service base but with only Coast Guard aircraft based there. We left one of our three B-17s in reserve at Elizabeth City, where it was also available for long-range search-and-rescue. Of extreme importance was the Navy **ground control approach** (**GCA**) team that talked inbound planes down a radar glide path to a landing.

Our arrival to start the iceberg season was sensational! And I don't know whether to be proud or ashamed, as I will explain. Captain Graves was the Ice Patrol Commander. He arranged for a Coast Guard **C-54 Skymaster** cargo plane to transport his office supplies, engineering parts for our aircraft, three ice observers, and his personal effects. I would fly one of the B-17s accompanying the C-54. He chose to fly in my plane. The second B-17 would come later.

The weather had a little of everything in it as we came north from Elizabeth City for a stop in Boston to pick up Captain Graves and the equipment mentioned. Since the weather forecast was good at Argentia, our two planes, the B-17 and the C-54, departed together for Argentia. The C-54 was a little faster and arrived first. We monitored the radio instructions being given by GCA as they picked them up and conned them onto the glide path. Passing snow showers were reported but everything was going smoothly. However, part way down the glide path, the C-54 aborted the approach. Still under GCA control, we heard them start the second glide path approach. Again we heard them say they were going around again.

On the third approach, we heard nothing for an agonizing minute, then the report "C-54 safely landed." Now it was our turn!!

I had the controls (left seat). Lieutenant Fred Raumer was copilot. GCA picked us up and talked us onto the glide path. We were in and out of snow showers and couldn't see a thing. But the reassuring voice gave us confidence as we started down the approach. Suddenly we entered turbulence, and we bounced around quite a bit. The minimum altitude was three hundred feet. If you aren't out of the soup by then you must take a wave off and go around again. At four hundred feet, we were still in snow with zero visibility. We could try again or fly to our alternate airport (with Captain Graves aboard and his personal gear aboard the other plane). Fred, an excellent and conservative pilot, favored another try, so I asked GCA to give us another approach.

On our second approach, we started down the glide easily with no turbulence. As we continued down it was solid as a rock. Still smooth. Passing four hundred feet. Fred said, "Keep going" and I did. It was still smooth as I looked up and saw one line of runway lights. I didn't know which side of the runway I was seeing. Anxious to get down, I cut the power and straddled the one line of lights! We were down!!! We stopped in the middle of the runway. The tower asked our position and sent a jeep to find us and lead us in. It was snowing quite heavily. When we reached the hangar and rounded one end of the open hangar door, we couldn't even see the other end of the door. There was a large gathering awaiting the Ice Patrol Commander, and with cheers for us making it in such a heavy snowfall.

For many nights, I lay in a cold sweat thinking about what I had done. Did I show great skill and judgment or was I stupid and too daring? I still have bad thoughts of what could have been.

Fortunately, we had very good weather as we flew orientation flights, standardized search procedures, and developed in-

**B-17 Bomber—the "Flying Fortress"—equipped with an experimental droppable lifeboat**

flight team work with the ice observers assigned to fly patrols with us. But about a month into patrolling, the weather caused a problem. A series of heavy snow showers descended from the north. One of our aircraft was caught on patrol when Argentia, our home base, shut down. Gander, in Labrador, opened and our plane diverted to there. No visibility problem. Since there was snow on the runway, our pilot planned to land short at the beginning of the runway. What he didn't know, and should have been told by the control tower, was that snowplows had cleared the runway by pushing the snow off the runway and piled it at the end. The result was that the plane hit the snow mound and "pancaked" on the runway. No one was hurt but the aircraft was "totaled"! (Time to call in the spare.)

By May, the bergs were no longer a hazard. They were trapped or grounded along the Labrador and Newfoundland shores. It was time for Captain Graves to end the Ice Patrol and send us home. But first, he was itching to fly "upstream" to where the biggest icebergs are calved and, in so doing, we would circumnavigate the whole of Baffin Bay on a sightseeing flight.

From our base at Argentia, we first flew to **Bluie West One** on southwest Greenland. I saw this base being constructed on the moraine of the Narsarsuaq Glacier when I was on the CGC *Mohawk* convoying cargo ships and engineers to build what would be the busiest airport for ferrying warplanes to Europe in World War II.

From there, we flew north to Bluie West Eight built on the moraine at Sondrestrom Fjord, and which is almost exactly on the Arctic Circle. The approach to land is a tricky one. You must land (and take off) to the west. The base leg is to the north, but straight ahead is an intimidating mountain! Nevertheless, this base became the major stop for commercial flights between the U.S. and Europe, with full accommodations for passengers and food services. We spent the night there in full comfort.

On our way to the U.S. Air Force Base at Thule, about six hundred sixty miles north of the Arctic Circle, we over-flew the village of Jakobshavn on Disko Bugt (Bay). The glacier there calves off the largest icebergs in the world. They can weight up to ten million tons!! Some of these same bergs may transit Baffin Bay counterclockwise all the way south to Cape Race and enter the shipping lanes between America and Europe, where the RMS *Titanic* met her fate.

Navigating from Jakobshavn to Thule was a unique first and last experience for me. We normally steer by magnetic compass, and we have a gyro compass we can set to help us stay on course. But the earth's magnetic pole towards which the magnetic compass points is located in northern Canada and was due west of us. In other words, it was useless. The north point on our compass was pointing west! Again, GCA took control of our flight pattern. They vectored us around with us setting the gyro compass as directed and using only it for our headings. They talked us right into the final approach for landing.

Thule Air Force Base is constructed to cope with the Arctic freezing weather. All the buildings are built like inside-out refrigerators (*i.e.*, warm air is kept in and the cold kept out). You pass through airlock doors to enter or leave. Even plumbing like head and septic tanks are in the warm zone. The buildings are built on stilts to keep the heat of the buildings from reaching and melting the permafrost on which they are built. Again, we had a comfortable night, Air Force-style.

Now it was time to head south. Apparently the weather had been bad, for planes were stacked up to get out of there. We joined the others and found that the problem was a strong crosswind for takeoff. When the wind moderated, planes were given departure clearance. For our turn, everything looked good except that two-thirds down the runway a breeze crossed from behind a little hill. Our B-17 had a vertical tail shaped like a weathervane. It depended on our takeoff speed at that point whether we would go or abort.

I used a short takeoff procedure of holding the brakes and revving up to full, then going for it. When the cross-wind hit us, the plane tried to turn to the right and run off the side of the runway. I called for *flaps!* The copilot said, *"What?"*

I said, ***"FLAPS**!!!"* We ballooned off the runway, picked up speed, and were out of there!

Going south, we went sightseeing along the east coast of Baffin Island, an area where the Coast Guard had built a chain of LORAN stations known as the Crystals. Captain Graves had been on that construction program. For support by water, the Coast Guard acquired a number of Grand Banks trawlers. Junior officers were given command, supported by Quartermasters. When I was on the *Mohawk*, we lost two Ensigns and one Quartermaster to the program. And I became master of mascot Rickey because we deemed the trawler life would be too hard for him.

Continuing southbound, we landed at Frobisher Bay, where Captain Graves met with the Canadians in charge of the Crystals. After a short stay, we were off for home base, and the end of a most interesting flight. We saw no threat to shipping as almost all areas were ice free. Captain Graves terminated the International Ice Patrol for the season, and we returned to CGAS Elizabeth City.

Since patrolling for icebergs was seasonal, we only worked as a team for about half of the year. For the rest of the year, we stood watches and integrated into the Air Station organization. I worked in operations—training pilots and crews and making my planes available for long-range searches. As it turned out, there was not enough ice to warrant patrolling by air, and we were never again activated. As a result, I was assigned permanent duty as Air Station Elizabeth City Executive Officer.

But first, I was sent to **Key West** for Anti-Submarine Warfare training. The family went with me. Biddie met her mate, as we found out some months later.

Elizabeth City was located just south of Norfolk and the Great Dismal Swamp, surrounded by cabbage and tobacco fields. We white folks were greatly out numbered by the blacks. Beet tops and collard greens were favorites there. Displayed under glass at the market meat counter were pickled pigs feet, snouts, and ears.

We found a great weekend retreat for summer months with our little trailer—Nags Head Beach, next to where the Wright Brothers made the first powered flight. The men at our Coast Guard Surf Station there gladly hauled our trailer to the top of the sandy beach, positioned to open to the sea. The Chief-in-Charge went home weekends, and we had use of his quarters for the toilet facilities. It was GREAT! Terry, Christy, and Biddie loved to run on the private beach, chasing sand crabs.

With limited recreational temptations and a long tour of duty, it was an ideal time to complete our family. Thus, daughter **Karen** (b. August 5, 1951) and son **Scott** (b. January 14, 1953) were born at the Albemarle Hospital, Elizabeth City. To add to the fun, Biddie had eight pups!

We no longer fit in the little trailer in which we had had wonderful times. We sold it to the Public Health doctor. His family had <u>four</u> children too! No, he wouldn't take the other pups. We kept one and found good homes for the others, amid tears.

Now we were getting ready for our next transfer: Dave, Mary, Terry, Christine, Karen, Scott, Biddie, and puppy Pretzel. Destination: San Diego, California. (Coast-to-coast, of

**Bayou Belle seaplane and crew. I'm in the back row, third from the right**

course). One change was to trade-in the Oldsmobile for a Ford station wagon. The Olds engine was acting up, and it only had the front seats and the rear seat. The station wagon, though smaller, had three rows of seats and a useful tailgate. We could all fit in (with the help of a shoehorn). Pretzel, who we thought was an awfully dumb dog, ran in front of the school bus and was killed. That was sad, but we hardly knew the pup, so we got over that quickly.

The driving plan was to go first to Mary's home in Abingdon, Illinois. There we would split up. I would take Terry, Christy, and Biddie with me in the Ford driving to my brother's home in Newport Beach, California. Mary would fly from Galesburg to Los Angeles with Karen and Scott. Families would help by putting them on and off at both ends.

The plan worked! With my charges, we stayed in motels. I remember an early morning start when I carried Christy from the bed to the car, and she never woke up until fifty miles down the road. We took a mini-vacation in Zion National Park, where we were treated royally.

As we left Ice Patrol behind us, it seemed as though I could hear my crew in the Officers' Club bar at the Naval Base Argentia, singing, as we often did, an ode to the great ship RMS *Titanic*:

> It was *sad*...yes, it was *sad*.
> It was *sad* when that great ship went down.
> There were husbands and wives,
> Little children lost their lives.
> It was *sad* when that Great Ship went down.

# SCENE 24

## CGAS SAN DIEGO—1953-1956 (SEARCH-AND-RESCUE)

The **PCS Orders** that brought me back to Southern California were my first return "on orders" since I left home to be a cadet in 1935! And what a GREAT LIFE I had during those eighteen years!

Finding housing, always the first order of business, was a little different this time.

We would not have to live temporarily in an auto court or someone's backyard. The officer I was relieving, a classmate, was breaking his lease on a rental. He said the aircraft industry workers had flooded the market and rentals were almost impossible to find. But the house he had rented would not do for us, except as a place to stay while we searched to buy. The landlord agreed on a monthly rental, and we took it.

The house was unfurnished until all our household shipment arrived. Then boxes were stacked everywhere. We couldn't unpack, for the permanent move to the house we would buy could come any day. Poor Mary had to live this way with four children and a dog. I had to peek in boxes to find what Mary needed. This was no picnic!

We found just what we needed in an upscale area known as Loma Portal. The homes were all built to early American/Spanish style with red tile roofs, thick stuccoed walls, large rooms, etc. Old but posh. A short ride down to the harbor and the Coast Guard Air Station. But the price was a scary $20,000! Remember, our first home cost $8,000. Our second cost $9,000. We lived in this San Diego house for three years and sold it for $25,000 when San Diego was in a local post-war depression. Now, in 2004, it must be worth close to $1,000,000!!

Santa Monica was only a little over one hundred miles from San Diego. An easy drive for visits. But with whom? After my mother died, my brother Porter sold the Santa Monica house, and the family members who had been living there found employment elsewhere. My close Scouting friends scattered (but not far from Southern California). (Through the years since then we had reunions, but no more. There are only five of us left now in 2004. **True friends for over seventy years!**)

My orders assigned me to the position of Executive Officer of the Air Station. In addition to a heavy administrative workload, I helped plan searches which mostly involved private yachts out of gas or breaking down offshore, but sometimes searching for lost hikers in Mexico, just across our border. These required diplomatic clearance, which was *pro forma*, but had to be obtained and quickly.

(I could now appreciate how the Exec at Port Angeles felt about finding enough time to fly.)

For our offshore search-and-rescue (SAR) cases, we flew the amphibious PBY-5A Catalina and PBM Mariner seaplanes. I remember one overnight flight south about three hundred miles down the Gulf of California to a fishing camp. I anchored in a little cove much like one would with a boat. There was an anchor in the bow. We took bearings to make sure it was holding. There were four double-sized bunks, a little mess table, and a butane stove. The patient was suffering from "Montezuma's Revenge." He could wait while we inspected the camp for contraband. No, it wasn't dope smuggling in those days. It was trade in smuggling lobster. We found none.

**Search-and-Rescue** has been a Coast Guard mission dating back to year 1790 when it was known as the **Revenue Cutter Service**. That mission was greatly expanded by addition of the **Life-Saving Service** in 1915, with its chain of Surf Stations specifically created to provide rescue services to ships that ran aground on the Outer Banks and other coastal shores.

And, in 1939, the **Lighthouse Service** was transferred to the Coast Guard for the establishment, maintenance, and operation of aids to maritime navigation. These were, of course, services to reduce accidents requiring rescue services.

New means of transportation were constantly being developed, requiring new SAR techniques and equipment. The changes which affected the Coast Guard mostly came from commercial aviation. World War II proved that land planes could replace the lumbering Pan Am Clipper seaplanes. Great Circle Arctic flight courses were shorter and feasible. And even ditching a land plane at sea need not necessarily mean a loss of all on board, provided the pilot and crew were trained and special flotation equipment was on board.

The post-war commercial aircraft, powered by rotary engines, were much more likely to have an engine failure than today's turbojets. The four-engine passenger planes could fly on three engines and, under favorable conditions, even for a while on two. But you can imagine how much better everyone feels if a Coast Guard aircraft intercepts and escorts the crippled plane, and is on-scene should a ditching be necessary? The rescue plane will accurately fix the position, drop rescue equipment, lead in rescue vessels, coordinate team effort, and keep the Rescue Control Center up to date.

When I reported to the San Diego Air Station, I found that a training course for airline flight crews was scheduled to be held in Pearl Harbor, where elaborate preparations were made for the training to be realistic. I asked to go before assuming the XO duties. It was granted, provided I could get a free ride. United Airlines flew from San Diego, so I tried them. They said I could have the "jump seat."

On departure day, I boarded the aircraft with the pilots and took my jump seat behind the pilot where I could observe everything the pilots did. That was great!

The pilots were only part way through the check-off list when the passengers began boarding. The pilot (UAL officer in charge of San Diego operations) was getting nervous because he didn't want to make passengers wait at the gate. And then he found that one engine showed a red light and wouldn't start. He radioed in to have a mechanic report *immediately*. One came running. He took one look at the switches, reached over the copilot's head and <u>flipped one on</u>, announcing, "You forgot to turn on the fuel pump!"

The flight was uneventful. The SAR course was very informative in use of equipment provided for ditching. Pilot instruction was based on offshore landings pioneered at CGAS San Diego in the PBM seaplane. The days were made brighter by watching the beautiful stewardesses ride the evacuation chute and bob around trying to swim in lifejackets. And then a dead-head flight back to San Diego.

**San Diego took the lead in developing safer techniques for offshore landings. Amphibious PBYs were used, for they were plentiful and "expendable"!**

I took my jump seat behind the grey-haired, distinguished, overweight captain. As he slid into his seat, the stewardess (as we called them in those days) placed a fresh white cloth across his lap to protect his uniform from soiling. He listened as the copilot went through the check-off list out loud. The captain then motioned to the copilot to taxi from the gate to the takeoff runway. There, on clearance from the control tower, he grasped the four throttles in one hand, accelerated down the runway, and took off for San Diego. When on course, he engaged the autopilot and gave control to the copilot.

We were a **young and healthy family**, and no more babies! Mary and I joined a square dancing group at our All Souls Episcopal Church. We dressed the part and had a caller who challenged us to keep up with his commands.

For enjoying the great "out back," I built three rain-proof boxes for the tail gate of our new Ford station wagon, one for cooking equipment, one for food, and one for camping accessories. And Terry was old enough to join the Cub Scouts, thus starting us on the Scouting Trail.

A very capable lady named Mary Wright became Den Mother. Somehow I got roped into what we jokingly called Den Father. "Cubs" is really a mother/son program and "Boy Scouts" a father/son program, as I view it. The Den Mothers tend to engage the little boys in handicraft activities which was not by the book, so I attempted to inject "manly arts," simple as they may sound, such as driving a nail with a hammer, tightening a screw or bolt, sawing a board, chopping with an axe, and physical acts like doing a somersault, judging the weight of a brick, height of a tree, sunrise (east), sunset (west), etc.

As the family grew older, I would find myself a Cubmaster and Scoutmaster, and Mary a Girl Scout Leader. Terry and Scott made Eagle Rank in the Boy Scouts; Christy and Karen were good Girl Scouts and have loved the out-of-doors ever since. Scouting was good for my family.

We had many other "firsts" for me and my family. We went south of the border to **Ensenada**, rode the horses on the beach, browsed the curio shops, and beat off the hawkers and the hookers. We attended the **Pasadena Rose Parade** and visited the floats being covered with flowers. But the biggest thrill for the family was to visit the just-opened **Disneyland**!

But transfer orders came all too soon. We were off for two years in Puerto Rico. We would take a Navy ship out of New York after driving cross-country. I don't remember any driving problems although it was years before the interstate freeway system was built. But the National Highways were pretty good. The northernmost east-west highway was Route 10. The southernmost was Route 90.

They were made of concrete and took square turns around land-grant property. North-south routes had a different one- or two-digit system, I believe. If the road was a diagonal, it had still another numbering system, like the famous road from Los Angeles to Chicago—**Route 66**.

Our route took us first to Mary's home in Abingdon, Illinois. It was a grand reunion with Mary's mother and father and a collection of Abingdon relatives.

But we were bound for overseas and a two-year assignment. A few tears were shed.

Our driving destination was the home of Mary's uncle George and aunt Bertha in Montclair, New Jersey, just a short distant to New York harbor where we would board a **Navy Sea Transport Ship** (**NSTS**) to San Juan.

We arrived in Montclair just in time for the village's Fourth of July celebration. The main event was the homespun parade. Various groups entered floats and piled on to hoop and holler. Mary's uncle George entered the centerpiece, a Wurlitzer automatic band! Lots of noise. Lots of fun!

George and Bertha raised their family in Abingdon. While there, as part of family fun, they made ice cream turning the crank by hand. It was so good and popular they decided to make ice cream to sell. When they moved to Montclair they decided to go into the business. They formed the **Bond Ice Cream Company** and opened several little outlets. Their milkshakes were the hit of the town. Someone said the milkshakes were awful big and awful good, from which came their trademark: "HOME OF THE AWFUL-AWFUL."

My next assignment was one of the very best. I can hardly wait to tell you about it! In the next Scene, I will reflect on my confession in Scene 7 of being a "milk thief" at Camp Emerald Bay, together with my assistant, Dickie Braun. (Albeit, we were stealing our own dinner ration of fresh milk.) Dickie surfaces in unbelievable circumstances.

# SCENE 25

## CGAS PUERTO RICO—1956-1958 (SEARCH-AND-RESCUE)

Another "Sea to Shining Sea" transfer, this time from San Diego to New York City with a sea voyage added on to complete the journey to San Juan, Puerto Rico.

I have a memory lapse on this trip. I know we went by car to New York because we had the same Ford station wagon in Puerto Rico. We sold it to become a "Publico" jitney when we left there for my next duty station. I don't recollect visiting parks en route, as we usually did, nor the paperwork involved, but we had orders where and when to report aboard a Navy Sea Transport Ship (NSTS) in New York harbor for the sea journey to Puerto Rico. Mary's Uncle George got us to the ship on time and promised to meet us on our return two years hence.

The big luxury **cruise ships** would appear years later to replace the **ocean liners** of the fifties. While the cruise ships offer constant entertainment with gambling, cocktail lounges, live bands and singers, swimming pool, gyms, and shore excursions, the primary purpose of ocean liners was to get the passengers from one place to another. Varying degrees of luxury were provided by classes such as First Class down to Steerage Class.

The NSTS ships could quickly be converted to troop ships in time of war, but the ship we took was in peacetime configuration like a poor man's cruise ship. No bucket seats, a good lounge, private staterooms, open seating mess hall, children's play room, nursery, some group activities, but <u>no</u> glamour.

This transfer was more like a Navy family transfer than what we had experienced in the Coast Guard, living on the economy as we did. It was one of the rare times when military housing was available to us.

**Housing**. We were assigned to one of the large, two-story separate houses on "Captain's Row." (No house hunting!) In addition to that, it was a Coast Guard tradition to put food and beer in the refrigerator as an arrival greeting!! We would for the first time have all the "On-Base" facilities such as Commissary, Exchange, schools, movie theater, medical clinic, Officers' Club (pool), gym, bowling alley, etc. And be qualified to participate in ongoing programs such as Boy and Girl Scouts, DeMolay, and Little League.

**Full-time Maid**. Our quarters had a Maid's Room attached for a full-time maid. We gave it a try and found we had taken on another "dependent" with bellyaches, scared of local lizards, lonesome, wouldn't answer the maid's buzzer to serve table until she felt like it, and worst of all she didn't recognize dirt!

**CGAS San Juan, Puerto Rico**. We made the most of the many programs and facilities available to us, but I had to remember that I was there to command the Air Station, which also served as the aviation facility for the Navy base. The Navy Admiral's responsibilities covered the Caribbean. Therefore, so did mine. My boss was the Commander, Greater Antilles Sector of the Coast Guard (primarily an aids-to-navigation responsibility). His headquarters were in San Juan; my station was on Isla Grande, actually a peninsula in San Juan harbor. I only saw him at staff meetings, which was fine with me. He kept his hands off, and I could do anything I wanted with my aircraft.

We flew the twin-engine amphibious **Grumman UF Albatross**. We were years before the Cuban and Haiti crises. There were not many search-and-rescue cases, so we had time for training flights. I saw an opportunity to visit several Caribbean islands by scheduling LORAN navigation flights to the islands, returning on airways under **Air Traffic Control**. By this means, we saw places the cruise ships and jet set would exploit in years to come, destroying a West Indies atmosphere I had enjoyed. More about this later.

At breakfast, all the talk was about a small **hurricane** headed our way. I called for a muster as a way to "install" myself. There would be no Change-of-Command Ceremony because the Commanding Officer I was to relieve had already departed to his new assignment. I read my orders and gave a little pep talk, then dismissed the crew and called for a briefing by the officers (I only had about ten).

I found out that our Coast Guard hangar was the only one of any size in San Juan, and everyone who had an airplane wanted to get into it for protection against a hurricane. The crew had been through this routine several times and knew how to pack in aircraft of many sizes. The largest was the Admiral's passenger plane. The smallest the Army cub-like spotter plane. The British West Indies commercial DC-3 was accommodated for goodwill. Our two amphibs were positioned for first out, should an emergency call come in.

The storm crossed over Puerto Rico from the southeast to the northwest and within a few hours it was gone, leaving good flying conditions behind. I was anxious to take a

**My little command consisted of three little amphibian seaplanes of the kind I have previously mentioned using to court Mary and get her to our wedding. Here my area of operation was the entire Caribbean, and we took advantage by sending training flights to many interesting islands for airways training. We had many memorable experiences such as attending a steel-drum competition and the Trinidad Mardi Gras**

look around and search for damage. I found that a village at the east end had been hit hard. The flimsy shacks had roofs missing, people waving as though in distress. Heavy rain made the roads look dangerous. While circling, to save time, I radioed the Air Station to notify the Red Cross so they could get a truck out there right away. I then returned to base to follow up on the situation.

Three days later the Red Cross phoned me and asked for a first hand report, as they were preparing a truck with emergency supplies! I was shocked. They were not. They knew that local country people would not suffer. They would just nail a few replacement boards on the roof. They could live on bananas, papaya, grapefruit, coconut, and plantain for a few days.

And now about those **training flights** as they apply to our primary search-and-rescue mission.

Military commanders have a responsibility to provide for the safety of their men, especially during military maneuvers. They will assign rescue facilities to meet that responsibility. The Air Force has what they call Air Sea Rescue (ASR) squadrons to cover their missions.

By contrast, the Coast Guard positions its **Search-and-Rescue (SAR)** equipment where the potential need is greatest. And, being a humanitarian service, the Coast Guard will give succor regardless of nationality, friend or foe. My Air Station was based in San Juan to best cover an area where American activity was the greatest. We could, however, be dispatched to any place within the Caribbean. The training flights gave us important local knowledge. I thought they were one of my "better ideas," as Mary would say. I thought so too.

Each Caribbean island had its own charm and something of special interest.

The **Dominican Republic** occupies the eastern two-thirds of the tropical island of Hispañiola. The western one-third is occupied by the Republic of Haiti. It was a short flight to **Ciudad Trujillo** (Santo Domingo today), recently named for their strict dictator. It was the neatest West Indies city we would see, excepted for Curaçao, which was Dutch. We walked the shoreline to see the tree stump to which they claim Columbus moored his *Niña*. Columbus' bones are buried in the Ciudad Cathedral, but were not available for public viewing.

**Haiti** had a separate airport serving **Port-au-Prince**, its principal city. It was a favorite because of the informality—there was voice radio that cleared us to land. That was all. We would taxi close to the terminal and go to the fence which was jammed on the other side by French-African (black) local spectators. They would be there to trade articles carved of West Indies mahogany! A t-shirt, a pair of pants, any article of clothing (never mind the condition) would get you a nice bowl, large or small, mask, or figurine. I came home loaded! Because of the swapping, this was a favorite flight destination.

But for fun, **Antigua** could not be beat. That was because my flight was there on Children's Carnival Day. Children of all ages dress in costumes depicting whatever they want. Everything from royalty to animals. One boy was in a green shroud from head to foot and he inched like an inchworm across the stage. While the pageant took place, they were accompanied by steel-band music!

Steel drums are said to have originated when African slaves stirred up their tribes to revolt by beating on skin drums. When skin drums were forbidden, their answer was to cut off the ends of empty oil drums and peen the surface to produce separate notes when tapped. Steel drums could play any kind of music if it had a good beat and soon became popular throughout the islands. Now steel-drum bands are formed in villages to keep the locals occupied and to compete with other bands on special occasions. The Navy Admiral was fascinated and the official Navy Band was soon equipped with steel drums. Its members played almost as well as the natives.

Antigua has history, too. In English Harbour is **Nelson's Dockyard**. Admiral Nelson's sail loft and storeroom stand in good condition as does the landing and bollards where he careened his ships for bottom cleaning and repair.

**Curaçao** is part of the southern Netherlands West Indies group which also includes Aruba and Bonaire. We landed at Curaçao and visited the capital, Willemstad. The harbor had all the atmosphere of the tropics, with inter-island native cargo sail boats, their bow sprits hanging over the docks, but the little city was in deep contrast with rows of spic-and-span Dutch-style buildings looking more like Europe than the West Indies. English was widely spoken, which added to the pleasure of this visit.

**Bridgetown, Barbados**, the eastern gateway to the Caribbean, was the busiest harbor we visited. European cargo was offloaded there for distribution throughout the Caribbean. It was all very primitive and picturesque but what I remember best is a little cottage-like building in the middle of the busy crowds clearly labeled "Château du Nécessité"!!

I remember the French island of **Martinique**, although I can't remember how I got there. It is noted for its many volcanic mountains, the highest of which is Montagne Pelée (4,600 feet). This mountain suddenly erupted in 1902. A ball of superheated gas rolled down over the city and killed an estimated thirty thousand people. Only one person survived. He was a prisoner locked in a dungeon-like jail in a deep cave.

I do remember the airport runway in the **Grenadines**. It ran east and west with a slight upward incline when landing to the west and a small hill directly ahead. That wasn't too bad to handle, but a downwind down-slope takeoff was scary! It was called a spice island, but all I remember were naked little black boys skinny-dipping in the little cove where fishing skiffs were being unloaded of the day's catch of good-size fish.

If this seems like a lot of "flights for fun," it was. But, over a two-year time span, it didn't seem very often. And there was a hidden mission we didn't talk about—**reconnaissance**. We reported anything out of the ordinary. These were peaceful times. Smuggling dope was not a problem, nor were there boatloads of people trying to escape their homelands to seek better lives in the United States. Those years were just over the horizon, so to speak.

This next flight was not for training but was a mission made easy and with confidence gained by the training flights we had.

It was **Mardi Gras** time. A great time of year for politicians and military top brass to make field inspection trips. And what better place to focus in on than the Caribbean, where every island was jumping to the native beat of **Carnival**!! The world's most famous Carnival celebration is in New Orleans and the next biggest (and most truly native) is in **Trinidad**. Local clubs are formed to come up with a theme and to work all year designing and creating costumes for their club to show off as they march and dance across an elevated stage to the shouts and cheers of the spectators.

The Commandant of the Coast Guard invited the Commissioner of Customs to accompany him to attend the Trinidad celebration. He would fly to our Air Station in San Juan in his **Lockheed C-130 Hercules** (with its customized posh interior insert) and requested the Air Station to provide the link between San Juan and Port-of-Spain. Needless to say, "We would be pleased!" And I assigned myself to pilot the plane. The flight was uneventful and successful in all respects, but our little twin-engine amphib must have seemed tiny to the Admiral and Commissioner.

**Receptions**. With so many European nations owning islands in the Caribbean Sea, it is not surprising that there were many protocol calls to be made and returned by senior government representatives. Less formal ones might just consist of a cocktail reception. The Coast Guard did not host one, but I will never forget this one:

The Commandant of the Marine Corps was passing through just long enough for an exchange of calls between the Navy Admiral and the Marine General. The senior Marine officer stationed in San Juan, a full Colonel, held a reception for him in his On-Base quarters, in Captain's Row like mine. The problem was that his quarters had settled through the years and the living room and dining room had a list to starboard of about three degrees. It was unnoticeable, except that after standing awhile nursing a drink one found himself amongst the gathering crowd at the lee edge of the room!

We guests were all dressed in our Service Dress Whites for the occasion. I was upwind observing the crowd when out of the mist a younger officer appeared staring straight at me. As he approached, I observed he wore the aiguillettes of an Aide and Naval Aviator Wings. By golly, he did look familiar! He couldn't be, but surely looked like **Dickie Braun** who was caught with me steeling milk in Camp Emerald Bay. (See Scene 7) **IT WAS!!!** Dickie recognized me from across the room. We had just about five minutes together when he had to depart, never to be seen by me again. "What's the big hurry?" I asked. He replied, "I am the General's personal pilot and we are flying out immediately. Let's hope our paths cross again sometime somewhere!"

# SCENE 26

## 11ᵀᴴ CG DISTRICT HQ, LONG BEACH—1958-1959 (JET FIGHTER QUALIFICATION / ROTATION TO SEA DUTY)

I had successfully avoided staff duty up to this point but Headquarters finally caught up with me. With my family, we were authorized commercial air travel from Puerto Rico to New York and mileage to Long Beach. Yes, we sold the Ford in San Juan, but there was a new, big, Mercury station wagon waiting for us in New York. How come, you ask?

An enterprising Air Force Colonel made a deal with most of the auto dealers in the area to sell new autos at inventory prices plus a small percentage markup for the dealer and the Colonel. The models would be exactly what you ordered. The car would be ready for the road: licensed, inspected, fueled, road maps, and keys. He would meet your arrival with transportation for the whole family. He had a good thing going with returning servicemen and <u>had to be reliable</u>. He was.

Our family now consisted of Mom and Dad, Terry, Christy, Karen, Scott, and Strudel, our dachshund. (She flew under our seats in the airline. But shortly after arrival she became paralyzed in the hind legs. We nursed her to health by rigging a sling under her hind quarters, but after two more episodes we had her put down.)

Our first stop was at the home of Mary's uncle George and aunt Bertha in Montclair, from where we departed for San Juan two years before. That was wonderful.

We took the southern cross-country U.S. Route 90 stopping at **Mesa Verde**, **Grand Canyon**, and **Bryce Canyon** among other places. We rented a cottage in Long Beach while we house hunted and bought a house (which Mary liked best), but after only one year we were moved on. It was an interesting year, however. Let me tell you about it.

I was assigned to the 11th CG District staff in Long Beach, California, as the Operations Officer. The **Rescue Coordination Center** (**RCC**) was my responsibility. It was very active finding overdue boats, enforcing motorboat equipment regulations (boarding), conducting safety patrols, and maintaining communication links with other available rescue facilities such as maintained by the Navy and Air Force.

I was still an aviator drawing hazardous duty pay for which I was required to fly at least four hours a month. To get my time in, I would have San Diego Air Station send up a plane, and I would maybe shoot a few touch-and-go landings or visit a nearby military base for lunch at the Officers' Club!

My tour in Long Beach was cut short for this reason: at Coast Guard Headquarters, the left hand didn't know what the right hand was doing. While I was selected for a Transition-to-Jet Training Course for senior aviators in Olathe, Kansas, a Board was meeting to thin out the senior aviators ranks, which over a period of time had gotten out of proper proportion. I was selected for rotation back to sea duty. On learning this, the District Commander asked me if I wanted my orders to jet training cancelled, as I would no longer be flying. I opted for the training because it would be good to have knowledge of jet operations, on which the future of aviation depended. He let the orders stand.

**Jet Flight Training**. First we were given a Flight Manual to study. Then a look at the **Grumman F9F Cougar** in which we would train. That was a little intimidating. I never dreamed of being a fighter pilot. I am certainly not the "hot dog" type. However, it was comforting to know there would always be the flight instructor in the forward cockpit, except on the final exam, the solo flight.

Now a **disclaimer** for the mistakes I may make relying on my memory. It has been forty-seven years, at this writing, since I took that course, and I was forty-three years old at the time. The age limit for fighter pilots was forty-five. But remember, this course was for senior aviators. The instructors were kind to us old fogies.

First, we were issued anti-gravity flight suits and shown how to plug them in. Then, the flight helmets with connections to oxygen and radio. Then, the parachutes in their ejection seats with instructions on how to eject (*scary thought*).

Next, we got the walk-around inspection of wheels and controls and finally the blind-fold cockpit check.

The flight is smooth without the engine torque trying to take control. It is weird to have only the throttle to push without the other levers of a "prop job."

**Maneuvers** were quiet (you hardly heard the roar heard by people on the ground). Without the torque, the flight controls moved easily. We did wing-overs, slow-rolls, Immelmanns, and loops.

We started the **loop** at about five hundred feet above the ground. Your eyes were glued to the artificial horizon to make a clean climb and passing over the top you were watching the altimeter to make sure you recovered level flight before hitting the ground. Most of us tightened the loop once we saw the earth coming straight up at us and leveled off about a thousand feet higher than we started.

**Breaking the Sound Barrier**!! If you think doing a loop is scary, you should try going faster than the speed of sound in a slow plane like the F9F. The instructor walked me through this maneuver.

We climbed to forty thousand feet, poured the coal to her, and rolled into a vertical dive towards the earth!!! At about thirty thousand feet, everything went quiet. I didn't hear any boom. We pulled out of the dive at about twenty thousand feet. Whew!!

**Landing a Fighter Jet**. Here is where I will probably get in trouble for not knowing what I am talking about. Well, here goes anyway.

You went through the landing check-off list, flaps and especially the landing gear down (meaning wheels), and you lined up with the assigned runway for your final approach to a landing. Now you did what we learned to do in our seaplanes—you maintained a nose-high attitude. You established a glide pass to land at the close end of the runway. You used power to control the rate of decent (slope of the glide path). Reduced power to steepen the slope. Added to lessen. Flew that way to touchdown with a three-point landing and down to stay.

I soloed!! **I made two touch-and-go's and a final, and not bad ones either. A couple of more flights in a San Diego plane and my aviation career was ended. The last takeoff and landing in my life was in the fall of 1958.** I was grounded.

**In pressurized flight suit for fighter jet training**

# SCENE 27

## CG ICEBREAKER *NORTHWIND*—1959-1960 (BERING SEA PATROL)

This transfer was going to be an easy one—only fifteen hundred miles from Long Beach to Seattle. We would use a procedure that worked well before. On moving day, when the house had been vacated and all our household possessions were in the custody of the moving van company, we would go to a nearby motel for a restful night and be fresh for hitting the road next morning.

Boxes of china and furniture of all sizes were on the front lawn and were slowly being swallowed up by that huge van. The driver took full responsibility and signed the inventory. There was nothing left for us to do, so we left for the motel. We had made a reservation at a resort motel high in the San Bernardino Mountains. We had just settled in when daughter Karen announced she didn't feel well...swelling in the throat. With driving instructions from the resort manager, Karen and I headed down the mountain. We found the doctor who gave us some pills and said he didn't think it was the mumps. The MUMPS!

Karen seemed okay the next day and off we went. After one night on the road somewhere, we arrived in Portland for a night with Mary's sister Helen and her husband John. After an early breakfast, we were off again, ignoring the fussy, whining little Scott. In just a few minutes, we were on the freeway, and Scott got even for the lack of attention—he upchucked all over the backseat! U-turn back to Helen's for cleanup detail.

We found a nice motel, and I reported for assignment to the **Coast Guard icebreaker Northwind** (WAGB-282). I complained of a sore throat and the Public Health doctor said I had the MUMPS and was "grounded." The ship would sail, and, when I was no longer contagious, I would be flown to Juneau to join the ship.

We had arranged to rent the house occupied by the officer I was relieving, and we moved right in. Now I would sail on a six-week cruise, leaving Mary on her own with four children and a dog. (Good luck, my love!)

---

At this point, I want to pay **tribute to Coast Guard wives**, who travel from station to station making homes for their families. Support facilities found on the bases of the large services are seldom available to Coast Guard families. They must utilize local facilities such as schools, doctors, grocery stores, pharmacies, churches, etc. Local neighbors are often vitally important and are usually very friendly thanks in no small part to the fact that the Coast Guard is a humanitarian service. (In this case, Mary went to the next-door neighbor and introduced herself. The lady was polite, but said she had become very fond of the preceding Coast Guard couples who had rented that house. But just when they became good friends they were transferred...and she wasn't going through that again!)

How do these women do it? Far from their homes, young women having first babies without their mothers being in attendance? Coping with illness and not knowing where to turn? Making the household furnishings somehow fit? And how frightening to be left ashore while their husbands leave on long sea patrols or fly a plane out of a hurricane's path, leaving the family to cope.

Those who have not lived the life of a service family will never really know how much credit the service wife deserves.

---

## Bering Sea Patrol

First, let me refresh your memory about the early history of the Coast Guard. Alexander Hamilton, the first Secretary of the Treasury of the United States, had ten ships built to enforce customs laws. His motive was, of course, to collect money. The vessels were called Revenue Cutters. They were assigned to the Treasury Department. Their flag was the Treasury Department flag with the Coast Guard shield mounted on it. The Coast Guard remained in the Treasury Department until the Department of Transportation was formed in 1965.

In 1867, the Revenue Cutter Service transported the first federal officials to the new territory of Alaska. The reason was to protect the northern fur seal. The Russians practiced a controlled harvest of the animals, and this procedure was continued even after the U.S. purchased Alaska. But pelagic hunting was threatening to lead the seals to extinction. The Secretary of the Treasury was the official who regulated the killing of the fur seals, as this was a source of income for the United States. He naturally ordered his Revenue Cutter Service to enforce the proper harvesting of the seals.

While cruising the Bering Sea and visiting its shores, the cutter men observed destitute villages in desperate need of food and medical care. Whaling and lawlessness was uncontrolled among the sailors and caribou herders. One unusual aspect of the Bering Sea Patrol was the **Court Cruise**. A cutter would be assigned the duty of transporting a judge, a public defender, court clerk, and a Deputy United States Marshall to hear criminal cases in the isolated region. Along with poachers, the court tried cases involving murder, arson, assault with a deadly weapon, and selling liquor to natives. The cutter's captain was made a Marshall and the executive officer a Deputy Sheriff. (On my cruise I was designated a Deputy Sheriff! But I never did get a case.)

The old **Coast Guard cutter *Bear*** participated in a project to bring reindeer from Siberia to Alaska and teach the North American natives how to herd and raise the animals to provide a steady and dependable food supply. The project started in 1892 with a small herd that grew to half a million by 1941.

A remarkable rescue mission took place in 1897 when eight whaling ships were trapped in the Arctic ice field near Point Barrow. There was great concern that the 265 men who

**For my rotation back to sea, I was assigned as Executive Officer of the CG Icebreaker *Northwind***

made up the crews of the whalers would starve during the long winter months. The *Bear* sailed north, but it was November and the ice pack was consolidating. There was no way the ship could get through. It was then decided to form the **Overland Relief Expedition**. They put ashore at Cape Vancouver and bought a small herd of reindeer. Using dog sleds pulled by reindeer, and on snowshoes and skis, the men traveled fifteen hundred miles fighting subzero temperatures, blizzards, and the long Arctic night. The party arrived at Point Barrow. The expedition managed to bring 382 reindeer to the whalers, having lost only 66.

**Icebreakers are working vessels, not set up for ceremonial duties. They are equipped to handle heavy cargo, and the crew was known as a "dungaree gang"**

The patrol I was on was very different. We cruised to designated villages. We were expected, and by radio we reported our pending arrival. The ship had a helicopter by which means the Dental Corpsman and I were flown in ahead of the ship's arrival. I would meet with the village leader and approve the place for the medical and dental exams. (Usually in the schoolhouse.) The Medical Doctor and the Dentist would follow.

Due to the introduction of candy bars, soft drinks, and sweets, the villagers had very bad teeth. Since the ship could not return for another year, the solution for diseased teeth was to pull them.

On one occasion, the prettiest native girl was in the chair. The Dentist pulled a tooth. It got away from his forceps and landed right square in the middle of her crotch. All eyes stared for a second or two, then the Corpsman said, "Do you need any help, Doctor?"

I will close this Scene with a Song of the Bering Sea Patrol:

> Full many a sailor points with pride
> To cruises o'er the ocean wide;
> But they cannot compare with me,
> For I have sailed the Bering Sea.
>
> While though you've weathered fiercest gale
> And every ocean you have sailed;
> You cannot a salty sailor be
> Until you've sailed the Bering Sea.

# SCENE 28

## CG CUTTER *WACHUSETT*—1960-1961 (WEATHER PATROL)

As I have mentioned before, most of my PCS Orders were long hauls. Those are not easy; however, they offered a unique opportunity to see much of our country. Our whole family (Mom & Dad plus four children plus dogs) has gone coast-to-coast on the northern U.S. Route 10, the southern U.S. Route 90, and zigzagged up the middle on the famous U.S. Route 66, among others.

Now, resting in Seattle after the end of the Bering Sea Patrol, I received orders to take command of the 255-foot **Coast Guard cutter *Wachusett*** (WPG-44), also based in Seattle. This change of command was executed with the standard ceremony—All Hands on the quarterdeck in Service Dress Blues. Officers with white gloves and swords. I tagged along as the District Commander, an Admiral, inspected the crew. Then I read my orders and I turned to the outgoing Commanding Officer, saluted, and said, "I am ready to relieve you, sir." He returned my salute and said, "Sir, I stand relieved."

The ship was in the shipyard and ready to leave. We would have to back into the channel and turn ninety degrees to port to depart. The *Wachusett* is a single-screw vessel which makes it hard to turn. Knowing this, I gave the conn to the Executive Officer who was familiar with the ship's characteristics. We backed away from the yard and started our turn. About halfway through, the XO could see he wasn't going to make it. He called for "all engines back one-third." The ship leaped forward. He called for "back full." The ship vibrated violently and stopped its forward motion very close to penetrating broadside a moored ship!!

I came very close to losing my newly earned fourth stripe of a Captain right then and there. This is known as the "**Hazards of Command**." I had watched the XO and saw no mistake. But the black gang stuck together, and I was happy we could *not* find who it was that turned the wrong valve.

*So stick to your desk and never go to sea,
And you may soon make Admiral in the USCG!*

Here is another example: I believed in helping junior officers learn through hands-on experiences. We had time to spare between Weather Patrols, so I scheduled little cruises around Puget Sound where they could learn to "read" lighthouses and buoys, keep running fixes by plotting bearings of fixed aids-to-navigation, etc.

**I had command of the 255-foot CGC *Wachusett*. Based in Seattle, the *Wachusett* was assigned to Weather Patrol in the Pacific, halfway between San Francisco and Hawaii**

We were cruising up a channel used by San Juan Islands ferries just outside Anacortes. Approaching a turn near a point of land on a small island, the Ensign Officer-of-the-Deck gave an incorrect command to the helmsman, namely, "Right three degrees!" The helmsman acknowledged, "Right three degrees," and put the rudder three degrees to the right. The Ensign went to the bridge repeater compass and bent over it to take a bearing. The ship turned to the right and continued turning, heading for the rocky island. I saw what was happening and, with my authority, counter-commanded the Ensign's order with, "As you were. Steady as you go." This gave us time to forget plotting and visually steer a safe course. What should the Ensign have said? Either: (1) "Right three degree rudder" (in which case he would expect the ship to keep turning until he gave a heading), or (2) "Come right three degrees" (which would be a small course correction by the steering compass).

I was lucky to be on the bridge and to catch that mistake. "The buck stops…with the Commanding Officer."

My first **Weather Patrol** in CGC *Wachusett* was to **Weather Station November**, halfway between San Francisco and Honolulu. I was given the date to relieve the **Coast Guard cutter Klamath** (WPG-66). Together with the XO and Navigation Officer, we decided to leave Seattle at night in order to arrive a little before schedule.

On the main channel just north of Seattle, the engine shut down without permission from or notice to the bridge. I was alarmed as I could see another ship standing out astern of us. I ordered the Quartermaster to turn on the breakdown lights and flash the searchlight aft and on our stern without shining on the following ship. This gave us time to find out what was going on. The engineering office came on the phone and reported the major circuit breaker kicked off without notice, and he was too busy supervising to call the bridge. We would be back to normal immediately. (And we were. But, obviously, the black gang needed more training.)

It was a beautiful clear night and interesting to identify the many lights of red, green, and white everywhere. Offshore there was a big, black Pacific Ocean ahead of us. My Night Orders directed the Officer-of-the-Deck to call me if any ships were sighted. None were.

The next night we were rolling gently with an ocean swell on our beam and a starry sky overhead. I was in my cabin when the messenger reported that the wing lookout had seen a rocket to starboard. Oh, my gosh! As a Coast Guard duty as well as a rule-of-the-sea, I would have to go and investigate. That would take time and I would be late relieving the *Klamath*. If it is a false alarm, they will be mad for having to stay overtime on station.

The Coast Guard quite often receives reports of flares from well meaning beachgoers that turn out to be false, and I suspected this might be the case. I summoned the XO and Navigator, and we broke out the star-finder chart. I thought we should look for a planet in that general direction. There was none, but we did find the constellation Orion in that direction. And in that constellation is Sirius, the brightest star in the heavens. THAT'S IT! The lookout must have seen Sirius!

I went to the wing of the bridge and stood beside the young seaman on lookout. As the ship gently but deeply rolled, I located Sirius and watched it appear to shoot straight up into the sky between scattered clouds. "Is that what you saw?" I asked the lookout, and he replied, "Yes, sir!" "That is Sirius," I told him. To which he replied, "Yes, sir. I'm *serious*."

We arrived at Weather Station November midmorning with beautiful sunny skies and calm seas. The *Klamath* lifeboat was alongside with a stack of official messages. Their CO got me on the radio and explained what was going on—President Eisenhower was on a diplomatic trip to Japan. He flew to Tokyo in Air Force One by the shorter northern route over Alaska and was returning direct to San Francisco over us.

The Navy stationed destroyers along the route which passed over our station. The first vessel in line would turn on its radio beacon at a given time and turn it off when **Air Force One** passed overhead. The next ship in line would listen and turn its beacon on when that ship turned its beacon off. The Klamath CO offered to remain on station until Air Force One passed over us as it was due soon. That was a *very* nice gesture, but I said we could handle it. He and his crew happily left for Seattle.

The specific instructions where carried out. When our turn came, our beacon was turned on. When Air Force One passed overhead we received this voice message: "Air Force One…Out." We were not to reply or acknowledge.

Our time on station was pleasant. We played volleyball with a fish line attached to the ball (to retrieve it if it went over the side). We held swim call. We played with the gooney birds that landed on deck and couldn't take off. We had pulling-boat races around the ship between the deck force and the black gang. On "Hump Day" (halfway through the on-station time), we had barbecued chicken and two beers each on deck and entertainment by a musical combo (guitar, trumpet, improvised drum, and timpani consisting of two GI-Can lids which ended each rendition with a bang and flair).

The **Coast Guard cutter Winona** (WPG-65) relieved us on schedule. We performed a risky transfer-at-sea drill, using a dummy. Had either helmsman gotten careless while we were underway close aboard, we could have had a serious collision. However, all went well, and we took departure for home.

Almost immediately an officer came down with **appendicitis**. We radioed the district to get us advice from the Public Health Hospital. As best I remember, they told our corpsman to use ice packs and penicillin, and to get him to a hospital as soon as possible.

Our choice was to cross the Columbia River bar (dangerous) and have the patient taken off at Astoria, or continue to the Juan de Fuca Strait and have the patient taken off at Neah Bay by CGAS Port Angeles. I chose the latter. My choice worked. The patient's appendix did not burst, although it was close to doing so.

Back in Seattle, after a reasonable rest period and time to catch up on mail and paperwork, we were given an assignment to take a **Reserve unit** for a week's cruise to meet their drill requirements. The District Commander gave me a choice of where to go. I chose the Inside Passage of southeast Alaska. And, as a perk, the CO may have a **Cabin Guest**. I selected my son, Terry. He slept in the Chiefs' quarters but took his meals with me in the cabin.

Halfway to Skagway, we ducked into an isolated little anchorage and repeated our on-deck barbecue routine. I granted liberty in Skagway.

After about a month in home port, I attended the District Commander's staff meeting of the Commanding Officers of his units. At the end of the meeting, the Chief-of-Staff called me into his office and said, "Your orders have just arrived." "Where am I going?" I asked. "To Tokyo!" was his reply. "What is the Coast Guard doing there?" I asked. He said, "It says here that you will be the Commanding Officer of the **Far East Section of the Coast Guard**." **WOW!!**

However, I had first to make another Weather Patrol. It afforded me a great time to read up about Japanese. I got an audiocassette made for our Occupation Forces that taught common phrases, a novel about a Japanese Inn, and a book titled "The Chrysanthemum and the Sword" on Japanese culture. My cabin was a great place to study in preparation for my forthcoming unique assignment.

I am not going to report on the second patrol because it was very similar to the first. But there was one interesting difference—the **Gemini** astronauts were dropping in near our line of ships, but not near us. It made interesting radio listening and made one wonder if we were ready for a pickup.

This was my last seagoing assignment by the Coast Guard. But before I say goodbye to the *Wachusett*, I would like use her to further illustrate **R.H.I.P.** (Rank Hath Its Privileges). But, don't forget, the saying is not complete until you add: "and its responsibilities." I believe the latter has been illustrated above, so let's look now at the privileges.

The CO is treated nicely by the crew. At the movies, the best seat is reserved for the Captain. On the bridge, you don't sit in the Captain's chair. When he enters "your space" you rise, and, if covered, you salute. On boarding the shore boat, an airplane, or an official car, the juniors board first and the ranking officer boards last. And it follows that disembarking the senior get off first. The junior officer walks on the left of the senior. These privileges are just protocol. And don't mean much. Well, how about the Captain rating a private cabin? Isn't that a super privilege? The answer is "yes" but often not as good as it sounds.

**Unlike the *Northwind*, the *Wachusett* was a spit 'n' polish operation**

Remember how the ship rolled deeply when the lookout reported a flare? The crew in their fore-and-aft-bunks down at water level had only to stick out a knee to stop the little rolling in their bunks. What was I doing in the cabin? In my fore-and-aft bunk, I was not just rolling. I was sailing through space on the end of a thirty-five-foot imaginary wand from thirty degrees one side to thirty degrees the other.

Ah, but the ship designers took care of that. They installed a settee mounted athwartship for such an occasion. Now, with your head to starboard, when the ship rolls to starboard you get artificial respiration as your guts press the air out of your lungs; and on the roll to port your reversed gut-pressure sucks in air. All you have to do is *relax*.

Well, the time has come. Goodbye, *Wachusett*. It was a wonderful tour and my last operational type. From here to retirement, it will be senior officer staff billets.

Cleaning out my "treasure drawer," among old ribbons, CG buttons, name tags, patches, shoulder boards, a fifty-year medallion, aviator's wings, and my Boy Scout Eagle badge, I found some certificates for some of my outstanding operational achievements. (Joke) What better place than here to brag about them?

Crossing Equator: Pollywog to Shellback, 1936, CGC *Bibb*
Crossing Arctic Circle: 66-33n/52-00w, 1942, CGC *Mohawk*
Honorary Submariner: Dunking, 9-11-50, USS *Sennet*
Coast Guard Aviator No. 179, December 7, 1943
Instrument Flying Qualification, CGAS St. Petersburg, 29 March 1944
Commercial Pilot, CAA, December 17, 1945
Member, International Ice Patrol, 1953
OMIAS, USNAS Olathe, KS, 48,000 ft, March 1, 1959
Qualified BOOMER, JTTU, Olathe, **smashed Sonic Barrier in F9F-8T**

# SCENE 29

## COMMANDER FAR EAST SECTION, USCG—1961-64

### Tokyo, Japan (Chain of LORAN Stations)

Every time I expressed enthusiasm about my forthcoming assignment to Japan, I received the same question: What is the Coast Guard doing in Japan? I didn't know either until I got my orders in hand. They contained <u>great news</u>. I would be in charge of five LORAN-A stations in Japan proper and three on outlying islands. AND it was a three-year assignment. I was authorized to take my family, selected household effects, our big new yellow Mercury station wagon, our piano (children of music-lesson ages), and our one dog, dachshund "Biddie."

The next most frequently asked question was: What is **LORAN**?

I will defer to The World Book Encyclopedia to explain: "LORAN stands for Long Range Navigation. It is a system of radio navigation that helps ships and aircraft find their positions. Two stations, known as the *master* and *slave* continually send out radio signals. The ship or aircraft receives these signals with special equipment. The receiver equipment measures the time interval between the pulses it receives from the stations. The difference in time between receiving the signals from one pair of stations places the ship or aircraft at some point on a *LORAN line of position* on a chart. In actual operation, two pair of operating stations are used. This allowed the navigator to *intersect two LORAN lines of position for a fix.* LORAN is effective up to about 800 miles during the day and 1600 miles at night."

From the beginning to the end of World War II, there was a requirement to send huge squadrons of warships, flights of military aircraft, and convoys of cargo ships across the vast expanses of the North Atlantic and western Pacific oceans. There are no lighthouses, landmarks, or buoys out there. Precision navigation was necessary for the safety of these movements. LORAN was the answer.

As it was being refined, surveys were made of suitable locations and construction teams were soon building stations up the Atlantic Coast of the United States and Canada, and westward across the northern Pacific and on scattered islands in the mid and south Pacific. As Japanese troops were driven off, stations on Okinawa, Iwo Jima, and the Japanese main islands were made part of the COMFESEC chain. Mobile LORAN units were placed ashore even as the military occupation was taking place.

Mobile units consisted of two semi trailers, one for the power plant and the other for the transmitter and receiving units. Two telephone poles were erected with an antenna between them and a copper wire ground plane around them. That unit would be in place as its slave was being built hundreds of miles away.

Now, let's take a look at one of my units. Niigata LORAN Station was typical. The personnel consisted of a Lieutenant Junior Grade in command. These young men were about three to four years out of the Academy. Typically, just off sea duty. Often married for about a year and proud fathers of first born children. They would command a unit with a Warrant Officer trained in electronics as Executive Officer and a dozen enlisted men. One would be a ship's cook. One Japanese male would be hired as a mess cook, but with time he would wind up as the No. 1 cook, and also as interpreter. The crew would chip in to hire a Japanese woman to do their laundry and polish their shoes.

These Coast Guardsmen would serve one year on station, without liberty except to visit a little farming or fishing village. No USO shows or other R&R. But, at the end of this "isolated duty," they would be granted thirty days of compensatory leave in addition to their thirty days earned.

Their orders were to report to COMFESEC for unit assignment. I had inherited the office staff, which I found _too_ efficient. These men would report aboard in the morning and by afternoon were on their ways to their remote stations...without even really seeing Japan! I changed that by keeping them at our office for two days of orientation and briefing and a liberty to see the Shibuya District with its fantastic neon displays, ancient lanterns, restaurants, and bars (and yes, barmaids!) just outside our base gates.

I remembered my family's first night when the FESEC officers took the six of us to dinner at a typical (shoes off) restaurant and the waitresses (in kimono) served the men first, the boys second, and the females last! Mary was shocked!

With this in mind, I usually took the incoming LORAN station CO to lunch as a good way to get acquainted.

As COMFESEC, I obviously needed to inspect "my" stations as soon as possible. How did my predecessors do it?

The Japanese Maritime Safety Agency assigned Mr. Ono to serve as liaison and interpreter. Together, they flew by Nippon Air to the closest field and went the rest of the way by Toyota or Nissan taxi. There was no easy way to go from one LORAN station to the next, so they returned to Tokyo and visited another station on another day.

I did that one time with Ono-san, but since I had learned enough Japanese to get by, and my secretary had written directions in Japanese using roman letters, I chose to go it alone. I traveled in uniform and found all the Japanese to be friendly and eager to help (and practice English). I loved that experience—traveling on the local economy, staying in Japanese Inns, dining on local cuisine, and bathing in an ofuro (public bath).

Mary didn't usually travel with me on inspection trips, but there were two occasions I recall. One was to the new LORAN-C station under construction. One of the contractor's men accidentally electrocuted himself, and I thought I should personally view the circumstances. In showing me around, they opened the reefer and there he stood! I'm glad Mary was elsewhere having tea!

When I was satisfied the investigation was complete, Mary and I joined a sightseeing bus 100% full of Japanese. The main attraction would be to see aborigine villages much like Americans visit Indian Villages. Yes, they sold souvenirs, posed for pictures, viewed craftsmen at work, etc. These were the Ainus. They were a white race, larger than the Japanese, with white skin and heavy black beards. Their women tattooed their faces. They lacked the oriental eyelid flap.

On the way home, we stopped at a huge public bath in Sapporo where you squat naked (except for a little towel) on a small stool to wash outside of the big pool. Then, <u>after</u> you are nice and clean, you enter the steaming hot pool with the others. Unisex, of course!

**We enjoyed the experience of staying in Japanese inns**

On the other occasion, <u>we got VIP treatment</u>. Mary and I and the U.S. consul and his wife were included in a small group invited to make the inaugural flight of All Nippon Airway's new route to Okinawa. The ladies were given big bouquets of flowers and we men were each given $20 in yen for spending money. And on arrival in Okinawa, we were all taken sightseeing in a small bus. Mary and I were the only "round eyes" on the bus. The Consul and his wife were making a call elsewhere. The usual little hostess in the front of the bus told us on the microphone how valiantly the Japanese had fought and showed us where Generals had committed hara-kiri by jumping over the cliff.

Then, we stopped at a cave of the type Japanese used to hide out. When flushed out by flame-throwers, they came out screaming and firing in all directions. During the war, at this cave they refused to come out and so were all killed by American flame-throwers! Investigation showed that the occupants were all young Japanese girls from a nearby school seeking shelter!

By the end of my third inspection trip, I had come to two conclusions: (1) **All Far East Section mattresses needed to be replaced!** (I sent a message to Commander 14th CG District and it was approved for them to implement.) (2) I declared the accommodations at the Far East LORAN stations to be inadequate for visiting officers. Let me explain. The choice for a bed at the unit was to displace the Commanding Officer from his private room (the only one at the station). Or sleep in the storeroom where a cot would be set up. My declaration was approved, and I received per diem. That permitted me to seek lodging in the little local inns, where I could host drinks and exchange little gifts with the mayors (the Japanese cook interpreting and the station CO attending). One time, the hors d'oeuvres were candied grasshoppers!

Another LORAN station story, and I will go back to Home Base.

My three years as COMFESEC were without any serious disciplinary problems. But while I was inspecting one station, the Commanding Officer told me he had one man who would not obey him. The culprit grew long hair that formed boat-tails in the back that were non-military in appearance.

I took the man aside and asked him why he refused a haircut. He said that, in his opinion, it was neat and looked military and did not violate military regulations. I looked him over and said that in <u>my</u> opinion it did not look military and violated military regulations by not being cut gradually up the sides and back. And then I asked him whose opinion did he think would prevail, his or mine? He agreed to get a haircut.

We were at the threshold of the Vietnam War. The Communist Party was staging rallies all over the place. They naturally loved red and waved large red banners to gather crowds.

One day, I received a phone call from the CO of a LORAN station on Kyushu saying he had been told by the cook that the Communists were going to protest the station because it would be used to direct bomber planes to attack them. We, of course, had no such intent or equipment to do so.

So I said for him to send word reminding the police chief that Japan had the responsibility to protect this station, and then invited the protestors to tour the station to show that LORAN is a passive system and unable to control air squadrons. Then, I invited them to the mess hall and treated them to cookies and coffee. The plan went over big. The protestors were satisfied and grinned ear-to-ear as they marched off, still waving their red banners and munching on American cookies!

**Scott learned to ride at the Imperial Stables**

Meanwhile, back on the base...life goes on American-style—American schools through high school, Little League football and softball, Girl Scouts with Mary a Leader, Cub Scouts with me a Pack Leader, and a joint program with a Japanese Cub Pack that tested our "protocol."

My Japanese secretary told me her Catholic church had a Cub Scout Pack and it would be nice to invite them to the base. From that suggestion grew this program.

In the base auditorium, we would seat the American Cubs on one half of the room and the Japanese Cubs on the other half. (Which side is the "honor side"? We are on an American base located on sovereign Japanese soil.)

Facing the stage, we put the Japanese Cubs on the right side and the Americans on the left.

Parading the Colors, we had the Japanese Cubs come down their side simultaneously with the American Cubs coming down their side. Both Color Guards mounted the stage and on meeting they crossed their flags, so now the honors were reversed! (The generals and admirals in the audience didn't say a word!)

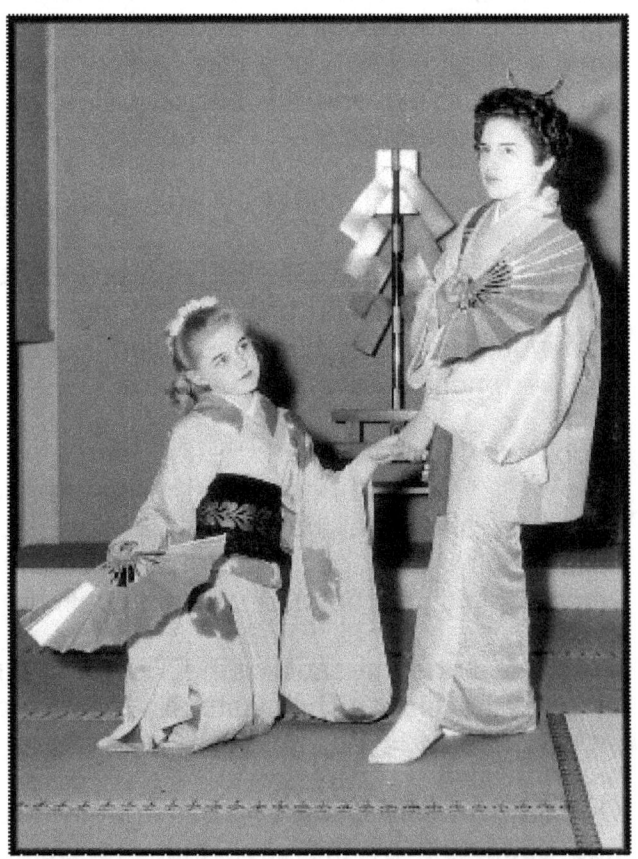
**Karen studied Japanese dance and performed at the Meiji Shrine**

Next, with recorded music, each side in turn sang their anthem.

I was next "on stage" to lead them in yelling. When I raised my right hand, that side of the room yelled. Ditto left side, with variations of long, short, unexpected reversals, etc. This lung exercise was concluded with singing a song both sides knew. (Can you guess?) "ABCDEFG, HIJK..." etc.

Now to end the joint meeting, the American boys were instructed to pick out a Japanese boy and lead him through the Cookie & Punch line and say "Sayonara." End of joint meeting...a great success.

Christy was elected Worthy Advisor in the International Order of the Rainbow for Girls

**Ancient Japanese.** Their history is loaded with old traditions that are often celebrated with parades in ancient costumes, with warriors in battle dress riding horses and a dozen or so men carrying a huge palanquin bearing three or four bass drummers, or a portable shrine, or even a newly trained Geisha.

New Year's Day celebrated firemen with a parade in traditional costume consisting of large white diapers and exposed tattoos covering their entire bodies. They drove modern hook-and-ladder trucks in addition to walking, and at a designated area performed handstands and other acrobatics atop extended ladders. Quite a show!

Another great tradition to watch was an archery-on-horseback contest. There was a runway for the horse to gallop past a mounted bulls-eye target. The mounted archer had to draw and fit the arrow to the bow and shoot at the target while at a full hands-off gallop! Very exciting!

I could go on, but suffice to say we made the most of absorbing a little of the Japanese culture. We read about the forty-seven ronin before visiting the Nagoya Castle. Mary, Terry, and I took a course in the ancient martial art of Aikido. Scott took judo. We all trained for and climbed Mt. Fuji! Scott learned to ride a horse at the Royal Emperor's Stable. They played "musical chairs" on horseback, and Scott made his mount jump a little fence!

Remember **R.H.I.P.** (Rank Hath Its Privileges)? There was a charter airline connecting bases where we could go to Manila or even Hawaii on space available. I was several times the ranking passenger. On deplaning, all passengers would be held back while an intercom announcement would state, "Captain Sinclair and family deplaning!" One Christmas, I took leave and we went as a space-available family to New Delhi and Thailand. It was wonderful!

Just one more story about my Far East Command: When the Commandant of the Coast Guard came through on his annual inspection trip, it was my responsibility to set up a reception for him. We always used the Sanno Hotel in Tokyo, which was a U.S. military billet. Ranking officers would be invited and cute waitresses would circulate with trays of drinks and snacks and they would take refill orders. It would be easy to drink too much, so we had trained the waitresses to recognize an order for "Mizu on the Rocks" (mizu meaning "water"). We could safely drink with our unsuspecting guests by drinking "water on ice."

For a great departure gift, the Japanese government presented me with a medal, ribbon, rosette, and a scroll with the Emperor's han stamp entitled the **"Third Order of the Sacred Treasure,"** for my work obtaining sites for the new LORAN-C system.

Our flight home completed our 'round-the-world flight, piecing together segments from Tokyo to Manila to Madrid to London to New York! A time break made a tour of Western Europe possible. There were only five of us rather than the usual six, because Terry was at the Coast Guard Academy. Upon arrival in the U.S., we stayed with Mary's aunt Bertha and uncle George as we had going and coming from Puerto Rico years before.

Now it is <u>Sayonara to Japan</u> as I turn my focus to my first "desk job."

**Terry graduated from Narimasu High School in Tokyo**

**Our family on Mt. Fuji, with nephew Roy Sinclair (seated second from left)**

**Scott, Mary, Karen, and Christy viewing the Taj Mahal, Agra, India**

# SCENE 30

## CG HEADQUARTERS—1964-1967 (CHIEF, RECREATIONAL BOATING SAFETY)

It was midsummer, hot and sticky in Washington, D.C., when I reported for duty in that old condemned Headquarters building at Twelfth Street and Pennsylvania Avenue, NW. The building was not air conditioned except for the private offices of senior officers, of which I was one. But my unit didn't do the job.

The uniform of the day was Service Dress Blue. (The short-sleeved summer uniform had not yet been invented.) The hot jacket could be removed while in the office, but had to be worn when in the hall, because when the jacket was removed there was no insignia showing rank.

I had found a parking space for my car behind the building, but it was "solid packed," meaning no entrance or departure during office hours. I had to register for a parking permit, and found I must form, or be in, a carpool of five. All meetings and conferences had to adjourn promptly at 4:30 p.m. so cars could leave and not "land lock" a line of cars.

The operations staff held a special briefing just for me to acquaint me with ongoing plans. I patiently listened to jargon splattered with staffanese. It was something about constructing a computer model of the Coast Guard. When they finished, they asked me if I had any questions. I said, "Yes. Would they mind briefing me again using plain language?…Perhaps at another time?" Agreed!

**I enjoyed my job**. I had a pretty free hand from the Commandant and the Chief of Operations because recreational boating didn't stack up as important as other missions.

Yet, it was a time when the boating industry was booming and needed safety regulations and standardization. There were new designs for boats and equipment, more regattas, more racing, and more challenging cruising. The basic federal regulation for recreational boats was the Motorboat Act of 1940. It was inadequate to meet the challenges of new federal waterways, new lakes built by the Bureau of Recreation, and use of federal waterways by fishermen and hunters. Numerous states had formed departments to manage the growth. Our concern was that the state regulations must not conflict with the federal. State Departments for Marine Navigation were formed, and it was our job to work with them. I traveled a lot and my assistant often traveled with me. It was a nice experience.

**Our home at 5800 Conway Road in Bethesda, Maryland**

To build staff positions at our Coast Guard District offices, we "stole" from other departments. Being new to staff work, I assumed that, since we were all Coast Guard, we would all work together. At one meeting in the Marine Inspection Office, my Admiral (operations) accompanied me. The Marine Inspection Admiral had one of his staff read a letter from a District Commander in which he declined to give up a billet. I had read the letter and knew that the reader had stopped right where the letter continued with a "however..." (followed by a condition we could easily meet!). I spoke up and called him on that. I was shocked! I grumbled to my Admiral as we walked back to his office. His reply, "Well, you called him on it, didn't you?"

An enhanced boarding program for my office to run was established before my arrival. It was to board boats underway for enforcement of safety equipment laws. Any Coast Guard officer had the authority, but to conduct a good and fair inspection considerable training was necessary. To provide good boats for boarding, the Coast Guard purchased a small fleet of seventeen-foot runabouts. To make it visibly clear when the vessel is on an enforcement or rescue mission, these little boats were equipped with a flashing blue light, as is the practice with police patrol cars. With blue about the only distinctive color left, I took the initiative to have the authority placed in the Federal Register and eventually made law.

I will close with the reminder that federal laws are far-reaching and must be carefully drafted to enhance safety, establish accountability, and be enforceable.

# SCENE 31

## 12<sup>TH</sup> CG DISTRICT HQ, SAN FRANCISCO—1967-1969 (CHIEF-OF-STAFF / RETIREMENT)

Coast Guard officers are required to retire on the completion of thirty commissioned years, unless selected for Admiral. That left me just two more years for active duty.

Accommodating my desire to leave Headquarters, the Personnel Office found two billets appropriate for my rank that would be available and offered me a choice. One was to San Francisco as District Operations Officer, the other to Cleveland as Chief-of-Staff. Which would you choose?

My principal responsibility as **Operations Officer** was the functioning of the **Rescue Coordination Center** (**RCC**). I found it well equipped for handling rescue cases and coordinating joint efforts with other agencies. The officers and men assigned to the RCC were well trained. There were many little cases but no major ones. That left me lots of time for working on inter-agency plans for coping with a major oil spill within the harbor, should one occur. Fortunately, none occurred.

In the corner of my little office, next to my desk, was a locked filing cabinet. I asked around but no one knew the combination or what was in it. I thought it might contain readiness plans, which were another officer's responsibility, and I forgot about it. It never was opened on my watch. My relief told me later that he never opened it either. Apparently it didn't smell???

The **Chief-of-Staff** retired and I moved up to fill that billet. The only noticeable change was that I now had to wear the aiguillette on my uniform. That is the gilt cord hung in loops from the left shoulder. It gave me prestige as next in seniority to the District Commander…or was I just the Admiral's "go-fer"?

Since the department heads knew vastly more about their jobs than I did, my duty was to keep order at staff meetings and, with the assistance of my secretary, keep the coffee urn filled.

**Living conditions** for my family were unusual yet excellent. Long before the Lighthouse Service joined the Coast Guard, they built two large houses high on Yerba Buena Island for their two most senior officers. That is the little islet on which the San Francisco Bay Bridge touches down between San Francisco and Oakland. Our Admiral

**Coast Guard Quarters B, Yerba Buena Island**

occupied the Lighthouse Keeper's Quarters (the light and fog signal having been automated). My family and I were assigned one of the houses.

For the 1939 Golden Gate International Exposition, the bay was dredged to form Treasure Island abutting Yerba Buena. On it, the Navy established a base with all the usual facilities—Exchange, Commissary, Officers' Club, and sailboat club. Also a sickbay, but no schools. The Navy bussed school children to San Francisco where they were a minority race among the Chinese-Americans. There was an academic high school to which Karen and Scott qualified. (Terry was moving about on CG orders. Christy was in college.)

Scott's bus took him down the row of North Beach nightclubs just at the time topless dancing was the latest attraction. He (a junior high kid) liked to report to me on the latest: "Hey, Dad. They now have topless shoeshine girls in North Beach!"

I had several relatives from my mother's side of my family living in the Bay Area, which also added to the pleasure of this assignment.

Captain Lynn Parker, a classmate of mine, was also on our district staff and also subject to retirement on June 30th. Admiral Bender, the District Commander, with whom we got along very well, arranged for us a joint Retirement Ceremony at the CG Base Alameda, with Rifle Drill Team, Base Band, and a Pass-in-Review to make us feel big. It was very nice of him.

So now I am retired, and have been for thirty-six years at this writing (2005), which tops my thirty-four years as a cadet and Commissioned Officer. **It was truly a GREAT LIFE!**

# SCENE 32

# RETIREMENT YEARS—1969 TO PRESENT

It has been a Great Life and it continues to be great in retirement. It took me **thirty-four years** to go from **Cadet Swab** to **Captain Retired** and already, in 2005, I have been **retired thirty-six years.**

In the following Scenes, I will separate activities by category and comment where I feel there is something special to say. But before I start on recreational activities, I want to try to describe how it felt to realize I was retired! I left Mary at home to sort things out while I went to the Naval Training Center to acquaint myself with the facilities available to us.

It was a warm sunny summer day. I said to myself, "This is it! **San Diego** is where I will spend the remainder of my life. I will probably wind up in the Navy Hospital on the way out!"

Then, I had an empty feeling when I realized I did not have to log in with anyone. For thirty-four years, the Coast Guard kept track of me. If I was late returning from liberty or leave, the Coast Guard would search until they found me. They cared! Now it seemed only my family cared. I felt cast adrift with no anchor to windward. My parents were long gone and so were Mary's. Neither of us had family relatives nearby.

**Terry**, our eldest, was serving on active duty in the Coast Guard (expenses paid).

**Christy**, second child, elder daughter, was enrolled at San Diego State University.

**Karen**, third child, younger daughter, was enrolled to start at U.C. Santa Barbara.

**Scott**, our youngest child, was enrolled at the Point Loma High School with two years to go before he would head to U.C. Berkeley and finally to graduate school at UCLA for his MBA degree.

As we met our neighbors and made new friends, they sympathized with us for the expense of putting four children through college in eight years' time. But they didn't know the half of it. On thirty-year retirement, I received 3/4 base pay. That sounds pretty good, but I lost allowances for housing, subsistence, and flight pay!

I thought we might be extending ourselves too much by the purchase of a nice small three bedroom, two bath house, in choice Point Loma for $47,000. (This house will sell now for in excess of $600,000!!!) We did have negative cash flow for awhile, but I was determined not to take a nine-to-five job or try to be a salesman. We dipped into the college funds we had set up for the children, and I took on the seasonal job of **income tax preparer**. A few years later, we bought a fixer-upper nine-unit apartment complex in Ocean Beach. I worked like a slave, and Mary helped me manage the headaches owners face. As it turned out, it was a lucrative investment.

It wasn't all work and no play. We got started with sailing right away, and went on to have an exceptionally full retired life of travels and adventures. The following Scenes will describe some of the highlights.

**I retired in 1969. By 1972, we were alone with our children in college or out on their own. Mary said, "If we are to do any traveling, we should start right now while we are in good health." And travel we did, starting with Europe. Little did we know how far our travels would take us. The following scenes and photos are just a sampling of what we did and saw.**

**At Stonehenge, 1975**

**Snorkeling in the Virgin Islands, 1976**

We learned to travel light. In this picture, our bags are packed for cruising, bicycling, hiking, birding, all kinds of weather, and even dressing for dinner. Europe, 1979

Hiking the Milford Track, New Zealand, 1982

Whitewater rafting, New Zealand, 1982

On safari in Africa, 1987

**Departing for Mexico, 1999**

**Biking the Netherlands, 1990**

**Taking a glider flight on my 90th birthday, Warner Springs, California, 2005**

**On a walking tour in Switzerland, 1998**

# SCENE 33

## SAILING

Ever since I learned to sail a little Snipe and <u>sail</u> a canoe, I have had a love for sailing. Owning a boat was impracticable while on active duty and being subject to transfer orders at any time and to any place, so I just kept saving and dreaming. Now was the time!

Years earlier, I had turned to my brother, Porter, for advice. He was a prominent yachtsman in Newport Beach, active in organizing sailing races such as the Newport to Ensenada and a longer one to Acapulco.

Porter had built from scratch the largest marine hardware store in Southern California. He knew the trade and recommended a "Cal Boat." He knew they were quality built boats. We selected the **Cal 34**, a boat not too big for the two of us to handle yet big and seaworthy enough for cruising Southern California offshore waters. He arranged for me to get a discount if I would install the hardware such as knot-meter, wind gauge, winches, cleats, and lifeline stanchions, and order sails separately. The boat price to us was $10,800.

Mary and I named the boat "*Ichiban*," which we learned when stationed in Japan means "Number One," or the best, also our first boat. We took possession in Long Beach in early 1970 for the **maiden voyage** to San Diego. I invited Porter's son, Roy (known to the family as Jeep), to be navigator, as he was a yachtsman too, and knew the coastal waters. And we invited Porter's widow, Jill, to join us. Son Scott was on as crew.

*Ichiban*, christened in 1970, has provided us with wonderful recreational and social opportunities for over thirty-six years

It was a foggy day with limited forward visibility. Shortly after sailing (powering), we passed through a yacht race in fairly thick fog. (First thrill in *Ichiban*.) Then, off Huntington Beach, we heard voices to starboard! Starboard?? As the shoreline was to port, where could the voices be coming from? Maybe men fishing in a skiff? A large dark form took shape. To starboard was the tee of the Huntington Beach Pier!!! My immediate command was, "Turn to port and let's get out of here!" Scott was on the tiller and did a one-eighty in record time!

As soon as *Ichiban* was ready, I gave Mary and her friend, Barbara Hood, sailing lessons. These made Mary feel safe, and she soon became my principal "sail trimmer." We raced locally in the Handicap Fleet for about ten years. We didn't win many races but usually came in second or third. The most strenuous were the races around buoy-marked courses where spinnakers were required. Offshore races as far north as Oceanside and south to Ensenada were more relaxing.

**Not a very enthusiastic sailor before *Ichiban*, Mary took on the job of "first mate" with gusto and developed a love of sailing that continues to the present**

I organized a small fleet of retirees we called the **Mid-Week-Cruisers** and had wonderful times doing crazy seamanship-testing challenges en route to a selected anchorage, shared meals, etc. This fleet only fell apart after about twenty years when its members died or got too old for sailing.

To expand our sailing experiences we also sailed "bareboat." That means we chartered a boat without a skipper or crew. I became fully responsible as skipper. We had terrific sailing experiences on each of these waters:

- San Juan Islands
- Chesapeake Bay
- British Caribbean
- Canada Gulf Islands
- Dalmatian Coast
- Penobscot Bay
- Lesser Antilles

**Chartering sailboats with friends, as well as joining friends on their boats, enabled us to combine sailing, travel, and friendship. Here, cruising the Antilles in the eastern Caribbean**

**Sailing in the San Juan Islands**

**Sailing with friends on their boat in San Francisco Bay**

**A black-and-white reproduction doesn't do justice to how beautiful *Ichiban* looks with her red, white, and blue spinnaker flying**

**Turns out we weren't the only ones who appreciated *Ichiban's* beauty. Imagine our surprise to see our very own *Ichiban* featured on billboards of "Home Federal Country"**

# SCENE 34

## BARGIN'

With the introduction of the railroad, the network of small canals in Europe became obsolete. Many are now maintained for the tourist trade. Some old work barges have been converted to what are called "hotel barges." The most interesting of which we have heard are the **Narrow Boats** of England that used to carry cargoes of coal. They are seventy feet long and only seven feet wide. The locks are about eight feet wide!

The skipper's barge, with an engine, works with a "butty" boat which is engineless, either towed alongside or astern. The skipper and his wife (with baby?) have a small cabin in the stern of the engine boat. Forward are single and double (believe it or not) staterooms. In the bow, there is a library with a few observation seats and a self-service bar and head.

The butty boat has the shower, staterooms, dinette with athwartship seats, a passageway, and galley. Galley maids are very busy maneuvering in that small space and turning out: 0700-tea, 0730-breakfast, 1100-coffee and cakes, 1300-lunch, 1630-tea and cakes, 1930-dinner. All on English china. It was something to see the galley slaves leaping from barge to butty boat with a full tray of tea and crumpets! Then, from 2100-2230, the barges were moored close to the local pub.

Comments:

It was great to observe the skipper align his barge behind the butty boat and thread them into the narrow locks.

We were the only Americans, but all the passengers spoke English and were very congenial.

**We enjoyed a canal cruise in England on a narrow hotel barge. The boats barely fit through the locks. One boat has an engine, the other—the "butty" boat—is engineless and is towed**

Passengers were invited to work the hand operated locks, giving the lock keepers a little rest. It was fun and good exercise. The gate is turned by pushing on a big long boom. When the water in the lock is <u>exactly even on both sides</u> the lock is easily opened. Until that last inch is matched, you can't budge the lock's gate.

## French Hotel Barge (1979)

Four years later, we were back to cruise French canals in the *Palinurus*, the first coal barge converted by the French for the concept of "holidaying" on a barge. She is one-hundred-feet long with a sixteen-foot beam, with two decks. The upper deck has a saloon and elegant dining room, and a sundeck forward. The lower deck contains four double

**Passengers were invited to operate the locks, as I am doing in this photo**

**A professional French lock keeper works the locks**

cabins, two twins, and five singles. There are three showers (douches), one bathtub, four WCs, the engine room, galley, and crew's quarters.

The vessel was named after Palinurus, the mythical navigator who fell asleep at the helm on a cool balmy night and was swept overboard by a sudden rogue wave!

Virgil, the greatest Roman poet, captured the moral to this story in these words from the "Aeneid":

"The masts are raised and sails stretched from the halyards…At the head of the fleet rides Palinurus…

"The God of Sleep speaks, 'O Palinurus, the fleet rides smoothly in the even weather. The hour is given for rest. Lay down thy head; rest thy tired eyes of toil. I will take over a

**Compared with the narrow hotel barge in England, the French hotel barge was quite spacious**

little while.'

"But Palinurus answered, 'Trust the waves, however quiet? Trust a peaceful ocean? Put faith in such a monster? Never!'"

There were bicycles available for our use. Mary and I had been biking with groups around San Diego, so we biked the towpath several times while the *Palinurus* went from lock to lock. That sometimes gave us enough time to pass through a canal-side village. But we had to catch up with the barge, or we would be in big trouble. We needed the exercise for we had a "Holiday on Two wheels" scheduled for the Netherlands.

## R/B *River Explorer* (1999)

The narrow boats described above are the smallest hotel barges we were to experience. I am skipping head now nineteen years to include in this section on hotel barges the largest hotel barge in the world. We were booked on it by Elderhostel for a birding tour of the Texas coast from Port Isabel to Galveston aboard this newly built composite of two 295-foot x 54-foot barges and a 140-foot pusher boat. They are chained together by cables to form one rigid vessel 682 feet long!

The *Miss Nari* pusher boat on the left is run by remote control from the bridge of the after barge. She is unmanned except for an engineman on watch when underway

The *Miss Nari*, the pusher boat, is powered by twin engines that can rotate individually 360 degrees. There is no need for a rudder, and there is none. The *Miss Nari* is unmanned, being completely under remote control from the bridge which is located on the sky deck of the after barge. Yes, there is a bow thruster.

The forward barge houses the public rooms (lounge, dining hall, auditorium, bar, etc.). The after barge staterooms accommodate 197 "barge mates."

The sky deck runs the length of both barges. It has a bar, weight room, hot tubs, shuffleboard, and a walking track. Birding was from the sky deck only and was poor.

**The above photo provides a good perspective of the size of the barges**

**We birded the Texas coast with an Elderhostel group on the R/B *River Explorer*, a huge hotel barge comprised of two huge barges and a pusher boat**

# Canal Boats (1985)

There are many yachts designed for cruising the minor canals of Western Europe. They must have low overhead clearance for bridges, hull strength for getting banged about in locks, and with enough power to proceed up river between some locks. Our San Diego boating friends, Clare and Loch Crane, bought such a boat thirty-six feet in length, with excellent accommodations for four persons. We joined them in Brussels for a two-week cruise of Belgium's lesser canals.

**Canal boats are built low to clear the bridges**

We experienced two most unusual locks. One, called an **"ascenseur,"** built in 1917, designed by Eiffel. It was built with two entire loch basins counter-balanced like the buckets on an old fashioned scale. When they are full of water, with or without a boat or barge floating in one or both, they are counter-balanced! Now you figure that out!

The other lock is, I believe, the only one of its kind. It is the **Incline at Ronquières**. Again, two lock basins are filled with water to counter-balance. One at the top of the incline and the other at the bottom. It doesn't matter how many boats or barges are floating in one or both of the basins as each boat displaces water equal to its own weight. The basins remain in balance. The vertical lift is sixty-eight meters on railroad tracks!!

Our friends, Loch and Clare Crane, invited us to join them in Belgium to cruise the canals on their yacht *Dolfin*. Of course, we accepted!

For overnight, we would find a soft bank of the canal and moor to it. Another safer way was to moor to a huge cargo barge that had moored to a dock built for waiting just outside the lock entrance. The friendly barge captain welcomed us but said they would enter the lock when it opened at 7:30 a.m. We should be ready to cast off at 7:15 sharp. We were ready, and, at exactly 7:15, the Captain walked forward, casting off lines. His wife entered the pilot house and took the conn at the six-foot helm. (There was no other

**Here, I am tending the locks again**

crew.) At 7:30, the big engine roared to life and immediately the propellers churned and washed us halfway across the canal. We were underway and headed for the biggest lock we were to see. Eight huge barges entered with us in the rear…and the lock was only half filled!

Cruising the labyrinth of connecting rivers and canals was challenging, reading foreign language charts, while complying with the European buoy system where the colors are reverse to ours. Giving sea room to the barges was exciting as they often changed sides of the canal!

A white-knuckled thrill came running the Lorelei where the Rhine River is swift and dangerous. A line of barges came down like running a slalom, sweeping from side to side. They did display a sign and a light signaling which side we should take! That helped!

**The *Dolfin*, on the left, waits its turn at the locks**

Now back to the *Dolfin* and the Cranes, where after two more locks we arrived at Brugge, one of Europe's more beautiful villages, known for its many bridges. We had just two weeks remaining before our date to meet John and Jean Krase in Venice to crew for them in their yawl *Nereid* for a trip down the Dalmatian Coast of Yugoslavia. "What can we do in two weeks?" we asked ourselves. The answer that came back, "Rent a car and see what is behind the **iron curtain**!" The time was right! The United States was in a cold war with Russia. The **cold war** was a conflict of ideologies between the free nations of the world and Russia and its communist allies. It was fought with economic and political weapons rather than with guns and explosives. The phrase "iron curtain" refers to Russia's isolation policy set after World War II when Russia set up trade barriers and rigid censorship that cut off Russia and its eastern European satellite countries from the rest of the world.

# SCENE 35

## BEHIND THE IRON CURTAIN

### Czechoslovakia (1985)

We flew from Brugge to Prague in a Russian-built jetliner much like a skinny Boeing 727. Although we called for reservations a week before, we had to wait for space to open up. It was reasonably comfortable. Male flight attendants served us a lunch of cold cuts and <u>beer</u>. No English was spoken, but that didn't matter. The paperwork took care of that. You could sense that the government was in control. In addition to our passports, we had a four-part visa on which was recorded our nightly hotel stops, conversion of money, boat tickets, purchases, etc. We could not take Czech money in or out of the country and were required to spend a minimum amount each day of our stay (a ridiculous $17 per person). Accommodations could only be made through CEDOK, the government travel agency. Our category-B hotel rooms were always clean and the beds comfortable. Tap water was good everywhere, but nearly everyone drank beer. The Czech food was inferior. The main dish would be a variety of goulash with yellow bell peppers, sauerkraut, potatoes, and a tasteless dumpling. Seldom any lettuce or fruit. No tourist menus. Everything à la carte, but very inexpensive.

We made a self-guided city tour of **Prague**, the "City of Spires." The architecture was very interesting. The Jewish Quarter was a sad reminder. We saw the St. Stephen Church from where "Good King Wenceslas looked out, on the Feast of Stephen; When the snow lay round about, deep and crisp and even."

We had made a reservation with Avis International to rent a car in Prague, to be returned in Bratislava (on the Danube opposite Vienna). When we called to pick it up, they had never heard of us. But they delivered a two-door stick shift, as we requested (Renault 9).

The car was just right for Mary and me. We drove through beautiful countryside on excellent two-lane roads with little traffic. There was a wide-open-spaces feeling looking across large cultivated fields. No fences! All land is government owned. Remember that Czechoslovakia was under Communist Russia's control.

**We rented this little Renault 9 from Avis for our self-guided motor tour from Prague to Bratislava**

**This dramatic monument near Bratislava honors the 6,885 Russian soldiers who died in two days fighting the Nazi. It is topped by a statue of a Russian soldier crushing a swastika**

One night, we were in a hotel built inside a medieval ruin. We dutifully turned in our passports as instructed and went to the police station to log in as required. The officer who greeted us said the chief was busy and to wait. We did, just a few minutes. He asked what we wanted. We told him. He answered with a "no problem" kind of answer and motioned us out.

The next day, we had a chance to observe a little of every day life in the village of Ceske Krumlov. Shopping for daily needs seemed quite a chore. One had to go to a variety of specialty shops, which appeared to be well stocked, but always with a waiting line. Meats and produce looked very poor. Wine was good and cheap. Bread was cheap but only white, uncut, and unwrapped. Milk came only sterilized and in boxes. Fruit juices only in boxes, too. Cheese was tasteless. We never found salted crackers to go with our scotch.

Lots of school children, all well dressed. No sign of poverty, but no opulence either. People were animated and pleasant!

Before returning the car to Avis, we drove around looking at dramatic monuments to many wars from Roman times that entered Eastern Europe through the ford across the Danube where **Bratislava** now stands. The most dramatic was a tall column with a Russian soldier on top stomping and crushing a Nazi swastika. Throughout Europe, the German Nazis were sending Jews to concentration camps and annihilation. Under the monument lay the graves of 6,885 Russian soldiers who died in two days of fighting liberating the city from the Nazis!

A self-appointed guide told us a lot about life in Czechoslovakia—alcoholism is a big problem. Liquor is cheap. Jobs are assured by the government so no fear by the workman of getting fired. Wages were about $250 per month. One third goes to rent, regardless of income.

We arranged through CEDOK in Bratislava to go to Budapest by hydrofoil. The ride was smooth and fast. The seats were upholstered, three to each side of the center aisle. The stewardesses wore dresses and high heels (and were also well upholstered!). The vessel carried

**The hydrofoil ride to Budapest was comfortable and fast. Standing in the aisle is the well-dressed stewardess**

about sixty passengers. We checked in at 0530. Paperwork to 0600 departure. Arrived Budapest at 0830.

## Hungary (1985)

We booked with IBUSZ (Hungarian Tourist Agency) into Hotel Erzsebet, just two-months old. Excellent appointments, good management, convenient downtown location, good food. Room on the quiet side. The rate was $44 with unlimited breakfast. Complete dinner for two with wine, soup, salad, and main dish (no room for dessert) was $7.07! Hungarian food was excellent everywhere.

We liked Hungary better than Czechoslovakia in spite of the fact the countryside was not as beautiful, the roads were not as good, and there were many more vehicles. The country seemed more prosperous. There were still tight controls on currency and on your whereabouts, but it was not as obvious. The ancient buildings had been scrubbed clean and the revealed masonry was fantastic.

**Touring Budapest**

**Budapest** is the capital and largest city made up of two former cities. Buda was established on the east bank of the Danube on the site of a Roman colony. Pest on the west bank. Which would you rather be, a Buda or a Pest? No matter, bridges join the two to make the one city of Budapest. During World War II, air raids destroyed the greater part of Budapest. The communists occupied Budapest and deported thousands of non-communists to Russia

**Relaxing in our cabin at Lake Balaton in Hungary**

for slave labor.

Again, we rented a car through Avis. Again, they had never heard of our reservation. Not to worry, they provided a brand new VW "Golf," like our "Rabbit."

**Lake Balaton** is a large lake with vacation facilities including nice clean little housekeeping cabins. We rented one for a couple of nights. We needed to slow down. The drive had been slow because of the heavy truck traffic to Yugoslavia and light rain. But when we turned west at Kecskemét, the driving through farm country was pleasant.

Now we had to watch the calendar to meet the Krases in Venice and become their crew on *Nereid*. After a frantic time in the Budapest bahnhof trying to find the correct ticket window, we had a pleasant train ride on the "Orient Express" **out from behind the iron curtain** and on to Vienna. There was a thirty-minute delay at the Austrian border while the Hungarian Army searched in and under the train.

## Austria (1985)

In **Vienna**, the first stop after "Exchange" was the Austrian Government Travel Agency.

They booked us at Hotel Wandl. Quiet room with breakfast for two for $46. It was Friday and all the museums were closed. We took the city tour and sloshed along in the rain with the multitude of tourists from the numerous tour buses. We felt the pressure of guided tour groups being herded about like cattle. We were glad to leave Vienna for charming **Salzburg**.

We booked two nights in a nice Pension Austria ($35/night). We walked to the Unterberg Mountain cable car. It was a clear day and the Alpine views were magnificent. We saw mountain goats, Alpine crows (choughs), local hikers in Alpine clothing, and views of the valleys below.

We attended an evening concert in the "Residenz" (palace). A quintet consisting of a piano, two violins, a viola, and a cello played pieces by Mozart, Schubert, and Dvorak. A brilliant performance.

The next day, we took a local train to **Bad Gastein** for a two-stage cable lift to a mountain-top restaurant. That evening we went to the Mirabell Palace to see the famous Salzburger Marionettentheater performance of "The Marriage of Figaro." We took another local train the short distance through a mountain pass to Venice. We had picked up some bread, meat, and boxed drink to have for lunch along the way. Seats on the train were in compartments for six passengers each. The one we got was, with us, overflowing with two men standing. Others were eating so, we unwrapped our snacks and I was reaching to deposit the papers in the trash basket located under the window when one of the standing gentlemen said (I presume), "Here. Give it to me. I'll deposit it." I gave the handful to him and he turned and threw it out the window! I was shocked!

**Enjoying a mountaintop view in Austria**

# SCENE 36

## COASTAL CRUISING

### Venice (1985)

Venice (Venezia) has been called the "Queen City of the Adriatic." It was not built on solid land but lies on a cluster of small mud islands. Venice has canals for streets and gondolas for taxicabs. The famous buildings that line the canals are built on posts sunk deep in the mud. Unfortunately, they are slowly sinking in spite of tremendous engineering efforts and millions of dollars spent trying to save the city.

This was our second trip to Venice. This time, it was our meeting place to begin our two-week cruise with the Krases

We stayed at the Gavalento Hotel where we made contact by telephone with John and Jean Krase, the owners of the *Nereid*. They asked for one more day to prepare the boat for us. That was fine with us. It gave us a day to see the sights by ourselves. We traveled the Grand Canal by vaporettos (high speed water "busses"). At one stop we saw the boat get out of control. The skipper brought her to the landing but couldn't back down. The deck hand threw the mooring line over the bollard but couldn't hold it as it went singing out. The vaporetto coasted on down the canal and crashed into a group of moored gondolas. The skipper got the engine stopped and his boat out into the stream, when another vaporetto came along going the other way and just grabbed the disabled one and deposited it back at the landing it had missed! The "rescue" was a smooth operation.

Following directions, we made our way by bus to Porto Turistico di Jesolo. There, waiting for us, was the *Nereid*.

The **Nereid** was custom built for the Krases in southern France. She was designed as a yawl but the masts could not be stepped until reaching the Mediterranean due to the low

**We enjoyed cruising the Dalmation Coast of Yugoslavia with John and Jean Krase on their yacht, the *Nereid***

profile required to pass under bridges and in some locks. When the rigging was completed in a Mediterranean shipyard, the *Nereid* became an oceangoing yacht ideal for coastal cruising.

## Yugoslavia (1985)

For the next two weeks, the *Nereid* was our home as we crossed the Adriatic Sea from Venice to Rovinj on the Istria Peninsula of Yugoslavia. We anchored or stopped at modern marinas of the Adriatic Club Yugoslavia. We sailed only in daylight, usually covering forty-five to fifty-five miles. The skies were always clear and the visibility unlimited. The winds were mostly from the northwest at five to ten knots. The only blow we had was a "bora" while we were tied up in Split. It blew about forty knots.

The west coast waters of Yugoslavia, known as the Dalmatians, are lined with many small islands with picturesque villages, many of which are stucco white with red tile roofs much like in early Southern California.

At the modern marinas, the challenging "Mediterranean moor" is used. You must back your unruly boat stern to the dock to receive a "sand line," while at the same time passing a stern line to the dock. The sand line is then pulled in hand-over-hand until the anchor line is reached and made taught.

If your assigned space is between two boats, numerous big fenders are rigged on both sides. The dockmaster and a miscellaneous assortment of idle boat neighbors join in pushing and pulling your boat into position, amid shouted commands and counter-commands from various directions and in several foreign tongues.

We rented a car to tour Yugoslavia by land. This was one off the beautiful waterfalls at Plitvice Lakes National Park

**Zadar** was one of the most interesting of old walled cities. The old city and the new city were connected by bridges and passenger ferries. The ferries consisted of twenty-foot (?) rowboats propelled by two oars and carrying up to twelve passengers, most standing. The city was built on the ruins of a Roman Forum.

**Split** is a major port for yachts and small ships, and is the port where the Krases spent the winter. Split is famous for Diocletian's Palace, built in the third century for the Roman Emperor by that name who lived in it until his death. It then served as residence for exiled Roman Emperors.

To sample the interior of Yugoslavia, we rented a car, a Zastava 128, from Hertz. Our destination was the **Plitvice Lakes National Park**. It was a lovely tree-filled area with beautiful waterfalls formed by a cascade of small lakes feeding their overflows from one lake down to the next.

At the check-in desk, we asked for a room with a bath...and that is what we got! A nice room with a very large tiled bathroom...but no wash basin! and no toilet!! (The WC was down the hall.)

In the breakfast room the next morning, a large group of country people were having a great time joking with each other. The women wore their babushkas. The men wore suit coats over shirts without ties. We saw them later on the trails walking in one tight bunch. They really stuck close together.

The park was so lovely that we stayed a second night. That gave us enough time to hike to those spectacular waterfalls and enjoy them up close.

The last leg of our voyage in the *Nereid* was to Korcula, a really neat medieval town. Its history takes it through all the migrations from the Stone Age and now is a popular resort. John and Jean returned to Split to spend the winter. We went on by commercial ferry to **Dubrovnik**.

**In Dubrovnik, we witnessed the pigeons flocking to the square when the bells rang at noon**

We took a guided tour of Dubrovnik with a small English-only group and an interesting guide. During the black plague, all things entering the city were held outside for forty days. From the word for forty comes the word "quarantine" now used universally.

In medieval times, an orphanage accepted unwanted babies by dark of night through a rotating blind window together with half a broken stick. If the mother later wanted her baby back she claimed it with the other matching half stick.

Legend has it that, in the mid-1600s, the pigeons suddenly left town. Viewed as an omen, many citizens left town too...and just in time to avoid a severe earthquake! As a tribute to pigeons, bells are rung at noon and flocks of pigeons come to the main square to be fed.

We flew home from Dubrovnik to Los Angeles to end a wonderful and extended vacation in Europe. I don't remember how we communicated in those days, but son Scott was waiting as we deplaned at LAX.

# SCENE 37

# BICYCLING—SAN DIEGO & BEYOND

## The Netherlands (1979)

As always, it was great to be home. We settled into our exercise routines such as walking before breakfast, and later we advanced to jogging (which was popular in those years). Soon we encountered beginning bicycle groups which were lead by volunteers and which we were free to join. Their routes were around the harbor and Mission Bay Park on mostly flat land, but there were a few easy hills and some breezes which gave us plenty of challenges. From these tours, we learned biking protocol and biking rules of the road.

It was during this time that Mary read in the newspaper travel section of a tour in the Netherlands called "**Holiday on Two Wheels.**" We bravely booked it through the Netherlands Travel Agency (VVV) starting in **Arnhem**, as an extension of our French Hotel Barge cruise. The booking included a walking tour of a forest in Luxembourg!

Our "Holiday on Two Wheels" in Holland (1979) turned out to be more "independent" than expected. We were provided with bikes, maps, and instructions, and off we went. It was a great way to meet locals and experience country inns

We arrived two days early and reported to the VVV. They were expecting us. We would find our bicycles waiting for us at the Haarhuis Hotel. (You said it?) They were new English three-speed bikes with upright handlebars. No bending forward for these old people. We were given saddle-bags for our rain suits, toilet articles, and change of clothes, and given route instructions.

"Where and when do we meet our biking group?" we asked. "Vot Groop?" was the reply, and then he explained we would travel alone. The bike trails were paved and well marked. Our overnight accommodations were in country Inns and prepaid. There was a clipboard on the handle bars for mounting the routing instructions.

The instructions for the first segment read: From VVV to traffic lights, turn left, Y1630 turn left, follow signs "doorgaand verkeer," direction Zevenaar. At H310B keep to right, through tunnel. Y7338-1 turn right, direction Westerwoort. (4 kms).

We got lost getting out of Arnhem and had to ask a truckdriver for directions. But since we were ahead of schedule, we decided to spend the day enjoying the Kröller-Müller Museum, which is located in **Hoge Veluwe National Park**, Holland's largest nature reserve.

In a modern building in this beautiful setting was a fabulous collection of paintings, sculptures, and drawings, but the central feature was an assemblage of 276 works by Vincent van Gogh (1853-1890).

We were also fascinated by the sculptures of Lipchitz, which were also in the well-manicured park around the museum. Sixty sculptures are displayed in lovely harmony with nature.

**Biking brought the sights up close!**

Finally, we hit the trail. Actually, we were right on schedule. Once across the Ijssel River things took shape. The end of the first day found us walking and puffing and pushing our bikes up what must be Holland's highest hill! To the old but luxury Hotel Erica.

We were surprised to find that large areas in central Holland are wooded, with extensive footpaths and bicycle trails through them. We had many rivers to cross. Some were by little ferries which were pulled across by cable. There were bridges for crossing railroad tracks. Steps were for bikers but smooth channels along side the steps were for the bikes.

It was market day in several of the villages along our route. Lots of interesting produce and clothing, but not many curios for souvenirs. This was serious business, not a tourist trap.

The village for our overnight was having a large party with a BIG Wurlitzer Electric Band! You know, the kind seen in big city parades. It played endlessly and stopped promptly at midnight.

Yes, the terrain was mostly flat. By searching the horizon, you could most likely spot the church spire of the next village. That can make for easy navigating, but there is no shelter from the wind. Bucking a headwind is like riding with the brakes dragging.

Each inn was different and all were cozy and warm. The food was delicious and cooked just for us. The problem was, there was much more than we could eat and it was embarrassing to waste food.

The weather was good, meaning a high overcast. It rained hard only on the last day. We put on our rain suits and pedaled along, dry inside! And behind the rain came spectacular clouds in dramatic shapes from stratus to cumulous, snowy white to threatening charcoal black.

It was, and remains, <u>the best bike ride of my life</u>.

## Holland with Elderhostel (1990)

There were twenty-two of us Elderhostelers over age fifty-five forming the tour group which was run by International Bicycle Tours, Inc. with a crew as follows: the leader, the historian, the Sag Wagon driver, and his helper. The leader set the pace and led the tour. If there was a sharp turn, the leader would pick a biker to stand on the corner and point the way. Before starting, the leader would select the sweep-of-the-day. That rider brought up the rear and never let any participant fall behind him. Thus, if the sweep doesn't show up at the next rest stop, the leader knows there is a problem and goes back to investigate. (No cell phones then.) The Sag Wagon was following as closely as roads allow for access to the bike trail. He was equipped to fix flats, even provide a spare bike which he carried, and could take into the wagon anyone injured or too tired to continue. The historian talked at rest stops. He told us about the flower industry, the history of Amsterdam, Noord Holland, and Zuid Holland. Also of the Fight Against the

Sea, history of Friesland, the Royal Dutch family, and Holland under Nazi occupation. All were well presented and very interesting.

**We enjoyed many years of bicycling both at home and abroad, including international Elderhostel bike tours in Europe. With Elderhostel bicycle tour in Holland, 1990**

**Flowers**. We visited the world's largest flower mart at Aalsmeer under the largest single-roofed building in the world (ten million square feet). Flowers from eight thousand nurseries all over the Netherlands and neighboring countries are auctioned five days a week. Three-and-one-half billion flowers and four hundred million plants are sold annually to the tune of about $1 billion. Trains of flower carts are paraded on rails before buyers where thirteen auction blocks operate simultaneously.

The landscape scenes were beautiful no matter which way you looked. In a polder, we saw a dairyman milking his cows with an electric milker powered by a portable generator. Nearby, one cow was getting a drink of water at a watering hole by stepping on a faucet made for that purpose.

**Wooden Shoes**. The dairyman was wearing wooden shoes called 'klompens." They are said to keep the feet warmer and drier than other shoes. We visited a factory that custom made wooden shoes to order. It was loaded with special kinds of woodworking machines.

**Steeples, Spires, and Bells**. Church steeples, clock towers, and bell towers were centuries old. All were topped with spires supporting an ornament significant to the town or edifice—in a canal town there was an anchor, in a fishing village a fish, for the Roman Catholic church a rooster. The latter is held over from the religious days when the Catholic church was forced underground and not allowed to display the cross.

The peal of bells was charming. Some were the call to worship. Some were hymns. Some chimed the time, though not accurately.

**Sailboats for Work and Play**. With the Netherlands drenched in water and wind, it is not surprising that the Dutch are famous for their water-oriented sports. Boats of all sizes and shapes are found in the most unlikely places, due to the network of canals. Most "romantic" are the heavy blunt-nosed barge-like sailing craft with their arched gaffs, oversized outboard rudders, huge leeboards, and retractable jib booms. They are classified by such lyrical names as "Boeier," "Botter," "Hoogaars," and "Tjalk." The word "yacht" is said to have been originated by Dutch sailing fishing vessels racing to market. (Herring, anyone?)

**Windmills**. The last Ice Age left the Netherlands a shallow drainage area for northwestern Europe. There was very little arable land. The earliest Germanic tribes that moved into Friesland built up high ground called "terps" for their buildings and built canals to drain the land. They imported the windmill principle from Turkey and began reclaiming land by pumping water from behind dikes and into drainage canals. Windmills also became the prime movers for industries, not only as pumps, grist mills, and saw mills, but to drive machinery in factories.

The "wings" are more scientifically designed than one would think. Each blade has a fixed edge shaped somewhat like a jib to direct the wind at proper angle to the canvas covering of the wings. The canvas "sail" can be reefed, furled, and trimmed and shaped like a canvas sail.

The highlight of this biking tour was to be invited to "board" a windmill/sawmill and examine "close up and personal" the features just explained. The wind power was turned into mechanical power and, through hoists, levers, and gears, the raw logs were hauled to the cutting board and pulled through four vertical oscillating saw blades to form planks.

There are two more biking tours coming up: France and the Danube River.

## Biking the Loire Valley, France (1992)

The Loire (lwahr) is the longest river in France (six hundred fifty miles). It flows northward from the Cevennes Mountains to Orleans where the river turns westward and flows through a beautiful valley with many famous châteaux and empties into the Bay of Biscay.

**Château** is the French word for castle. Our Elderhostel biking tour would take us to visit several of these fortresses. But first, we had to return to Avis the rental car in which we made a nonstop drive in clear weather to Chinon, where we checked into the Hotel Cheops to meet our biking group at the welcoming dinner.

**Biking the Loire Valley in France with Elderhostel, 1992**

Taking a *douche* (shower) before dinner became a challenge. The bathroom was typical of those we found in the country—the bathtub was long, deep, and narrow. A real struggle for weak knees trying to emerge. Fat ladies would require assistance. Then there were the shower wands with personalities all their own. This one fit into an inadequate bracket from which it fell and thrashed about like an untamed fire hose, indiscriminately rinsing down the walls.

The tour was run by the same International Bicycle Tours so we already knew the rules and procedures.

The biking trails were not as good as in the Netherlands. There were several hills that we had to dismount and push over the crest that first day. Then, an easy glide (whee!) down to the Loire River. But there were some roads shared with auto traffic so close alongside one could reach over and touch them. I didn't like that!

Château d'Ussé was the first we encountered, followed closely by Château de Villandry. We marveled at the sculptured gardens of flowers, vegetables, and herbs. Looking like fairy story castles, we photographed wildly. Farther along we came to the little roadside Hôtel des Cèdres where we stayed for two nights. Charming accommodations, great French cuisine, and <u>quiet</u> sleeping!

An easy ride took us, in the rain, to Château d'Azay-le-Rideau. The douche in this hotel had the unique feature of being in a two-foot square enclosure. If you dropped the soap you had to do a deep knee bend to retrieve it!

We biked through large fields of corn and sunflowers, both grown for their oil, on a route that took us to the Château de Chaumont-sur-Loire. This was a smaller château and our favorite. The stables were famous in their day for their luxury—tile- and carpet-lined stalls!

The highlight and last château visit was to the huge Château de Chambord.

## Biking the Danube River, Munich to Vienna (1994)

This will be a report on our third Elderhostel biking tour in Europe run by International Bicycle Tours. We biked the dikes of the Danube River from Munich to Vienna. To get there from home, we drove a rental car to the Los Angeles airport for our 9 p.m. departure on Lauda Air (an Austrian airline booked by Lufthansa) nonstop to Munich. It was a long eleven hours. The food was superior, however, with wine before and with meals and Drambuie for the asking afterwards.

Lauda Air uses triangular dishes which help you trap the food. The British technique of fork in left hand and knife in right corralling the morsels is a better straight-forward approach than our covert method of giving reluctant bits a nudge with a sneaky finger.

Our hotel was the Dorint, in the little village of Freising, where they have a unique work schedule. A flurry of traffic activity took place from 3 to 3:30 a.m. as a medley of cars, trucks, and the local motorcycle idiots drag-raced in the alley below our room.

The bells in the charming medieval church belfry keep you posted on the time all night long, in case you are interested. One clang for each quarter hour and four clangs on the hour followed by bongs counting which hour! The chimes somehow lose their charm at midnight with four clangs and twelve bongs.

Our group met the next day at the Munich airport and was taken by bus to Hotel zum Burgwirt in the village of Natternberg, just outside Deggendorf. There was great similarity in room layouts but not so with bathrooms. There we were issued our bikes.

## Epilogue on Elderhostel Biking

How better could we visit the beautiful Loire Valley of France, the favorite area of French Kings? How better could we see the famous châteaux? At our ages, with our limited biking skills, Elderhostel was the way to go. The biking was slow even for us. The rest stops too frequent. The group of twenty-one too large. But the comradeship was good, the small hotels quaint and to our liking, and how else could we come by four-course gourmet meals every night? And the biking just makes one feel good all over! However, those hand-held French showers are incorrigible! Besides, I never did figure out how to wash one hand while holding the shower in the other!!

**Biking the Danube with Elderhostel, 1994**

# SCENE 38

## BIRDING HITHER AND THITHER

Humans have been fascinated by birds from ancient times, for their ability to fly, for their keen eyesight, for their beauty, their behavior and survival skills...and the list goes on and on. The eagle serves as an icon for *bravery,* the dove for *peace.*

When we hear the term "birdwatchers," we tend to think of little old ladies from the Garden Club visiting the local park lake to feed stale bread to the ducks or birdseed to the pigeons.

At the top of the list of observers are the professional ornithologists. They study birds in depth to determine the health and growth or decline of flocks, the effect of environment loss. They become experts in locating single birds by bird calls, knowing where on trees and bushes to look. Their studies lead to laws and regulations to protect certain species.

Between these groups are the "birders," which was our category. We equipped ourselves with top quality binoculars and a birding scope with an exceptionally broad and clear field of view. We always carried a field guidebook and usually had lists of sightings by others that we hoped to find.

We were not good birders and never would be for three age-related reasons:

- ➢ Hearing is poor at the high frequencies of bird calls.
- ➢ Color quality declines and there is some shifting of hue dominance.
- ➢ Memory loss shows up trying to remember a bird's specie name.

We found it best to go with a group of birders if we wanted to see lots of birds (let the good birders find the bird and point it out to us for a sighting to enjoy). The professional tours were best because the other birders were always congenial and helpful. The tour company billeted us in the best available country inns, which was part of the pleasure. It was great to see the "out back" of so many countries, and yes, we got plenty of exercise hiking back roads and trails seeking rare birds.

Listed below, to show the extent of our birding days, are most of the birding tours that we took, in addition to our own independent birding.

## Birding Tours

- 1975  Highlands of Scotland
- 1986  Costa Rica
- 1987  Malheur, Oregon
- 1988  Oregon Coast
- 1988  Galapagos Islands
- 1989  South Texas
- 1990  Eastern Canadian Islands
- 1991  Venezuela
- 1992  Trinidad & Tobago
- 1994  Belize &Tikal
- 1995  Hawaii & Kauai
- 1996  Southern Brazil
- 1998  Klamath Falls, Oregon
- 1999  Copper Canyon
- 2000  Ecuador
- 2001  Sea of Cortez

**In Costa Rica, 1986**

**In the Netherlands, 1990**

**In Venezuela, 1991**

**On birding trip to Belize & Tikal, 1994**

**In the tropical rainforest—with bug protection—Brazil, 1996**

**Mary birding by a mangrove swamp near San Blas, 1997**

**Mary straddles the equator on a birding trip to Ecuador, 2000**

**In Haines, Alaska, 2004**

# SCENE 39

## TOURING THE BRITISH ISLES—1975

**England**. By happenstance, we were in London for the dress rehearsal of the Queen's birthday celebration. We saw the Trooping of the Colors at Buckingham Palace with the Guards in their red coats and black bear fur hats. The Queen's Own Horse Guards exquisite with a band mounted on white horses. We visited the infamous Tower of London and its White Tower where Lady Jane Grey came up through Traitor's Gate to be beheaded.

We went by bus to Stonehenge, the finest Bronze Age sanctuary in Europe, believed to date back to 2800 BC.

And, of course, we went to Trafalgar Square to salute Admiral Nelson as he stood on top, guarded by two bronze Lions who **roared** when a virgin passed by!

(Our first **animal antic**?)

**Scotland**. Our first focus in Scotland was the **Isle of Skye**. We found an excellent guest house which was a converted crofter's farmhouse. It was a small rectangular cottage with walls three feet thick. A bedroom, fireplace, and kitchen are at one end and a family room at the other. Opposite the front door is a play area for the children. They burn peat for fuel.

If you think the White Tower in London is cruel, witness the dungeon in the **Dunvegan Castle**. You go up to see the "Prisoner's Exit," which is a three-foot-square hole with a twenty-six-foot drop to the rocky river below. If not killed in the fall, the prisoner starves!

We were delighted to see the Trooping of the Colors by the palace Guards at Buckingham Palace—a dress rehearsal for the Queen's birthday celebration

Mary read in a birder's magazine of a new little lodge in the highlands of Scotland that offered a four-day nature study course. That sounded just right for us—and it was. There were just nine participants: an English couple, a Dutch couple, an English woman, a Welsh woman, a New Zealand girl, and Mary and me.

Our base was at Guischan House in a remote and lovely valley west of Loch Ness. Our host and naturalist was Sir John Lister-Kaye (who birded in kilts). We hiked six hours or so each day to see endangered species of birds nesting, red and roe deer, waterfalls, burns (creeks), fords, glens, moors, etc.

Sorrel, John's wife, ran the lodge. She cooked delicious meals and fed us at a huge round table that seated twelve! Dining together family style were the host, helpers, and guests. You can imagine that table talk was very interesting.

Oh, did I mention? Sorrel was also raising a toddler!

**Wales**. We arrived by train completely disoriented with no maps and the Welsh signs were long (like this) and unpronounceable. We hailed a taxi and asked the cabby could he recommend a B&B. He, of course, had just the place. We had him take us there. The proprietress was out sweeping her walk. Yes, she had a room, and it would be ready "just as soon as she finished hoovering it out."

Our reason for wanting to visit Wales was really to visit Chester which is just across the border in the northwest corner of England and is the ancestral home of my mother's family line, named "BIRD." The lineage traces back to John Bird, bishop of Chester in 1541. A William Byrde [sic] was mayor 1557-8. A William Bird was mayor 1580-1, and Richard Byrd [sic] was mayor 1654-5. They all served first as sheriff. (I got the above from the archives I asked to see. My request was cheerfully granted!)

We visited Chester, England, the ancestral home of my mother's family, the Birds. The lineage traces back to John Bird, bishop of Chester in 1541

Chester is the only walled medieval city in Great Britain, and it is very much alive with modern stores within the ancient half-timbered buildings. The stables and craftsmen's shops are on the street level, stores and offices were on the second floor, and living quarters were on the top floor.

In the countryside, there were lovely glens, ancient Roman bridges, waterfalls, lakes, and rivers. Mt. Snowdon, not far from Chester, is the highest mountain in the United Kingdom. We were surprised to see the mountains treeless. However, that allowed us to see the *miles* of rock fences, all hand laid. (Oh, my aching back!)

**Ireland**. We flew from London's Heathrow airport to Dublin where we stayed three nights at Mrs. Geoghegan's guest house. We were disappointed in Dublin, famous for its singing bars. Those we visited were stoic. But we did enjoy the excellent acting at the Abbey Theater and the bus tour to **Glendalough**. It is amazing that the Round Tower erected in the monastery by Saint Kevin around 1000 AD has stood without reconstruction for over one thousand years!

We rented a car to drive the Ring of Kerry in the southwest corner of Ireland near Killarney. It is a beautiful drive, if it isn't raining. And it was a perfectly clear day! We stopped overnight at the Falcon Inn at Glenbeigh, and the next day continued to Macgillycuddy's Reeks and Dingle Bay.

**Caernarfon Castle** kept the Welsh in check during their wars for independence from the English. King Edward I built it on the shores of Menai Strait in 1280. He then won over the Welsh chieftains with a ruse— he promised to name as Prince of Wales one born on Welsh soil who spoke no English. With this agreed, King Edward dispatched his pregnant Queen to Caernarfon to deliver a son, who was born in 1284 and was invested there as the first Prince of Wales in 1301.

We discovered that B&B lodging is wonderful in Europe. We enjoyed the hospitality of our hosts and sharing experiences with the other guests

The present Queen of England, Elizabeth II, crowned her eldest son, Charles, there as the 21$^{st}$ Prince of Wales on July 1, 1969.

# SCENE 40

## VIGNETTES OF ANIMAL ANTICS

**Highland Horses.** One day at a rest break, I was admiring the landscape and was especially intrigued by a large snow field, pure white and undisturbed, except for a rock out-cropping near its center. As I looked I thought I saw one rock move. Looking through binoculars I confirmed that the rocks were moving, and I told Sir John what I had seen. He put his high-powered birding scope on target. What did he see? Two young horses romping in the snow like children on their first encounter with snow. Their **antics** spelled enjoyment!

**Cavorting Sea Lions.** We moved aboard the sixty-six-foot luxury yacht *Mistral* for cruising the Galapagos Islands, fabulous birding, and study of marine life. We went ashore in pongas (skiffs), leaping ashore for a dry landing or wading ashore for a wet landing. For snorkeling, the skipper chose the "Devil's Crown," a small crater open to the sea. We were dressed with goggles, snorkels, swim fins, and lifejackets. We went to the crater and slipped over the side. Immediately, the "welcoming committee" of young sea lions arrived, coming at us with great speed, and, at the last instant, they split to go one side or the other. From then on, they did backward loops, barrel rolls, deep dives, and never touched a soul. By reaching out, one never could touch them either. It was just Great Fun!!

**Boobies.** There are Blue-Footed, Red-Footed, and Masked Boobies. Only the Reds have feet with sufficient flexibility to roost in trees. The Blues feed in close to shore, the Masked in waters between islands, and the Reds far offshore. An interesting relationship exists between the Frigate Birds and the Boobies—the Frigates cannot dive for food, although they might pick something eatable from the surface. A principal source of food for them is to harass a Boobie that has just been fishing. The Boobie gets so nervous it upchucks. The Frigate catches the fish as if falls!

**Three-Toed Tree Sloth**. Usually they are seen as just a ball of fur high up in a tree, but this one was working his way down "his tree," in ultra slow motion, searching for tender leaves on nearby plants. He had a firm grip with his left hand and outstretched arm, and, with his right arm fully extended, he was trying for a nice tender leaf on an adjacent tree. He was one foot short.

A male member of our party rushed to his rescue. He grabbed the branch with the "forbidden fruit" and pushed it into range for the thankful sloth!

The naturalists say that the sloth comes down from "his tree" once a week to defecate and "fertilize" it!

**Body-Surfing Sea Lion**. When we reached the north-facing sandy beach of Venezuela, we found that the "Christmas winds" had been blowing long enough to create long parallel rows of small breakers, just big enough for body-surfing. The beach was unused by people but occupied by a big bull sea lion, which we called "the beach master," and his harem. The swell carried him in until he was grounded, at which point he flapped his way back into deep water to ride another swell. "Surfing, anyone??"

**Migrating Gray Whales**. Each year, thousands of gray whales leave the ice packs of the Arctic to journey six thousand miles to southern Baja California. Throughout the spring months, these lagoons and bays are filled with gray whales—breeding, calving, and nursing. To watch whales anywhere is exhilarating, but in San Ignacio some of these whales have gone one gigantic step further—they come to us to rest their heads, tails, or flippers alongside our skiffs, enabling us to reach out...and touch...to cross a barrier to their world, on their terms. One cow whale brought her newborn calf to be admired (or for reasons known only to her). My wife, Mary, and I each kissed the whale wishing her and her baby good luck!

**A Scarlet Ibis Sunset**. The grand finale of our Neo Tropical Birding was the return of the Scarlet Ibis at sundown to roost on trees in the Caroni Swamp of Tobago Island. In flights of thirty or more at a time, these gorgeous birds flashed their brilliant iridescent red wings in the light of the setting sun as they circled to perch on the top of bushes and trees across the water from our boat. This roost, one of four or five, numbers some fifteen hundred birds. One-by-one they landed and remained fully exposed in contrast to the green foliage behind them to form nature's most exquisite Christmas tree. It is one of the most spectacular sightings a birder can have!

# SCENE 41

**FAREWELL**

### Let Me Go

When I come at last to the end of the road
And the sun has set for me,
I want no rites in a gloom-filled room.
Why cry for a soul set free?

Miss me a little, but not too long
And not with your head bowed low.
Remember the love that we have shared.
Miss me—but let me go.

For this is a journey we all must take
And each must go alone.
It's all part of the master plan
A step on the road to home.

When you are lonely and sick at heart
Go to the ocean we know,
And bury your sorrow among the waves.
Miss me—but let me go.

**Author Unknown**

**Drifting off among the bluebells of Scotland**

# EPILOGUE

(to follow)

www.ingramcontent.com/pod-product-compliance
Lightning Source LLC
Chambersburg PA
CBHW081128170426
43197CB00017B/2786